Pro Silverlight for the Enterprise

Ashish Ghoda

Apress®

Pro Silverlight for the Enterprise

Copyright © 2009 by Ashish Ghoda

ISBN-13 (pbk): 978-1-4302-1867-8

ISBN-13 (electronic): 978-1-4302-1868-5

9 8 7 6 5 4 3 2 1

Trademarked names may appear in this book. Rather than use a trademark symbol with every occurrence of a trademarked name, we use the names only in an editorial fashion and to the benefit of the trademark owner, with no intention of infringement of the trademark.

Lead Editors: Matthew Moodie, Ewan Buckingham
Technical Reviewer: Fabio Claudio Ferracchiati
Editorial Board: Clay Andres, Steve Anglin, Mark Beckner, Ewan Buckingham, Tony Campbell, Gary Cornell, Jonathan Gennick, Michelle Lowman, Matthew Moodie, Jeffrey Pepper, Frank Pohlmann, Ben Renow-Clarke, Dominic Shakeshaft, Matt Wade, Tom Welsh
Project Manager: Kylie Johnston
Copy Editor: Ami Knox
Associate Production Director: Kari Brooks-Copony
Production Editor: Kelly Gunther
Compositor and Artist: Kinetic Publishing Services, LLC
Proofreader: Patrick Vincent
Indexer: BIM Indexing & Proofreading Services
Cover Designer: Kurt Krames
Manufacturing Director: Tom Debolski

Distributed to the book trade worldwide by Springer-Verlag New York, Inc., 233 Spring Street, 6th Floor, New York, NY 10013. Phone 1-800-SPRINGER, fax 201-348-4505, e-mail orders-ny@springer-sbm.com, or visit http://www.springeronline.com.

For information on translations, please contact Apress directly at 2855 Telegraph Avenue, Suite 600, Berkeley, CA 94705. Phone 510-549-5930, fax 510-549-5939, e-mail info@apress.com, or visit http://www.apress.com.

Apress and friends of ED books may be purchased in bulk for academic, corporate, or promotional use. eBook versions and licenses are also available for most titles. For more information, reference our Special Bulk Sales–eBook Licensing web page at http://www.apress.com/info/bulksales.

The source code for this book is available to readers at http://www.apress.com.

I dedicate this book to my grandparents (Nayansukhray and Kumud Ghoda, Mahavir and Sarla Majmudar), parents (Jitendra and Varsha Ghoda), sister (Kruti Vaishnav), and lovely family (Pratixa, Gyan, and Anand Ghoda) whose blessings, sacrifice, continuous support, and encouragement enabled me to achieve this dream.

Contents at a Glance

Contents

PART 1 ▪▪▪ Exploring Silverlight

PART 2 ■ ■ ■ Enterprise Application Development with Silverlight

PART 3 ■ ■ ■ Silverlight for Mobile

PART 4 ▪ ▪ ▪ **Final Words**

About the Author

 **ASHISH GHODA** is a customer-focused and business values–driven senior IT executive with more than 12 years of IT leadership, technical and financial management, and enterprise architect experience. He is founder and president of Technology Opinion LLC, a unique collaborative venture striving for strategic excellence by providing partnerships with different organizations and the IT community. He is also associate director at a Big Four accounting firm.

Ashish Ghoda actively contributes to the IT community in the following ways:

- Provides strategic advice to achieve IT goals and define the product and the technology roadmaps of organizations
- Provides training and speaks on IT leadership areas and Microsoft technologies
- Architects and develops customer-centric software services
- Has authored not only this book but also several articles on Microsoft technologies and IT management areas for *MSDN Magazine*, TechnologyOpinion.com, and advice.cio.com
- Reviews research papers submitted for the Innovative and Collaborative Business and E-Business Tracks of the European Conference on Information System (ECIS)

About the Technical Reviewer

A prolific writer on cutting-edge technologies, **FABIO CLAUDIO FERRACCHIATI** has contributed to more than a dozen books on .NET, C#, Visual Basic, and ASP.NET. He is a .NET MCSD and lives in Milan, Italy.

Acknowledgments

It has been a nice journey and a pleasant experience writing my first book.

First of all, I would like to thank the chief .NET editor of Apress—Ewan Buckingham—for keeping trust in me and giving me an opportunity to write this unique book on Silverlight. Special thanks to Kylie Johnston for keeping this aggressive project on track; to Matthew Moodie and Fabio Claudio Ferracchiati for their thorough technical review, technical editing, and valuable guidance; to Ami Knox for copyediting; to Kelly Gunther for shepherding the project through production; and to the other Apress team members who worked on my book. Without positive support from the Apress team, I could never have achieved this goal.

I would also like to thank Jay Nanavaty, an independent senior consultant and my brother-in-law. Without his significant contribution and dedicated support in the development of the Silverlight Rich Internet Applications (RIAs) for Chapters 2 and 5, it would be very challenging for me to finish the book in the given timeframe.

With blessings from God and encouragement from my grandparents, parents, and in-laws, I was able to accomplish this task successfully. My wife, Pratixa, and two little sons, Gyan (5 years old) and Anand (8 months old), have positively supported my long hours of work (including most of the weekends). I thank my family for their unbelievable cooperation and encouragement and for keeping their faith in me during this challenging time.

Introduction

Microsoft Silverlight is a cross-browser, cross-platform, and cross-device plug-in for delivering the next generation of .NET-based media experiences and Rich Internet Applications (RIAs) for the Web.

If you want to learn how Silverlight can fulfill an organization's need for an enterprise-level technology platform for RIAs, you need to understand how Silverlight can be applied in today's business environment rather than simply delving into the syntax and grammar of Silverlight in isolation.

This book is a one-stop guide to understanding Service-Oriented Architecture (SOA), Web 2.0, Enterprise 2.0, and enterprise mobility concepts. You will learn how you can adopt Silverlight in your organization and remain ahead of the competition by developing Silverlight-based simplified, rich, interactive, and loosely coupled RIAs and deploying them as Software as a Service (SaaS) in a secured environment.

I will demonstrate the enterprise capabilities of Silverlight for developing service-oriented RIAs. You will get hands-on experience by developing a Silverlight-based enterprise training portal integrated with WCF, LINQ, and external data sources. The developed RIA also demonstrates how you can utilize advanced features of Silverlight such as Deep Zoom, custom controls, and externalized dynamic user interface definitions. We will explore different deployment options (same-domain vs. cross-domain) to deploy Silverlight-based RIA in a secured, supportable, and maintainable environment.

Finally, I will discuss the future of Silverlight for Mobile and how to plan for its release. You will learn the basics of developing for mobile applications, including coverage of common pitfalls and traps you may encounter, and you will explore the key architectural considerations for developing mobile applications.

Who This Book Is For

This book is for enterprise architects, IT executives, IT professionals, the developer community, technical and project managers, and anyone who wants to start using Silverlight in a corporate environment as well as understand SOA, Web 2.0, Enterprise 2.0, and enterprise mobility concepts.

This book assumes that you are familiar with Silverlight and its syntax, .NET Framework 3.5 components (WPF, XAML, and WCF), C#, ASP.NET, and development tools such as Visual Studio and Expression Blend.

How This Book Is Structured

This book is mainly divided into four parts. Part 1, "Exploring Silverlight," details how Silverlight is capable of supporting the Web 2.0 concept through rich, interactive RIAs and builds the foundation for the rest of the chapters by showing you how to develop an example RIA, named My Album. This part contains the following two chapters:

- Chapter 1 defines the Web 2.0 concept and discusses the architecture and available technologies for developing advanced RIAs. It also provides a detailed overview on Microsoft's Silverlight technology architecture and the components of Silverlight that allow organizations to develop advanced enterprise RIAs.

- Chapter 2 serves as a foundation for the rest of the book. In this chapter, I show you how to develop a quick but sound and attractive Silverlight RIA, the My Album application. In Chapter 5, you see how to extend the architecture of the My Album RIA to develop an enterprise-level training portal RIA.

Part 2, "Enterprise Application Development with Silverlight," is the heart of this book. This part defines Enterprise 2.0 and SOA in the context of Silverlight capabilities and provides hands-on experience by walking you through the development of an enterprise-level, service-oriented, Silverlight-based RIA, the Enterprise Training Portal. This part contains the following four chapters:

- Chapter 3 defines the Enterprise 2.0 concept and the key objectives of an enterprise-ready technology platform. Here I also explain what makes Silverlight an enterprise-ready technology platform.

- Chapter 4 focuses on defining the SOA concept in detail, which involves the seven key principles—usability, flexibility, simplicity, reusability, scalability, maintainability, and security—of the SOA concept. This chapter also covers Silverlight's enterprise capabilities for integrating with WCF/Web Services and LINQ by developing a sample Silverlight application with dynamic UI creation and dynamic content population.

- Chapter 5 provides hands-on experience by showing you how to transform the My Album RIA developed in Chapter 2 into an enterprise-level RIA, the Enterprise Training Portal, utilizing Silverlight and its service-oriented features and capabilities.

- Chapter 6 defines the deployment process in general. Here you explore Silverlight deployment features and Silverlight application deployment options/approaches such as Silverlight in-package and on-demand deployment, and same-domain and cross-domain deployment. The chapter also discusses embedding the Silverlight plug-in into a web page, custom error handling, and Silverlight support for globalization and localization features.

Part 3, "Silverlight for Mobile," takes a look at the future of Silverlight for Mobile with the following chapter:

- Chapter 7 explains enterprise mobility and its key components so you can understand the role of mobile applications in Enterprise 2.0. Here I outline the basics of developing enterprise-level mobile applications, main architecture components, key design considerations, and different data synchronization models for mobile applications. This chapter also provides the latest updates on Silverlight for Mobile and potential capabilities of Silverlight for developing RIAs for the mobile platform.

Part 4, "Final Words," wraps up the book with one last chapter, which provides practical advice on how to adopt Silverlight in your organization.

- Chapter 8 discusses current challenges posed by Silverlight and key considerations and practical advice for organizations deciding whether to adopt Silverlight as part of their technology and product roadmaps.

Prerequisites

The design theory and Silverlight enterprise capabilities I discuss apply to Silverlight 2 and future versions (Silverlight 3 is planned for release later in 2009).

I developed the example Silverlight RIAs in this book with the following tools, which you may want to use as you follow along:

- Microsoft .NET Framework 3.5 SP1
- Microsoft Silverlight 2
- Microsoft Visual Studio 2008 SP1
- Microsoft Silverlight Tools for Visual Studio 2008 SP1
- Microsoft Expression Blend 2 SP1
- Microsoft Expression Encoder 2 SP1
- Microsoft Deep Zoom Composer

Downloading the Code

The source code for this book is available to readers at www.apress.com by clicking the Source Code link on this book's details page. Please feel free to visit the Apress web site and download all the code there. You can also check for errata and find related titles from Apress.

Contacting the Author

I really enjoyed writing this book and actually learned a lot. I am sure you will feel the same when you read about the enterprise-level design concepts for Silverlight RIAs presented herein and how to develop enterprise RIAs using Silverlight.

I appreciate your continuous comments and feedback. You can send them to me, as well as any questions, via e-mail at AskAshish@TechnologyOpinion.com.

You can also visit my web site, http://www.TechnologyOpinion.com (an enhanced version of the Enterprise Training Portal developed in this book), to access my latest articles, instructor-led onsite training information, and news on different IT areas including Silverlight.

PART 1

Exploring Silverlight

CHAPTER 1

■ ■ ■

Understanding Silverlight

The Web 2.0 concept drives enterprises to develop browser-based Rich Internet Applications (RIAs) that support different market needs, such as platform (operating system, browser, and device) independence, information collaboration, social-networking, rich user interfaces, high performance, and high security. Silverlight 2 is a Microsoft .NET Framework–based technology platform enabling us to develop loosely coupled plug-ins and RIAs at the enterprise level. Silverlight helps enterprises to achieve the Web 2.0 concept by implementing RIAs in a very agile and cost-effective way that can provide maximum customer satisfaction and thus can drive enterprises to transform information system centers from cost centers to profit-making centers.

This chapter is divided into two major sections. It starts by explaining concepts of Web 2.0 and RIAs. I will discuss the architecture and available technologies in the market that basically drive the development of advanced RIAs. The latter part of the chapter focuses on introducing and understanding Microsoft's Silverlight technology and its components that allow organizations to develop advanced enterprise RIAs.

Web 2.0 and RIAs

Today users' expectations are increased in terms of collaboration, usability, performance, flexibility, user-level customization, and security for two reasons. The first reason is the use of the Internet and web-based applications have become part of users' day-to-day life. The second reason is the use of IT to execute and integrate business processes within and across organizations is extensive. Additionally, in today's digital economy era, the increased use of digital media makes all types of information available in digital format and can easily lead to information overload if organizations don't manage that information properly. Organizations also need to implement governance policies for data retention and government compliance. Innovative Web 2.0 and RIA concepts drive organizations to develop and deploy second-generation cross-platform and cross-device web applications meeting many of today's market needs.

Figure 1-1 presents a view of the Microsoft Surface home page (http://www.microsoft.com/surface), which basically demonstrates the different opportunities of Web 2.0 and RIAs by providing a rich, interactive user interface to explain how the new Microsoft Surface platform can deliver rich services.

Figure 1-1. *Microsoft Surface home page: an example of an RIA*

Key Attributes of Web 2.0

Although there is no specific definition for Web 2.0, one of the most accepted definitions is by Tim O'Reilly:[1]

> *Web 2.0 is the business revolution in the computer industry caused by the move to the Internet as platform, and an attempt to understand the rules for success on that new platform.*

As shown in Figure 1-2, the following are key attributes of Web 2.0:

- Improved usability via *rich and creative user interface* that provides an interactive rich experience, which is very similar to desktop rich client applications. Web 2.0 applications *process audio and video seamlessly*.

- *Modular* and loosely coupled web-based application architecture that supports flexibility, user-level customization, and seamless content and process integration.

- *High-performing* rich and interactive web-based applications due to the following capabilities:

    - Separation between the *loosely coupled presentation layer and the data access layer*. This enables client-side processing and reduces overall server-side processing by avoiding round-trips.

---

1. Tim O'Reilly, http://radar.oreilly.com/2006/12/web-20-compact-definition-tryi.html, 2006

- *Asynchronous communication* in the background to process different data process–related requests between client and server.
- *Metadata management and data indexing* capabilities to structure and organize data that help to overcome information overload by providing the right information at the right time.

- *Collaboration platform* to share information among diverse and geographically separate groups.

- *Simplified and standard distribution protocols* and *metadata management* enables secured social-networking.

- *Platform-independent* technology that is cross-platform (i.e., available on different operating systems—Microsoft Windows, Apple Mac, Linux), cross-browser (i.e., available on different Internet browsers—Microsoft Internet Explorer, Mozilla Firefox, Apple Safari, Google Chrome), and cross-device (i.e., available on computers, mobile devices).

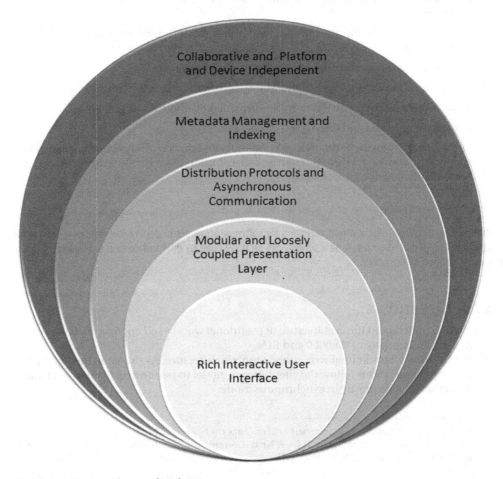

Figure 1-2. *Key attributes of Web 2.0*

Rich Internet Applications

RIAs are web-based applications incorporating the previously described key attributes of the Web 2.0 concept. Following is a simplified definition of RIA:[2]

> *Rich Internet applications (RIAs) are web applications that have the features and functionality of traditional desktop applications.*

From the end users' perspective, RIAs enable end users to collaborate information (content and media) securely and provide effective data search and social-networking capabilities with rich user interface. RIAs' user interfaces are usually high performing, interactive, and intuitive, and as such deliver rich user experiences.

As defined in a white paper published by Macromedia in 2002,[3] RIAs from a technology perspective should have the following capabilities:

- Provide an efficient, high-performance runtime for executing code, content, and communications.

- Integrate content, communications, and application interfaces into a common environment.

- Provide powerful and extensible object models for interactivity.

- Enable rapid application development through components and reuse.

- Enable the use of web and data services provided by application servers.

- Embrace connected and disconnected clients.

- Enable easy deployment on multiple platforms and devices. If designed correctly, RIAs can support the concept of development and distribution of service-oriented software applications as software as a service (SaaS).

■**Note** SaaS is a software deployment approach for software providers to deploy software as a service for public consumption. The deployed software as a service can be consumed by different consumers based on the subscription policies defined by providers.

RIA Architecture

It is essential to understand the architecture of traditional web-based applications before you understand the architecture of Web 2.0 and RIAs.

Figure 1-3 shows a traditional web application's architecture. As shown in the figure, these traditional client applications follow the client-server model to perform all the user requests and actions on the server side mostly in synchronous mode.

---

2. Wikipedia, http://en.wikipedia.org/wiki/Rich_Internet_application
3. Jeremy Allaire, "Macromedia Flash MX—A Next-Generation Rich Client," http://www.adobe.com/devnet/flash/whitepapers/richclient.pdf

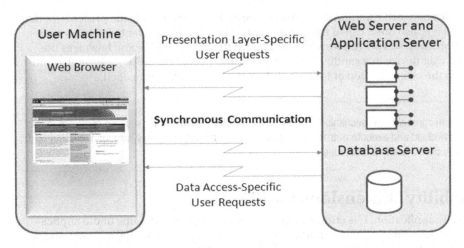

Figure 1-3. *Traditional (thin client) web-based application architecture*

Due to the sequential execution model and limitations of the rendered HTML user interface, traditional web applications lack the rich, creative, and interactive user interfaces of desktop applications. They lack the high-performing and modular application design that allows asynchronous communication between client and server in the background.

Figure 1-4 shows the typical RIA architecture. RIAs follow a hybrid approach to process user requests and actions. The presentation layer–related user requests and actions are performed at the web client side, and the data process–related user requests and actions are mainly performed at the server side asynchronously.

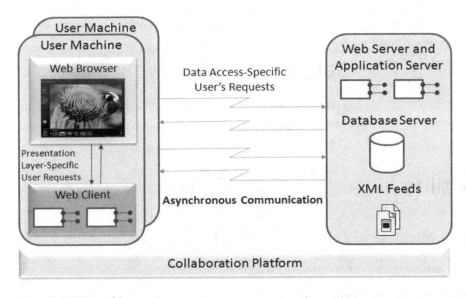

Figure 1-4. *RIA architecture*

The key difference between traditional web-based applications and RIAs is the presence of the web client layer, which is also often called the *client engine*. The web client layer helps to process the RIA's presentation layer–related requests and actions on the user machine and leverages the resources of the end user device in a sandbox environment. It also enables the asynchronous communication between the client and server to fetch and cache data before it is needed.

Note The *sandbox environment* is a mechanism to provide a restricted, isolated, and secured environment on the client machine to download and execute untrusted RIA components and code securely without accessing and having an impact on key client machine resources.

The Five Usability Dimensions for RIAs

Before developing any application, it is critical to understand the vision and scope of the application. In addition, especially for RIAs, it is important to choose the right technology platform and set of technology components because RIA technology is evolving all the time.

A paper published by Keynote Systems[4] defines four key dimensions of application usability that are essential for measuring the success of a web application—*availability, responsiveness, clarity,* and *utility*. I would add *safety* as a fifth usability dimension. Figure 1-5 shows the five dimensions of application usability.

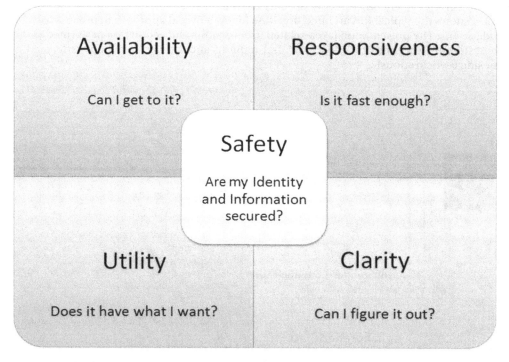

Figure 1-5. *The five dimensions of application usability*

---

4.   Chris Loosely, "Application usability dimensions—Rich Internet Applications: Design, Measurement, and Management Challenges," http://www.keynote.com/docs/whitepapers/RichInternet_5.pdf, 2006

I will cover the five dimensions of application usability in Chapter 4 in more detail. However, I wanted to mention them in this first chapter because I think it is important to know and keep in mind these usability dimensions before you really start exploring the Silverlight technology platform.

Technologies That Support RIAs

So far we have discussed the high-level vision and key attributes of Web 2.0 and the key features of RIAs. Unfortunately, there is no single technology available in today's market to develop RIAs fulfilling the Web 2.0 vision. This section of the book provides a high-level overview of the available technologies supporting the development of rich, interactive RIAs.

Microsoft ASP.NET AJAX

As described on the Microsoft ASP.NET web site:[5]

> *ASP.NET AJAX is a free scripting framework for quickly creating efficient and interactive Web applications that works across all popular browsers.*

Microsoft ASP.NET AJAX is an enhanced version of JavaScript. Its client- and server-side libraries are tightly integrated with Visual Studio 2008 and is included as part of the Microsoft .NET Framework 3.5 SDK. The client-side library allows you to implement client-level processing such as end-user-entered information processing and validation, refreshing a portion of the web page and developing rich, interactive user interfaces. You can also efficiently integrate the client-side library components with the server-side ASP.NET controls library in asynchronous mode.

However, ASP.NET AJAX is not an ideal solution for developing enterprise-level RIAs. The key technology driver of ASP.NET AJAX is scripting. In general, script-based web applications face several challenges due to different browser settings (e.g., JavaScript is not enabled by default) on PCs and mobile devices. ASP.NET AJAX supports only limited features of RIAs and does not support effective multimedia integration, managed code-behind integration, or metadata and information management.

ASP.NET AJAX does have asynchronous communication capabilities. However, due to the nature of the implementation, the web application must continuously pull data from the server to get the latest updates, which ultimately slows down overall application performance.

In conclusion, ASP.NET AJAX is a good place to start to transform your traditional web-based applications to RIAs. Often scripting is not always the best strategy for enterprises to develop secured and scalable RIAs. ASP.NET AJAX's script-based approach and the previously mentioned limitations raise many concerns about the security, compatibility, and maintainability of ASP.NET AJAX web applications. Thus many enterprises may hesitate to develop enterprise-level RIAs using only ASP. NET AJAX technology.

The PageFlakes web site (http://www.pageflakes.com/Default.asp) is a very good example demonstrating the use of ASP.NET AJAX. This page demonstrates key RIA features like modular design, asynchronous communication, and user customization with the use of ASP.NET AJAX.

---

5.   Microsoft ASP.NET AJAX Definition, http://www.asp.net/ajax/default.aspx?wwwaspnetrdirset=1

Java Applets

As described on the Java Sun web site:[6]

> *[A Java] applet is a special kind of Java program that a browser enabled with Java technology can download from the Internet and run. An applet is typically embedded inside a web page and runs in the context of the browser.*

A Java applet is a browser plug-in that is cross-browser and cross-platform. Java applets use the Java Virtual Machine (JVM) incorporated within the end user browser to execute and run in a sandbox environment on the end user machine.

Using the Java platform, it is possible to develop interactive and heavy graphical RIAs with offline capabilities. With the use of Java server-side component libraries, they can perform asynchronous communication.

Java applets have limitations similar to the ASP.NET AJAX technology. Users' browsers should be Java enabled, and the Java Runtime Environment (JRE) needs to be installed on users' machines to run Java applets successfully. Java applets support only limited features of RIAs. It would be challenging to develop a rich, interactive user interface with the media streaming and metadata management capabilities of RIAs in rapid application development (RAD) mode using the Java applets and supporting Java technology components.

Adobe Flash, Adobe Flex, and Adobe AIR

As described on the Adobe Flash product site:[7]

> *[Adobe Flash] software is an advanced authoring environment for creating rich, interactive content for digital, web, and mobile platforms.*

Adobe Flash is one of the most popular web browser plug-ins for displaying animation and audio and video streaming on web sites. Adobe Flash provides ActionScript—a scripting language—for developing animation and multimedia streaming.

Adobe Flash does not provide an efficient development platform to build interactive and complex RIAs, but it is the most suitable tool for creating interactive plug-ins for web applications.

To meet the need for an efficient development platform for enterprise-level RIAs, Adobe has developed Adobe Flex, which basically is an enhancement to Adobe Flash. As described on the Adobe Flex product site:[8]

> *[Adobe Flex] is a . . . free open source framework for building and maintaining expressive web applications that deploy consistently on all major browsers, desktops, and operating systems.*

The Adobe Flex development platform provides a rich UI component library and uses MXML, a declarative XML-based language to develop rich, interactive user interfaces. The ActionScript programming language is used to implement the business service layer.

Adobe is making some serious moves to enhance its platform so you can use it not just for developing rich, interactive user interfaces and integrating multimedia elements, but also for

---

6. Java Applet Definition, http://java.sun.com/docs/books/tutorial/deployment/applet/index.html
7. Adobe Flash Definition, http://www.adobe.com/products/flash/
8. Adobe Flex Definition, http://www.adobe.com/products/flex/

developing desktop applications that can seamlessly integrate with RIAs. In addition to Adobe Flash and Adobe Flex, in February 2008 Adobe introduced Adobe AIR for developing desktop applications that we can extend as RIAs. As described on the Adobe AIR product site:[9]

> *[Adobe AIR] lets developers use proven web technologies to build rich Internet applications that deploy to the desktop and run across operating systems.*

Figure 1-6 shows the eBay desktop application developed utilizing Adobe AIR and Adobe Flex. The eBay application demonstrates the power of the offline capabilities of the RIA.

Figure 1-6. *eBay desktop application developed using Adobe Flex and Adobe AIR*

Microsoft Silverlight

As described on the Microsoft Silverlight web site:[10]

> *Microsoft Silverlight is a cross-browser, cross-platform, and cross-device plug-in for delivering the next generation of .NET-based media experiences and rich interactive applications for the Web.*

Microsoft Silverlight is a subset of Windows Presentation Foundation (WPF), which is part of .NET Framework 3.5. Silverlight is integrated with the broad range of Microsoft tools and services

---

9. Adobe AIR Definition, http://www.adobe.com/products/air/
10. Microsoft Silverlight Definition, http://silverlight.net/

like Microsoft Visual Studio 2008, Microsoft Expression Blend, Microsoft Deep Zoom Composer, and Microsoft Silverlight Streaming by Windows Live for the easy development and deployment of Silverlight-based multimedia RIAs.

Microsoft partnered with NBC Universal for the Beijing 2008 Olympic Games[11] and successfully demonstrated the capabilities and power of the Microsoft Silverlight technology in the commercial RIA market. NBC's Olympics web site (http://www.nbcolympics.com) featured more than 2,000 hours of live content and 3,000 hours of on-demand video for Olympics lovers. The Silverlight technology enabled NBC to develop the Control Room feature, presenting video picture-in-picture capability that let viewers watch up to four events at the same time.

Figure 1-7 presents a page from the NBC Olympics web site featuring Silverlight-based video streaming.

Figure 1-7. *Beijing 2008 Olympics game videos on NBC's Olympics web site featuring Microsoft Silverlight*

---

11. Ina Fried, "What It Takes to Bring the Olympics to the PC," http://news.cnet.com/8301-13860_3-10003752-56.html?tag=nefd.lede, 2008

Figure 1-8 shows the Silverlight Olympic 2008 plug-in on the MSN web site (http://www.msn.com) during the Beijing 2008 Olympics.

Figure 1-8. *Olympics Silverlight plug-in on the MSN web site*

Applying a Balancing Act When Selecting Technology Components

It is very clear from the discussion in the preceding sections that one technology is not enough to develop intuitive RIAs. Although I will cover this in more detail in the later part of the book (in Chapters 3 and 4), in summary it is recommended you apply a balancing act (see Figure 1-9) in the selection of the right set of technology components to develop and deploy RIAs successfully. The selection of technology components must align with your organization's strategic vision, your customers' requirements, the product roadmap, and the technology roadmap for long-term success and to gain maximum ROI.

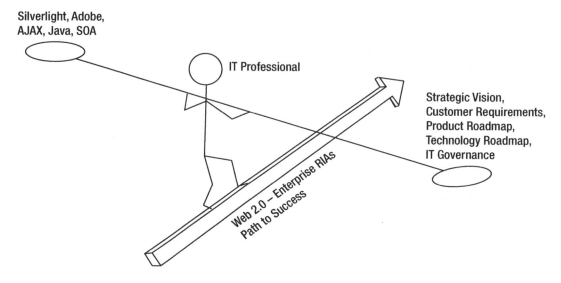

Figure 1-9. *Applying a "balancing act" in the selection of the right Web 2.0 technologies to develop Enterprise RIAs*

Examining the Silverlight Platform

This book is mainly focused on the Microsoft Silverlight technology. You will see how Silverlight can be utilized to develop service-oriented enterprise RIAs that fulfill the Web 2.0 vision. Before we dive into the details of Silverlight for the enterprise, let's take a high-level look at Silverlight and its available versions and key components. This book assumes that you are already aware of the Silverlight technology and how to build basic applications using Silverlight 2. If you are a newcomer to Silverlight and the following section is not sufficient to get started with Silverlight 2, please read the online materials and books mentioned in the "Additional References" section of this chapter.

As described earlier, Microsoft Silverlight provides a platform to develop cross-browser, cross-platform, and cross-device RIAs. All versions of Silverlight are a subset of WPF and use XAML (Extensible Application Markup Language), an XML-based language that facilitates externalized and loosely coupled definitions of the user interface and related style sheets.

Different Versions of Silverlight

At present, two versions of Microsoft Silverlight—Silverlight 1 and Silverlight 2—are available.

Silverlight 1

After having a great showcase at Mix 2007 in May 2007, Microsoft Silverlight 1 (earlier known by the code name WPF/E—Windows Presentation Foundation/Everywhere), along with Microsoft Expression Encoder 1.0, was released in September 2007 as the first version of Silverlight. Silverlight 1 is a very rudimentary release of the product and mainly focuses on the development of Rich Media Internet Applications (RMIAs). It contains rich media presentation framework–related core components like UI controls handling the rendering of 2D vector graphics, media, animation, and simplified user input management. The Silverlight Media Player controls support the WMA, WMV, and MP3 formats of media files. Silverlight 1 is also capable of using JavaScript with Document Object Model (DOM) integration to manipulate the UI.

■**Note** The RMIA is a type of RIA containing a subset of RIA attributes. RMIA-type applications/plug-ins are mainly focused on media (audio and video) streaming features.

Even though Silverlight 1 has limited features and limited support for development, when it was released, it was highly respected in the commercial market and created a buzz. Along with the Major League Baseball web site (http://www.mlb.com), many major commercial sites adopted Silverlight 1 to provide rich media experiences. Microsoft also provided some great sample sites like the Tafiti search front end (http://www.tafiti.com/), powered by the MSN search engine to explain the Silverlight technology and RIA concepts.

Silverlight 2

The next landmark version of Silverlight was released as Silverlight 2 in October 2008. It is a big leap from the first basic version to version 2. Silverlight 2 is enhanced in the following areas:

- Enhanced support for the Microsoft .NET Framework 3.5 with the Common Language Runtime (CLR). The support for the CLR enables the integration of Microsoft .NET managed code-behind using default Microsoft .NET class libraries in Silverlight 2 projects.

- Enhanced Base Class Library (BCL) and Language-Integrated Query (LINQ) integration to develop complex enterprise RIAs.

- Additional UI components to support the development of RIAs featuring rich multimedia functionalities.

- Enhanced media management supporting secured multimedia streaming.

- Enhanced networking support including policy-based cross-domain networking to support different types of application deployment.

- Support for the open source and cross-platform Eclipse development platform via Eclipse Tools for Microsoft Silverlight: eclipse4SL (http://www.eclipse4SL.org).

- Improvement of the interoperability features of Silverlight due to the Silverlight XAML schema vocabulary specification (MS-SLXV) released under the Open Specification Promise (OSP) (http://msdn.microsoft.com/en-us/library/dd361850(PROT.10).aspx).

Silverlight 2 and Development Tools Quick Links

Along with Silverlight 2, you can download the following supporting development tools from `http://silverlight.net/GetStarted/`:

- *Microsoft Silverlight Tools for Visual Studio 2008 SP1* enables you to develop Silverlight 2–based applications using Visual Studio 2008 SP1 IDE.

- *Microsoft Expression Blend 2 SP1* is tightly integrated with Visual Studio 2008 SP1 and allows artists and designers to create rich XAML-based user interfaces for Silverlight applications.

- *Deep Zoom Composer* allows professionals to create and prepare images to implement the Deep Zoom feature within Silverlight applications.

- *Microsoft Expression Encoder 2* contains Silverlight Media Player templates to author, manage, and publish media for Silverlight applications. Visit `http://www.microsoft.com/expression` and look for the Microsoft Expression Encoder within the Express product suite.

- *Eclipse Tools for Microsoft Silverlight (eclipse4SL)* enables development of Silverlight applications using the Eclipse open source and cross-platform development platform. You can install this tool set by visiting `http://www.eclipse4sl.org/download/link`.

Silverlight 3

Microsoft never stops improving its technology. By the time you have this book in your hands, it is very likely that the Silverlight 3 beta release will be available.

As mentioned by the corporate vice president of Microsoft's developer division on his blog,[12] Silverlight 3 is to be released in the latter part of 2009. Based on the currently available knowledge, the new version will mainly include enhancements in graphics capabilities (support for 3D graphics), media management (support for H.264 video), and application development areas (additional controls and enhanced data binding support). There are also plans for the enhancements of the Visual Studio and Expression Blend development tools to develop Silverlight RIAs more effectively.

A few introductory sessions on Silverlight 3 are planned for the MIX09 conference (`http://visitmix.com/News/Silverlight-3-Sessions-at-MIX09`).

Note This book is written in the context of utilizing enterprise capabilities to develop Silverlight-based service-oriented RIAs and adopting Silverlight in your organization. All technical concepts are Silverlight version (specifically, Silverlight 2 and 3) agnostic. Based on the current knowledge on the enhancements in Silverlight 3, the RIAs developed in this book should work with minimal or no changes.

---

12. Scott Guthrie, "Update on Silverlight 2—and a Glimpse of Silverlight 3," `http://weblogs.asp.net/scottgu/archive/2008/11/16/update-on-silverlight-2-and-a-glimpse-of-silverlight-3.aspx`

Silverlight Architecture

Figure 1-10 shows the architecture of Silverlight. It also highlights new enhancements introduced in the Microsoft Silverlight 2 version.

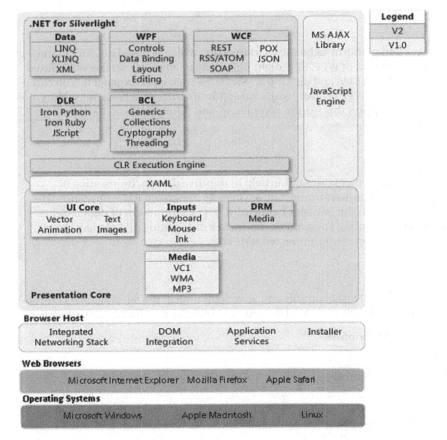

Figure 1-10. *Silverlight architecture[13]*

Note Figure 1-10 is modified from the original diagram to demonstrate the concept of platform independence.

Silverlight Is Platform Independent

Silverlight is a lightweight, platform-independent technology. Silverlight applications are

- Cross-platform and can run successfully on different operating systems—Microsoft Windows and Apple Mac
- Cross-browser and can run successfully on different well-known web browsers—Microsoft Internet Explorer, Mozilla Firefox, Apple Safari, and Google Chrome
- Cross-device and can run successfully on PCs and handheld mobile devices

13. Silverlight Architecture, http://msdn.microsoft.com/en-us/library/bb404713(VS.95).aspx

Presentation Core

Compared to Silverlight 1, Silverlight 2 includes significant enhancements in the areas of UI framework, media management, user controls and graphics, and animation support to implement the rich, interactive presentation layer of RIAs.

UI Framework

Silverlight 2 delivers a robust and platform-agnostic UI framework, which is based on .NET Framework 3.5, WPF, and XAML. As a subset of WPF, Silverlight ultimately enables us to reuse WPF-based components for web browser–based RIAs and desktop applications such as Vista gadgets. You can also convert Silverlight 2 projects to WPF projects with some effort in order to achieve reusability. However, Silverlight 2 does not support this feature completely, and future releases may possibly extend this reusability feature.

Media Management

Silverlight's capabilities for adaptive media streaming help to improve the synchronization of media, which ultimately provides high-performing and seamlessly integrated RMIAs by automatically adjusting the bit rates based on the network bandwidth. The introduction of digital rights management (DRM) for media streaming encourages enterprises distributing digital media to utilize Silverlight applications to develop media-protected RMIAs.

User Controls

As part of the default Silverlight XAML user controls and Silverlight toolkit, the Silverlight UI controls library contains a set of basic and advanced XAML UI controls, which fall into four main categories:

- Layout management XAML controls
- Form XAML controls
- Data manipulation XAML controls
- Functional XAML controls

These controls are available with full source code and with an OSI license that allows professionals to modify them to meet their expectations.

Note The Open Source Initiative, or OSI (http://www.opensource.org), manages the Open Source Definition (OSD) and provides open source licenses to the products that pass the OSI approval process and comply with OSD.

You will see more details in the "Quick Overview of Silverlight 2's Key Components" section, which will walk you through development of a simple and basic user interface to reinforce some key concepts.

With the help of Expression Blend, Silverlight 2 supports user control templates, which allow us to modify the shape and look of control templates very easily. Silverlight 2 also enables the Visual State Manager (VSM) feature with the help of Expression Blend. The visual state and state transition features of VSM enable us to customize the interaction of the Silverlight control templates with their Normal, MouseOver, Pressed, Disabled, Focused, and Unfocused events.

Silverlight 2 downloads the core UI controls as part of the initial application installation to minimize runtime downloads. This feature improves overall application performance. However, you can decide during the design phase how and when to download components. Applying a balancing act, enhanced UI controls like `DataGrid` and `TabControl` can be referenced and downloaded at runtime when they are referenced.

Graphics and Animation Support

The Microsoft Silverlight Deep Zoom feature provides us the ability to smoothly present and navigate large amounts of visual information regardless of the size of the data, and optimizes the bandwidth available to download it.[14] A very good example of Deep Zoom is available on the Hard Rock memorabilia web site (`http://memorabilia.hardrock.com/`), developed by Vertigo and presented during the Microsoft Mix 2008 conference in March 2008.

Along with the Deep Zoom feature, Microsoft Silverlight supports object animation and embedded code-based animation to provide high-performing graphics and animation support.

Microsoft .NET for Silverlight

Compared to Silverlight 1, Silverlight 2 introduces tight .NET integration by providing support for the CLR. This support allows professionals to implement managed code-behind .NET integration and support for WCF/Web Services, LINQ, and service-oriented features.

Managed Code-Behind .NET Integration

Support for the .NET Framework 3.5 with the CLR, and thus support for .NET managed code-behind code using the default .NET class libraries, is a key enhancement in Silverlight 2. The CLR basically provides memory management, garbage collection, type-safety checking, and exception handling. Additionally, the BCL contains a set of components that provide basic programming capabilities like string handling, regular expressions, input and output, reflection, collections, and globalization.

The Dynamic Language Runtime (DLR) supports the dynamic compilation and execution of scripting languages like JavaScript and IronPython to develop Silverlight-based applications. It also includes a pluggable model for adding support for other languages to Silverlight.

Note IronPython is an implementation of the Python programming language integrated with the .NET Framework, which is compatible with the Python language. For more details, visit `http://www.codeplex.com/IronPython`.

Data/Information Integration

Silverlight 2 provides us with asynchronous, loosely coupled data-integration capabilities. The rich user controls library is capable of binding and presenting data in a rich manner. It is capable of integrating with WCF and Web Services via REST, WS*/SOAP, POX, RSS, and standard HTTP, enabling us to perform various data transactions with external data (e.g., XML, relational databases). And last but not least is its integration with ADO.NET data services, LINQ, LINQ to XML and XLinq for data transformation, and local data caching with isolated data storage capabilities, which empower the Silverlight technology platform to develop high-performing data and media-centric RIAs.

---

14. Jaime Rodriguez, "A Deep Zoom Primer," `http://blogs.msdn.com/jaimer/archive/2008/03/31/a-deepzoom-primer-explained-and-coded.aspx`

Networking Support

Silverlight applications are capable of background threading and asynchronous communication, which helps to separate user interface interaction from other server-side processes to improve the overall application performance and provide a rich user experience.

Silverlight also supports JSON-based service integration. LINQ to JSON support enables us to query, filter, and map JSON results to .NET objects within a Silverlight application, which makes integration with existing AJAX-based applications and services easy.

Silverlight supports policy-based application development and deployment with cross-domain networking using HTTP and sockets.

Note JSON (JavaScript Object Notation) is a lightweight data-interchange language-independent text format language. It is based on a subset of the JavaScript programming language, Standard ECMA-262 Third Edition, December 1999. For more details, visit http://www.json.org/.

Quick Overview of Silverlight 2's Key Components

Before we develop our first basic application in the next chapter, I want to give you a quick overview of key components of Silverlight 2.

Defining User Interfaces in Silverlight

As Silverlight is a subset of WPF, the key technology for defining Silverlight application user interfaces is WPF and XAML. XAML UI controls are the building blocks to develop RIAs.

Figure 1-11 shows all the default basic Silverlight XAML UI controls available in Visual Studio as part of Silverlight 2. The same controls are also available in Expression Blend.

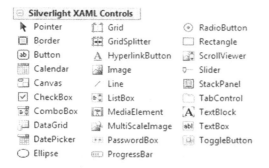

Figure 1-11. *Microsoft Silverlight 2 XAML UI controls*

As described earlier, we can divide the default XAML UI controls into four categories:

- *Layout management XAML controls* are the key basic controls of any Silverlight application and act as the containers for hosting and positioning different UI controls including other layout controls (as subcontainers). Three types of layout controls are available in the XAML controls library:

  - Canvas is a very basic and straightforward layout control that hosts user controls with absolute position relative to the canvas area.

- `StackPanel` layout controls are used to stack/group user controls horizontally or vertically in relative position.

- `Grid` layout controls are the most commonly used layout control and can group user controls in defined row and column positions (the same as tables do in HTML).

- *Form XAML controls* help users to perform different actions like entering text or selecting options. `TextBox`, `RadioButton`, and `CheckBox` controls are examples of form XAML controls.

- *Data manipulation XAML controls* manage data manipulation, and you can use them to display data in whatever format you choose. `DataGrid` and `ListBox` controls are examples of data manipulation XAML controls.

- *Functional XAML controls* help end users display information in a usable manner to perform different actions such as date selection to control application behavior (using the Slider UI control). `Calendar`, `DatePicker`, `ScrollViewer`, and `Slider` XAML controls are examples of functional XAML controls.

You can extend the scope of the Silverlight XAML controls library by using the Silverlight toolkit (downloadable from `http://www.codeplex.com/Silverlight`) and third-party controls (explained later in this chapter).

I'm assuming that you know how to create and test a Silverlight project. However, let's create a very simple Silverlight application as an example just to illustrate the different types of XAML user controls to get you up and running. Figure 1-12 presents the simple Silverlight survey application user interface we are going to develop. Hopefully, the question shown in the figure will also refresh your memory about the discussion we had on the use of which technology to develop RIAs with.

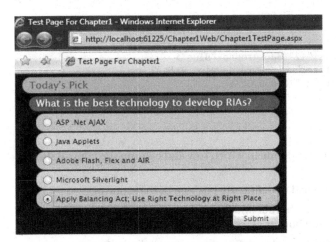

Figure 1-12. *XAML voting screen of the Silverlight web application*

For any Silverlight application, we need to select the main layout XAML controls. For this application, we have options to use the `StackPanel` or `Grid` layout control. In this case, let's use the `Grid` control. The following code snippet defines these aspects of the application:

- The background of the main `Grid` container is black.

- We need seven rows in the `Grid` each of height 30, which we define with the `RowDefinition` control.

- Each row will have one column with a width of 400 defined by the `ColumnDefinition` control. Since our sample application needs only one column, the width of which is also matched with the main user control's width, the column definition is optional for us.

```
<Grid x:Name="LayoutRoot" Background="Black">
    <Grid.RowDefinitions>
      <RowDefinition Height="30" />
      <RowDefinition Height="30" />
      <RowDefinition Height="30" />
      <RowDefinition Height="30" />
      <RowDefinition Height="30" />
      <RowDefinition Height="30" />
      <RowDefinition Height="30" />
      <RowDefinition Height="30" />
    </Grid.RowDefinitions>

    <Grid.ColumnDefinitions>
      <ColumnDefinition Width="400"/>
    </Grid.ColumnDefinitions>

  </Grid>
```

Now we have to define in each row the other XAML controls that we need for our sample application.

The first two rows contain simple text with different background colors. For that we use the TextBlock XAML control to display text as demonstrated in the following code snippet:

```
<Grid Grid.Row="0" Margin="10,5,10,0">
  <Border Grid.Column="0" CornerRadius="12" Background="Aqua">
    <TextBlock Text="Today's Pick" Foreground="Blue" Margin="10,2,0,0"/>
  </Border>
</Grid>

<Grid Grid.Row="1" Margin="20,5,10,2">
  <Border Grid.Column="0" CornerRadius="12" Background="Blue">
    <TextBlock Text="What is the best technology to develop RIAs?"
               Foreground="White" Margin="10,0,0,0"/>
  </Border>
</Grid>
```

As shown in the code snippet:

- The Grid.Row and Grid.Column attributes define in which row and column the control should be placed.

- The Margin property of the control is used to define the position of that control.

- The Border control is used to provide the border and/or background of the other control. Here we have used Border to define the border of the TextBlock control.

- The TextBlock control's Text property is used to define the static text in the first two rows.

- The CornerRadius property of the control is used to define the rounded angle of the control.

We'll use the RadioButton control to define all the options. These options are grouped within the Group1 named group by using the GroupName property of the RadioButton. Each option's description is defined using the Content property of the RadioButton control.

The following is a sample snapshot of the first option in our application. You can define the other options in a similar way.

```
<Grid Grid.Row="2" Margin="30,2,10,0">
  <Border Grid.Column="0" CornerRadius="12" Background="LightGreen">
    <RadioButton Content="ASP .Net AJAX" GroupName="Group1" Foreground="Black"
  Margin="10,0,0,0"/>
```

```
    </Border>
</Grid>
```

Finally, we need a button to submit the user's selection. For that we'll use the `Button` XAML control and name it with the `x:Name` property. The value defined in the `x:Name` property will be used to identify the control in the code-behind file.

```
<Button x:Name="btnSubmit" Content="Submit" Grid.Row="7" Width="70"
        Height="25" Margin="310,5,0,0"/>
```

Third-Party Silverlight Controls

In addition to the broad range of XAML controls provided by Microsoft, a number of well-known third-party Microsoft Partners have developed extended Silverlight XAML controls. This section provides information about Microsoft Partners providing extended XAML controls for Silverlight.

ComponentOne

ComponentOne has released Studio for Silverlight, providing enhanced controls covering layout, navigation, data input, grids, charts, data binding, data compression, and enhanced functionality (e.g., `MessageBox`, `ImageRotator`, `Book`, `Map`, `DragDropManager`). You can get more details on these controls by visiting `http://labs.componentone.com/`.

Infragistics

Infragistics' NetAdvantage for Silverlight Data Visualization provides about 28 chart types (including area, bar, column, line, spline, scatter, point, pie, doughnut, and stack charts) and gauges to enable data-driven RIAs. You can get more details on these controls by visiting `http://www.infragistics.com/` and clicking "Experience Silverlight."

Telerik

Telerik provides about 19 extended Silverlight controls to feature enhanced layout, form input, and data binding to help with rich user experiences and data virtualization. You can get more details on these controls by visiting `http://www.telerik.com/products/silverlight/overview.aspx`.

Developer Express

Developer Express (Devexpress) provides the enhanced Silverlight `Grid` control, which provides rich data integration. You can get more details on this control by visiting `http://www.devexpress.com/Products/NET/Controls/Silverlight/Grid/`.

Event Integration: Managed Code and Scripting Programming Models

XAML is a declarative language defining objects and related attributes/properties for the application user interface. In addition, it is capable of integrating event handling as JavaScript or code-behind managed code. `x:Class` is the key attribute for defining the attached programming model of a XAML-based page. If the `x:Class` attribute is defined at the root level of the XAML page, the managed code-behind file must exist and contain the event handlers related to the XAML user controls defined in the XAML page. If you don't define the `x:Class` attribute at the root level, there is no need for a code-behind file, and the application will use JavaScript. In this case, the event functions are not compiled at design time like managed code, but the function will be called at runtime when the end user initiates the event. You'll see an example of each of these approaches in the upcoming text.

The x:Class attribute at the root element of the XAML page defines the CLR namespace and class name to implement the code-behind event integration. In the preceding example, we use a managed code-behind file for event integration. To achieve that, the x:Class attribute of the root-level element UserControl is defined with the Chapter1.Page value, defining the CLR namespace as Chapter1 (see the following code snippet).

```
<UserControl x:Class="Chapter1.Page"
    xmlns="http://schemas.microsoft.com/winfx/2006/xaml/presentation"
    xmlns:x="http://schemas.microsoft.com/winfx/2006/xaml"
    Width="400" Height="250">
```

As an example, the Submit button would need to have a button click event to submit the user's entered information. To achieve that, you can add the Button "btnSubmit" Click event in the XAML code as shown in the following code snippet:

```
<Button x:Name="btnSubmit" Content="Submit" Grid.Row="7" Width="70"
        Height="25" Margin="310,5,0,0" Click="btnSubmit_Click"/>
```

Following is the code snippet of the associated Submit button click event, btnSubmit_Click, of the associated Page code-behind class:

```
private void btnSubmit_Click(object sender, RoutedEventArgs e)
{
    //Your Custom Code Goes Here.
    //=============================
}
```

You can achieve the same type of functionalities using the JavaScript. Let's see how the JavaScript event handling works. The following code snippet shows that the Canvas layout control is at the root level and there is no x:Class attribute. The function name getUserProfile() is defined in the JavaScript file HandleXAMLEvents.js linked to in the <script> tag. The getUserProfile() function will be called on the Loaded event of the TextBlock XAML user control.

```
<html>
    <head>
        ----

        <!-- JavaScript File Managing XAML Controls Events -->
        <script type="text/javascript" src="HandleXAMLEvents.js"></script>

        ----
    </head>

    <body>
      ----

      <!-- Define XAML content. -->
      <script type="text/xaml" id="xamlContent"> <?xml version="1.0"?>

        <Canvas xmlns=http://schemas.microsoft.com/client/2007>

          <TextBlock Canvas.Left="10" FontSize="12" Loaded="getUserProfile"/>

        </Canvas>

      </script>
```

```
    ----
    </body>

</html>
```

Data Binding

The data binding feature of Silverlight enables data display and user interaction with that data for Silverlight applications. Figure 1-13 shows the conceptual flow of data binding between the data object and a Silverlight control's data-bound property. Based on the value of the binding Mode property, the flow of the data between the data object and control is determined as follows:

- OneTime binding updates the control (the binding target) with the data object (the binding source) only when the binding is created.

- OneWay binding updates the control (the binding target) with the data object (the binding source) when the binding is created and in the future whenever the data is changed at the binding source level.

- TwoWay binding updates the control (the binding target) and data object (the binding source) whenever the user changes the data at the binding target level or data changes at the data source level.

For OneWay and TwoWay bindings, the binding source object must implement the INotifyPropertyChanged interface in the System.ComponentModel namespace for it to notify the binding target of any changes. The default value of the binding mode depends on the control type. For most form XAML user controls that are usually user-editable, the default binding mode is set to TwoWay. The XAML user controls that are not user editable have the default binding mode set to OneWay.

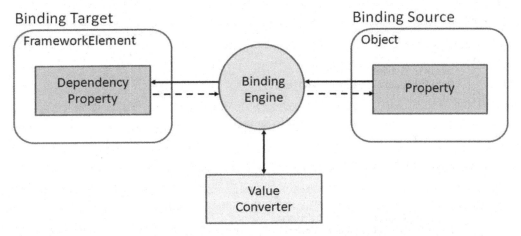

Figure 1-13. *Silverlight data binding[15]*

Note Figure 1-13 is modified from the original diagram to demonstrate TwoWay data binding.

---

15. Data Binding for Silverlight, http://msdn.microsoft.com/en-us/library/cc278072(VS.95).aspx

The following code snippet demonstrates OneWay data binding with the TextBlock control and its Subject type field. The Text property is bound to the Subject value.

```
<TextBlock Name="Subject" Grid.Row="0" Grid.Column="0"
        Text="{Binding Path=Subject, Mode=OneWay}"/>
```

The following code snippet demonstrates OneWay data binding with the ListBox control. The ItemsSource property is bound to the Courses collection.

```
<ListBox x:Name="Courses" ItemsSource="{Binding Path=Courses, Mode=OneWay}"
        Height="60" Width="200" Grid.Row="1" Grid.Column="0" />
```

As explained earlier, for OneWay and TwoWay bindings, the data source object must implement the INotifyPropertyChanged interface. The following code snippet presents the implementation of the INotifyPropertyChanged interface for the properties Subject and Courses used for the data source binding in our preceding example:

```
using System;
using System.Collections.Generic;
using System.ComponentModel;

    public class Training : INotifyPropertyChanged
    {
        private string trainingSubject;
        private List<string> trainingCourses;
        // Declaring PropertyChanged event
        public event PropertyChangedEventHandler PropertyChanged;

        //Properties used for Data Source Binding

        public string Subject
        {
            get { return trainingSubject; }

            set
            {
                trainingSubject = value;
                NotifyPropertyChanged("Subject");
            }
        }

        public List<string> Courses
        {
            get { return trainingCourses; }

            set
            {
                trainingCourses = value;
                NotifyPropertyChanged("Courses");
            }
        }

        //Raise the PropertyChanged event passing
        //the source property that is being updated.

        public void NotifyPropertyChanged(string propertyName)
        {
            if (PropertyChanged != null)
            {
```

```
            PropertyChanged(this, new PropertyChangedEventArgs(propertyName));
        }
    }
}
```

Microsoft Tools to Developing Silverlight Applications

The main goal of the Microsoft Silverlight technology platform is to develop RIAs in the RAD mode, making the lives of developers, designers, and artists easier. This section will give a high-level overview of the different development and designer tools provided by Microsoft to develop Silverlight-based RIAs.

Microsoft Visual Studio 2008 SP1

Microsoft Silverlight Tools for Visual Studio 2008 SP1 enables developers to develop Silverlight 2–based applications using the very familiar Visual Studio 2008 development platform. Microsoft Visual Studio 2008 allows you to develop Silverlight applications using the following templates:

- *The Silverlight Application project template* is used to develop Silverlight 2–based applications and includes all the required configuration, assembly references, and code-behind files to support development, testing, and deployment of Silverlight applications.

- *The Silverlight Class Library project template* is used to develop reusable user interface and code-behind components as library assemblies that can be included and deployed in multiple Silverlight applications as in-package (included in the Silverlight application deployment package) and on-demand (referenced assemblies downloadable at runtime upon request) files.

Microsoft Expression Studio 2 SP1

Microsoft Expression Studio is a set of graphical tools for graphical designers and artists to manage and develop digital media and content and present it in Silverlight-based RIAs. It has the following components:

- *Microsoft Expression Blend* helps user interface designers and artists to develop vector-based 2D and 3D XAML-based web and desktop user interfaces (for inclusion in Silverlight applications). It is also integrated with Visual Studio, enabling designers and developers to rapidly develop, debug, and test Silverlight applications in integrated mode.

- *Microsoft Expression Design* is a vector and raster graphic design tool that can be well integrated with Expression Blend.

- *Microsoft Expression Media* is a media management tool that allows users to build and track a digital media catalog. It also enables professionals to edit, tag, archive, back up, and deploy digital media, as well as transform it from one format to another. The deployed digital media can be used within Silverlight applications.

- *Microsoft Expression Encoder* contains several Silverlight Media Player templates to write, manage, and publish media in VC-1 quality for Silverlight applications.

Note VC-1 is a SMPTE (Society of Motion Picture and Television Engineers) standard codec that is a part of both HD-DVD and Blu-ray high-definition optical disk specifications.

- *Microsoft Expression Deep Zoom Composer* allows professionals to create and export high-resolution Deep Zoom composition tiled image files that can be deployed to enable in-place zooming and panning features for images in Silverlight applications.

Microsoft Silverlight Streaming by Windows Live

The Microsoft Silverlight streaming service is a free service for media streaming and hosting solutions (up to 10GB) for Silverlight-based applications provided by Windows Live. You can visit http://silverlight.live.com/ for more details.

Summary

This introductory chapter started with details about the next-generation Web 2.0 technology platform and RIAs. RIAs are

- Digital multimedia and content rich, with seamless multimedia and content integration providing desktop application–like rich, interactive user interfaces
- Platform independent (cross-operating system, cross-browser, and cross-device)
- Modular, loosely coupled, flexible, and customizable
- Metadata rich
- Collaborative
- High performing (with client-side processing and client-side local caching and asynchronous communication capabilities)

It is crystal clear from the preceding discussion that, just as the Internet (Web 1.0) and globalization impact broke the boundaries between countries, Web 2.0–based RIAs break the barrier between web-based applications and desktop applications and empower different communities to collaborate on digital information (content and multimedia) in the most user-friendly and secured way.

Microsoft Silverlight is one of the most promising technology platforms in the rising era of Web 2.0 and RIAs. After releasing a very basic scripting-oriented Silverlight 1, Microsoft made a giant leap by delivering Silverlight 2 with support for Microsoft .NET Framework 3.5 with the CLR, and thus support for .NET managed code-behind using the default Microsoft .NET class libraries. Silverlight provides a platform to develop cross-browser, cross-platform, and cross-device RIAs and is a subset of the WPF. As such it uses XAML, which facilitates an externalized and loosely coupled definition of the Silverlight application user interface and related style sheets.

To support an agile rapid application development model, Microsoft provides seamless and fluent integration between Visual Studio 2008 SP1 as the developer's tool and Expression Studio 2 (including Deep Zoom Composer) as the designer's tool to support development of Silverlight RIAs.

In the next chapter, we will create a Silverlight-based RIA, My Album, as a base application for this book. In Chapter 5, we will revise the My Album application to make it suitable to deploy at the enterprise level, and then we will transform it into an Enterprise Training Portal RIA.

Additional References

Links from the Microsoft Web Site

- Silverlight home page, `http://silverlight.net/default.aspx`
- ASP.NET AJAX Overview, `http://msdn.microsoft.com/en-us/library/bb398874.aspx`
- Events and Delegates, `http://msdn.microsoft.com/en-us/library/cc189018(VS.95).aspx`
- Data Binding, `http://msdn.microsoft.com/en-us/library/cc278072(VS.95).aspx`
- Developing a Silverlight Library Assembly, `http://msdn.microsoft.com/en-us/library/cc296243(VS.95).aspx`

Apress Reference Books

- *Silverlight 2 Visual Essentials* by Matthew MacDonald (2008)
- *Beginning Silverlight 2: From Novice to Professional* by Robert Lair (2009)
- *Foundation Expression Blend 2: Building Applications in WPF and Silverlight* by Victor Gaudioso (2008)
- *Pro Silverlight 2 in VB* 2008 and *Pro Silverlight 2 in C#* 2008 by Matthew MacDonald (2008)

■ ■ ■

CHAPTER 2

Setting Up: Developing a Simple Silverlight Application

Before you get a deep-dive detailing of advanced features, design concepts, and implementation approaches of Silverlight and developing an enterprise service-oriented training portal using Silverlight, it is important you understand the key differences between developing an enterprise RIA and developing a quick (by breaking some traditional design rules), but very impressive, rich application using the Silverlight technology. This exercise will also help to demonstrate how easy it is to develop Silverlight applications in a short time, and how Silverlight is scalable and can fulfill the needs of a broad audience ranging from individuals to enterprises.

This chapter serves as a base for the rest of the book. In this chapter, we will create an application concept for our end game—developing an Enterprise Training Portal using Silverlight. We'll use an individual application-centric development approach to develop an RIA named My Album. Using the same My Album RIA concept, we will build the Enterprise Training Portal RIA following an enterprise application–centric development approach in Chapter 5.

Without wasting any further time, let's start with defining the My Album RIA to develop a quick but very sound and attractive Silverlight RIA.

Defining the My Album RIA Project

The My Album application will have rich presentation capabilities to display videos and images with proper categorization, just as a traditional desktop application would have. Figure 2-1 shows a sample screen of the My Album RIA.

Figure 2-1. *My Album RIA*

I'll assume you are familiar with the Silverlight technology and tools and have some experience with the development of Microsoft Silverlight–based applications using Microsoft development and design tools.

Now let's consider the details of the application.

Application Features

The application has the following features:

- Desktop application–like, individual usage-centric rich user interface and functions
- Presentation/slide show capabilities for image files
- Play and stop capabilities for video files
- Video and image file preview capabilities using thumbnails
- Categorized presentation of images and videos to show a collection of images and videos belonging to the same group/category
- Easy jumping from one image/video to another
- Full-screen view option

Design and Development Considerations

When developing the application, you need to bear the following goals in mind:

- Rapid development (finishing development in minutes)
- Lightweight
- Easy to deploy and maintain
- Easy to use to categorize pictures and videos
- Pluggable into an existing web application
- High performing

Supported Media Types

The application will support the following types of media:

- *Pictures (Images) file types*: JPG, PNG, BMP, GIF (other file types should be supported but not tested) with a minimum resolution of 800×600 to ensure image files are of good quality
- *Video file types*: WMV (compressed broadband version)

Technology Platform Used to Develop the My Album RIA

The application will be based on the following platforms:

- Microsoft Silverlight 2
- Microsoft .NET Framework 3.5 SP1

Development Tools Used to Develop the My Album RIA

We'll use the following tools to develop the application:

- Microsoft Visual Studio 2008 SP1
- Microsoft Silverlight Tools for Visual Studio 2008 SP1
- Microsoft Expression Blend 2 SP1
- Microsoft Expression Encoder 2 SP1

My Album RIA Design Considerations

One of the key aspects of designing RIAs is creating a fluent user interface to provide high-application usability. As a result, your first design consideration when developing any RIA is to understand the scope of the application and user requirements and expectations, and then define the application capabilities aligning with the application features (defined during the scoping phase).

Application Capabilities

We can define the following application capabilities based on the application features discussed earlier in this chapter:

- Desktop application–like richness
- Categorized (three categories for this sample application) image files with "play slide show" functionality
- Presentation/Slide show mode for image files and play/stop mode for video files
- Categorized (three categories for this example application) video files with "play video" functionality
- Preview list functionality with scrolling list capability to display thumbnails of a list of image and video files of the selected category
- Selected image or video from the preview list displayed within the application
- Full-screen view functionality

User Interface Framework

The next action item is to define the user interface framework of the RIA that can support the defined application capabilities. The definition of the user interface framework will also help us with the implementation of the refactored application user interface design, which is aligned with the enterprise strategies.

It is critical to consider capabilities and limitations of the technology platform that will be used for application development as well as the deployment strategy before finalizing the user interface framework of the RIA. For the My Album RIA, we are going to use the Microsoft Silverlight technology as the development platform and Microsoft Silverlight Streaming provided by Windows Live to deploy the application and media files.

Figure 2-2 shows the user interface framework definition for the My Album application. As shown in Figure 2-2, the theme for the My Album application is a single *center stage* page user interface, where the majority of the page displays the selected image or plays the selected video.

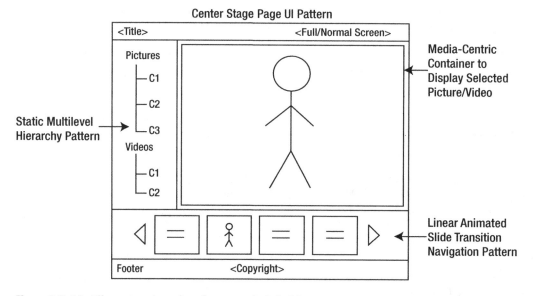

Figure 2-2. *My Album user interface framework definition*

Supporting the center stage theme, we have two types of *visual hierarchy* navigation patterns: first for the selection of image or video category, and second for the selection of a particular picture or video from the selected category.

Now let's take a look at the navigation patterns used in different areas of the application interface:

- Since we are going to simplify the categorization for this sample application and have only one level of category for images and one for videos, we can follow the *static multilevel hierarchy* navigation pattern to display various categories for images and videos.

- We will follow the *linear animated slide transition* navigation pattern to preview collections of images or videos based on the selection of the category.

- The application window layout will be configured as a *liquid layout* to enable us to resize the application when the user resizes the browser window to match the browser window size.

Defining User Controls

User controls are Silverlight's basic unit for defining XAML-based user interfaces and code-behind files. For this version of the My Album application, we will use the default Page class (containing an XAML markup file and code-behind file) as a main user interface, which is derived from the UserControl.

Defining Code-Behind Scope

We will keep the custom managed code-behind to a minimum and will define most of the functionality within the XAML markup file.

Other Considerations

We want to keep the first version of the My Album application simple and straightforward. As a result, we'll stick to the following restrictions for our application, considerations which are normally realized during the design and implementation process:

- No custom user control or class library
- Minimum code-behind
- Media files defined and embedded within the project
- Predefined categories
- No use of major enterprise application design concepts such as abstracted presentation layer, externalization of media source definition, externalized files, and so forth
- No use of Web Services or other service-oriented application architecture

We will reconsider the preceding concepts in Chapter 5 during the design of the Enterprise Training Portal RIA.

Microsoft Expression Blend

Microsoft Expression Blend is the tool for helping user interface designers develop rich, interactive WPF- and XAML-based user interfaces. It is also tightly integrated with Visual Studio, enabling designers and developers to rapidly develop, debug, and test Silverlight-based rich, interactive applications in integrated mode.

We will utilize Expression Blend to develop rich user interface. I assume that you are familiar with the Expression Blend tool, so this book will not focus on explaining it in detail.

Microsoft Expression Encoder

Microsoft Expression Encoder contains several Silverlight Media Player templates to create, manage, and publish media in VC-1 quality for Silverlight applications. We are going to use Expression Encoder to develop the thumbnail images for the video files, which will appear in the My Album application preview pane.

I assume that you are familiar with the Expression Encoder tool, so this book will not focus on explaining it in detail.

Developing the My Album RIA

Now that the scope and high-level application design for the My Album RIA have been determined, our next task is to develop the Silverlight-based My Album RIA. Figure 2-3 shows the application in full-screen mode.

Figure 2-3. *My Album RIA in full-screen mode*

As shown in Figure 2-3, the My Album RIA follows the *center stage theme* to display the selected picture and video in the main container.

Figure 2-4 defines the My Album RIA layout and its specifications. We will accommodate different parts of the application in a 2×2 grid, which will ease the work of designing and placing the controls. Here we set the width of the first column and height of the second row to 128 pixels (px), and the width of the second column and the height of the first row to * to cover the remaining portion of the window. This allows the application to resize according to the browser window's size and also maintains the original aspect ratio of the different parts of the application.

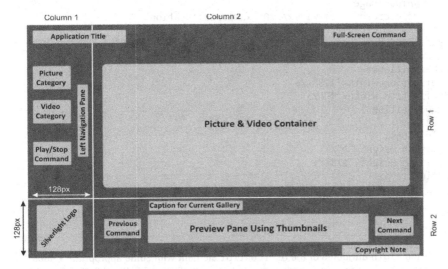

Figure 2-4. *The My Album RIA layout design and specifications*

The left navigation pane helps the user to find and select a category of picture or video. As you saw in the "User Interface Framework" section earlier, it follows the static multilevel hierarchy navigation pattern to display different categories (i.e., Nature, Beach, and Cartoon for pictures and Cartoon, Sports, and Pets for videos) under two main categories—*Pictures* and *Videos*.

A Play Presentation button, which is available in the left pane and applies to pictures only, runs the slide show of pictures in the selected category.

On the bottom is the preview pane with Next and Previous functionality. The selected picture/video will be animated and highlighted, and the rest will be dimmed slightly. As discussed previously, the preview pane follows the linear animated slide transition navigation pattern.

You can visit the following link to get access to the My Album application: http://www.technologyopinion.com/myalbum.aspx.

Creating the My Album Silverlight Project Using the Silverlight Application Project Template

Create a myAlbum Silverlight application project by selecting the Silverlight Application project template with a web project to host the Silverlight control for testing.

We need to make a couple of changes in the default main user interface UserControl element:

1. Set Height to 600 and Width to 800. Later we will remove the Height and Width attributes to align/adjust the application window size with the browser window size.

2. Set Background to red (#FF000000) and Foreground to white (#FFFFFFFF).

3. Set the Grid's Background value to #FFB7BB57.

4. Define two rows and two columns of the Grid using Grid.ColumnDefinition and Grid.RowDefinition elements, as shown in the following snippet:

```
<UserControl x:Class="myAlbum.Page"
    xmlns="http://schemas.microsoft.com/winfx/2006/xaml/presentation"
    xmlns:x="http://schemas.microsoft.com/winfx/2006/xaml"
    Width="800" Height="600" Background="#FF000000" Foreground="#FFFFFFFF">
    <Grid x:Name="LayoutRoot" Background="#FFB7BB57">
        <Grid.ColumnDefinitions>
            <ColumnDefinition Width="128" />
            <ColumnDefinition Width="*" />
        </Grid.ColumnDefinitions>

        <Grid.RowDefinitions>
            <RowDefinition Height="*"/>
            <RowDefinition Height="128"/>
        </Grid.RowDefinitions>
    </Grid>
</UserControl>
```

Tip Keeping the Height and Width attributes of the UserControl element with some appropriate values (say, Height = 600 and Width = 800) will ease your work at design time using Expression Blend 2 SP1. Once the application is designed, you can remove them, allowing auto adjustment of application window size to the browser window size.

The following sections will start defining the application with the simple XAML code generated with the help of Visual Studio 2008 SP1. Then we'll use Expression Blend to create the rich user interface, where the XAML code will be created automatically and integrated with the myAlbum Visual Studio project.

Defining the Left Navigation Pane

With the help of IntelliSense, it is very easy and quick to set up user controls. First create a Rectangle XAML control with the name mainBack that occupies about 95% of the area of the user interface (achieved by setting its Margin value and the RowSpan and ColumnSpan properties of the Grid) with the background color set to Red by using the Fill attribute.

```
<Rectangle
    x:Name="mainBack" Margin="8,8,8,8" Fill="Red" Grid.ColumnSpan="2"
    Grid.RowSpan="2">
</Rectangle>
```

The Width and Height attributes of the Rectangle are not hard-coded; this allows the application window to resize automatically to fit the browser window size. You can see this within the design window of the Visual Studio IDE, as shown in Figure 2-5; the user interface of the myAlbum application will change to the Red color.

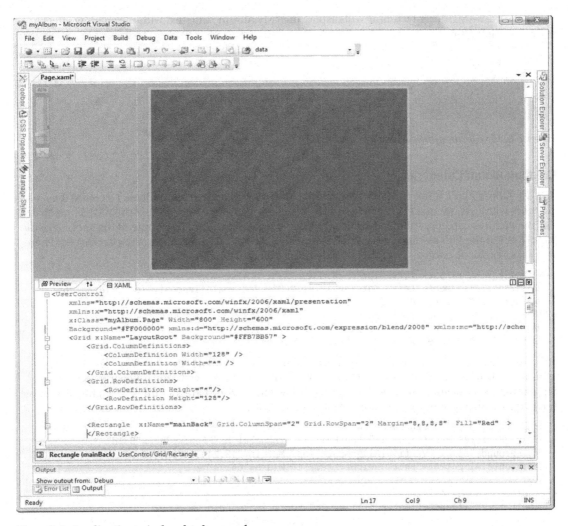

Figure 2-5. *Application window background*

Adding the Application Title

To add the title "My Album" at the top-left corner of the window, we will use two TextBlock XAML controls. For the first TextBlock, named title_shadow, and the second TextBlock, named title, specify the Text, Background, Foreground, FontSize, FontWeight, Margin, and Grid.ColumnSpan values shown in the following code snippet. The shadow effect will appear for the title text by having two TextBlock controls overlapping by setting the Margin property.

```
<TextBlock x:Name="title_shadow" Grid.ColumnSpan="2" FontFamily="Trebuchet MS"
        FontSize="32" FontWeight="Bold" Foreground="Black" Text="My Album"
        Margin="18,15,0,0"></TextBlock>

<TextBlock x:Name="title" Grid.ColumnSpan="2" FontFamily="Trebuchet MS"
        FontSize="32" FontWeight="Bold" Foreground="Yellow" Text="My Album"
        Margin="17,17,0,0"></TextBlock>
```

Now the XAML design window will display the "My Album" title text with the shadow effect as shown in Figure 2-6.

Figure 2-6. *My Album application title screenshot*

Creating Album Categories

The My Album application contains two album categories—Pictures and Videos. To create the category windows, we need to create two sections using Rectangle and TextBlock XAML controls. For the Pictures category (named backGroundBlue), we will set the Fill attribute of the Rectangle to DarkBlue. For the Videos category (named backGroundGreen), this attribute is set to DarkGreen. Then we place TextBlock controls over them for defining different categories.

```
<Rectangle x:Name="backGroundBlue"
    HorizontalAlignment="Left" Margin="12,97,0,0"  VerticalAlignment="Top" Width="76"
    Height="112" Stroke="#FFB7BB57" Fill="DarkBlue"    />
<Rectangle x:Name="backGroundGreen"
    HorizontalAlignment="Left" Margin="12,225,0,0" VerticalAlignment="Top" Width="76"
    Height="112" Stroke="#FFB7BB57" Fill="DarkGreen"  />
```

Now we create the album category titles "Pictures" and "Videos" the way we created the My Album application title using the TextBlock XAML controls, as shown in the following code snippet. Similar to the application title, we create the shadow effect of the category titles by slightly changing the Margin property of two overlapped TextBlock controls.

```
<TextBlock x:Name="cPicturesShadows"
    Text="Pictures" FontSize="16" FontFamily="Trebuchet MS" FontWeight="Bold"
    Foreground="Black" VerticalAlignment="Top" Margin="18.249,107.204,0,0"
    HorizontalAlignment="Left" Height="23.751" Width="66.74" / >

<TextBlock x:Name="cPictures"
    FontFamily="Trebuchet MS" FontSize="16" FontWeight="Bold"
    Margin="17,107,0,0" Text="Pictures" Foreground="Yellow"
    VerticalAlignment="Top"HorizontalAlignment="Left"/>

<TextBlock x:Name="cVideosShadows"
    Text="Videos" FontSize="16" FontFamily="Trebuchet MS" FontWeight="Bold"
    Foreground="Black"    VerticalAlignment="Top"
    Margin="22.2199993133545,235.404006958008,0,0"
    HorizontalAlignment="Left"   Height="23.751" Width="65.772" />

<TextBlock  x:Name="cVideos"
    FontFamily="Trebuchet MS" FontSize="16" FontWeight="Bold"
    Margin="21,236,0,0" Text="Videos" Foreground="Yellow" VerticalAlignment="Top"
    HorizontalAlignment="Left"/>
```

For the sake of simplicity, the My Album application has a total of six categories hard-coded (three categories for each album category—Nature, Beach, and Cartoon for the Pictures album category, and Cartoon, Sports, and Pet for the Videos album category) within the application by using six TextBlock XAML controls as shown here:

```
<TextBlock x:Name="catNature"
    Foreground="White" Text="Nature" Height="27" Width="65"
    HorizontalAlignment="Left" Margin="22,131,0,0" VerticalAlignment="Top"
    Cursor="Hand" />

<TextBlock x:Name="catBeach"
    HorizontalAlignment="Left" Margin="21,153,0,0" VerticalAlignment="Top"
    Cursor="Hand" Text="Beach" Foreground="White" Width="102"  Height="27" />

<TextBlock x:Name="catCartoon"
    HorizontalAlignment="Left" Margin="21,177,0,0" VerticalAlignment="Top"
    Cursor="Hand" Text="Cartoon" Foreground="White" Width="102"  Height="31.2" />

<TextBlock x:Name="vcatSports"
    Text="Sports" Foreground="White"  HorizontalAlignment="Left"
    Margin="22,282,0,0" VerticalAlignment="Top" Width="83" Cursor="Hand"/>

<TextBlock x:Name="vcatCartoon"
    Text="Cartoon" Foreground="White" HorizontalAlignment="Left" Margin="22,260,0,0"
    VerticalAlignment="Top" Width="83"  Cursor="Hand" Height="27" />

<TextBlock x:Name="vcatPets"
    Text="Pets" Foreground="White"  HorizontalAlignment="Left" Margin="22,304,0,0"
    VerticalAlignment="Top" Width="83" Cursor="Hand"  Height="27"/>
```

Please note that the Cursor property of the TextBlock XAML control is set to Hand to control the mouse cursor.

Now the design window will look as shown in Figure 2-7.

Figure 2-7. *My Album application with categories*

As I explained earlier in Chapter 1, Microsoft provides tight integration between Visual Studio and Expression Blend. Expression Blend is a designer's tool and mainly used to enhance and develop rich navigation through its user-friendly IDE.

If Expression Blend is installed and set up properly on your development machine, you will be able to access the Open in Expression Blend option, shown in Figure 2-8, by right-clicking the Page. xaml file within Visual Studio's Solution Explorer window.

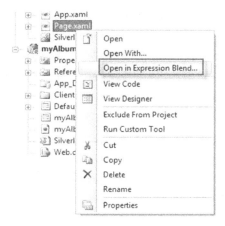

Figure 2-8. *Accessing Expression Blend within a Visual Studio Silverlight project*

You can use this option to switch to Expression Blend at any time from Visual Studio. In this book, we are going to use this option frequently as we build the rich user interface of the My Album application and the Enterprise Training Portal application.

After successfully opening the project in Expression Blend, we are ready to design the application interface. We will alter the red background in such a way that it changes from red to black in a linear gradient. You can achieve this by navigating to the Properties tab of the mainBack XAML Rectangle control, choosing the Gradient Brush under the Brushes category, and adjusting the two colors as shown in Figure 2-9.

Figure 2-9. *Setting up* Rectangle.Fill *with* LinearGradientBrush

The following XAML code is generated and integrated with the myAlbum Visual Studio Silverlight project as we design with Expression Blend.

```
<Rectangle.Fill>
  <LinearGradientBrush EndPoint="0.5,1" StartPoint="0.5,0">
    <GradientStop Color="#FF5C0505" />
    <GradientStop Color="#FF000000" Offset="1"/>
  </LinearGradientBrush>
</Rectangle.Fill>
```

Similarly, enhance the "My Album" title of the application (the TextBlock XAML control with title name) by setting the TextBlock.Foreground property with the Gradient Brush under the Brushes category to give it a metallic look, which will generate the following XAML code:

```
<TextBlock x:Name="title"
    Grid.ColumnSpan="2" FontFamily="Trebuchet MS" FontSize="32" FontWeight="Bold"
    Text="My Album" Width="202" Height="43.2" RenderTransformOrigin="0.5,0.5"
    VerticalAlignment="Top" HorizontalAlignment="Left" Margin="17,17,0,0"  >
      <TextBlock.Foreground>
        <LinearGradientBrush EndPoint="0.5,1" StartPoint="0.5,0">
          <GradientStop Color="#FF191804"/>
          <GradientStop Color="#FFFFFD28" Offset="1"/>
        </LinearGradientBrush>
      </TextBlock.Foreground>
</TextBlock>
```

To give a metallic look to both category titles—"Pictures" and "Videos"—we will use the same approach that we used to give a gradient metallic look to the application title. For the Pictures category, the following is the revised XAML code:

```
<TextBlock x:Name="cPictures"
    Text="Pictures" FontSize="16" FontFamily="Trebuchet MS" FontWeight="Bold"
    RenderTransformOrigin="0.5,0.5" VerticalAlignment="Top"
    HorizontalAlignment="Left" Margin="18.7110004425049,105.199996948242,0,0"
    Height="23.755" Width="67.254"  >
    <TextBlock.Foreground>
      <LinearGradientBrush EndPoint="0.5,1" StartPoint="0.5,0">
        <GradientStop Color="#FF000000"/>
        <GradientStop Color="#FFFAFF77" Offset="1"/>
      </LinearGradientBrush>
    </TextBlock.Foreground>
</TextBlock>
```

For the Videos category, the following is the revised XAML code:

```
<TextBlock  x:Name="cVideos"
    Text="Videos" FontSize="16" FontFamily="Trebuchet MS" FontWeight="Bold"
    RenderTransformOrigin="0.5,0.5" VerticalAlignment="Top"
    HorizontalAlignment="Left" Margin="22.7110004425049,235.399993896484,0,0"
    Height="23.755" Width="66.279"  >
    <TextBlock.Foreground>
      <LinearGradientBrush EndPoint="0.5,1" StartPoint="0.5,0">
        <GradientStop Color="#FF000000"/>
        <GradientStop Color="#FFFAFF77" Offset="1"/>
      </LinearGradientBrush>
    </TextBlock.Foreground>
</TextBlock>
```

Within Visual Studio, the design window should look as shown in Figure 2-10.

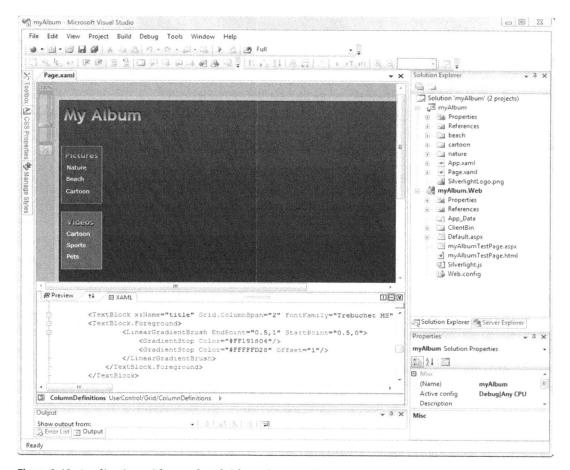

Figure 2-10. *Application with populated title and categories*

▉**Note** I started with some simple XAML to define the left navigation pane for demonstration purposes only. As a matter of fact, it would be much simpler to use Expression Blend directly to define the UI.

Defining the Preview Pane

The My Album application contains a horizontal preview pane at the bottom center where we display thumbnails of items from the selected category. On both sides of the thumbnails, Previous and Next commands let the user navigate through the content of the selected category. To implement such behavior, we'll use a StackPanel XAML control named thumbBar. At both ends of the StackPanel, we'll draw a triangle-shaped symbol to indicate Previous and Next navigation as shown in Figure 2-11.

Figure 2-11. *Designing the preview pane using Expression Blend*

We will place the StackPanel in the second row and second column of the Grid named LayoutRoot. For a horizontal view of thumbnails, set the thumbBar StackPanel XAML control's Orientation property to Horizontal along with the Name, Width, Height, Grid.Row, and VerticalAlignment properties as follows:

```
<StackPanel x:Name="thumbBar"
    VerticalAlignment="Bottom" Height="52.754"  Orientation="Horizontal"
    Margin="59,0,71,29.246000289917" Grid.Row="1" Grid.Column="1"/>
```

In the "Defining Application Behavior Through the Code-Behind" section of this chapter, we will use image controls to populate images of the selected category using the managed code-behind file for the Page.xaml file.

The Pen tool of Expression Blend, shown in Figure 2-12, enables us to draw lines that appear in the XAML as <Path> elements. We need to use the Pen tool to implement the Previous and Next commands.

Figure 2-12. *Pen tool of Expression Blend*

Adding the Previous Symbol

Before we start drawing the Previous symbol, we need to make sure that we draw it right in the cell in the second row and second column of Grid as shown previously in Figure 2-11. Expression Blend makes a designer's life very easy because, as shown in Figure 2-13, it highlights the rows and columns so you can position controls without worrying about properties.

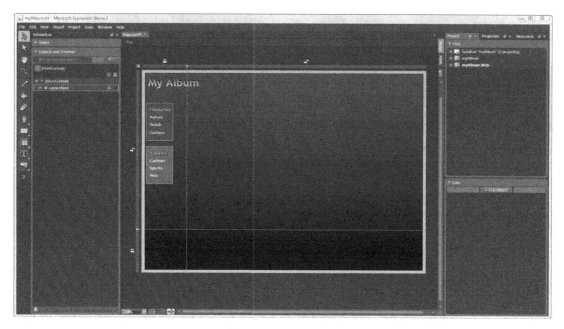

Figure 2-13. *Expression Blend Designer displays grid lines to define the control position easily.*

Let's first create the triangle shape for the Previous symbol using the Pen tool. To draw a tri-angle shape, you need to click three points. Based on those three points, the Pen tool will generate an opaque triangle with a default Fill color of White. The following is the XAML for the Previous command:

```
<Path x:Name="prev"
   Height="23" HorizontalAlignment="Left" Margin="106,0,0,45"
   VerticalAlignment="Bottom" Width="17.827" Stretch="Fill" Stroke="#FF000000"
   Data="M239.33333,359.33334 L279.33334,396.66666 L278.66702,320.00107"
   Cursor="Hand" >
  <Path.Fill>
    <LinearGradientBrush EndPoint="0.5,1" StartPoint="0.5,0">
      <GradientStop Color="#FF747272" />
      <GradientStop Color="#FFFFFFFF" Offset="1"/>
    </LinearGradientBrush>
  </Path.Fill>
</Path>
```

We also set the Name property to prev and Cursor property to Hand using Expression Blend's Properties tab.

Figure 2-14 shows the Layout and Common Properties tabs for the Previous symbol that we just drew. The figure includes the highlighted properties—HorizontalAlignment, VerticalAlignment, and Cursor—that we set for our application.

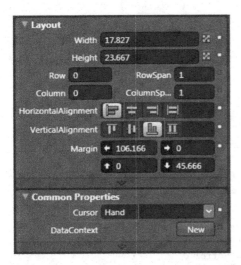

Figure 2-14. *Setting up the Previous symbol's properties using Expression Blend*

Adding the Next Symbol

Rather than making the Next symbol from scratch, we'll use the Previous symbol as a shortcut. Create a copy of the Previous symbol. Within the Transform category, flip this object to the x axis to make the Next symbol, as shown in Figure 2-15. Then you need to change the name to next for this Path object. Place the Next symbol at the right end of thumbBar StackPanel in the same cell (i.e., the second row and second column) as the Previous symbol.

Figure 2-15. *Transforming objects using Expression Blend*

Adding the Selected Gallery Display

Now just above the left corner of the thumbBar StackPanel control, we need to add two TextBlock controls that will display the current gallery selected by the user.

We want to show the check mark before the name of the selected gallery. For that we use the Webdings font type for the first TextBlock XAML control (named Symbol) and set the Text property to a, which is equivalent to the check mark symbol, as shown in Figure 2-16.

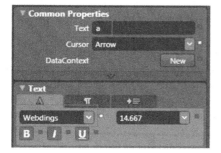

Figure 2-16. *Setting up common properties of the object using Expression Blend*

The following is the related XAML code snippet:

```
<TextBlock x:Name="Symbol"
    Grid.Column="1" Grid.Row="1" HorizontalAlignment="Left"
    Margin="28,0,0,91.1370010375977" VerticalAlignment="Bottom"
    Foreground="#FFFFFF00" Width="29" Height="24" Text="a"
    FontFamily="Webdings" FontSize="24"/>
```

On the right side of this symbol we put another TextBlock XAML control to display the name of the currently selected gallery. We name this TextBlock XAML control currentView. The following is the XAML code that is generated upon designing the TextBlock XAML control using Expression Blend:

```
<TextBlock x:Name="currentView" ↖
    Grid.Column="1" Grid.Row="1" HorizontalAlignment="Left"
    VerticalAlignment="Bottom" Margin="50.8269996643066,0,0,86.1370010375977"
    Text="Nature" Foreground="#FFFFFF00" Width="79.339" Height="27"/>
```

The application, which now includes the preview pane, should look as shown in Figure 2-17.

Figure 2-17. *Application with the preview pane*

Defining a Container for Pictures

We want to display selected pictures of various categories in the center (slightly floated to the right) of the application. We also need to take care that the picture container is of the same width as the thumbBar StackPanel XAML control and exactly aligned with it. Our aim is to create a neat, good-looking application and align with the window size when the application resizes or when in full-screen mode.

It is very easy to achieve this functionality using Expression Blend. We just need to select the Image control from the Asset Library of the Expression Blend. To bring up the Asset Library, click the >> symbol in the toolbox (as shown in Figure 2-18). By default the toolbox is located at the left side of the Expression Blend IDE.

Figure 2-18. *The Asset Library button displays the Asset Library in Expression Blend.*

Upon clicking the Asset Library button, you will see a window containing different system controls within the library. Select the Image control (make sure Show All is checked at the top right of the window) as highlighted in Figure 2-19.

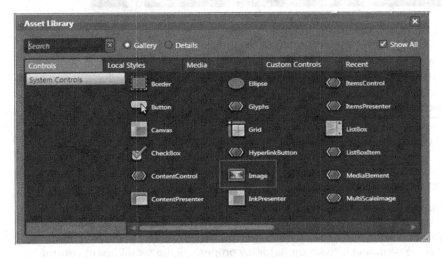

Figure 2-19. *Asset Library controls in Expression Blend*

Now you can start drawing an Image control right on the center area of the application window. When doing so, you will notice that Expression Blend will guide you so you can draw a picture container that is properly aligned on the x and y axes to the thumbBar StackPanel XAML control. It implements this by showing a red-white dotted line as you design the control (see Figure 2-20).

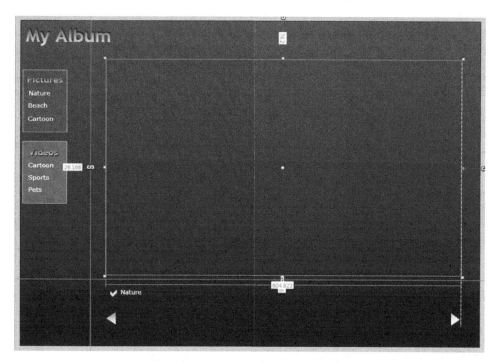

Figure 2-20. *Drawing a picture container using the* Image *control*

After successfully drawing the picture container, we will name it imgStage to identify it in the code-behind when we dynamically load images into it. We also need to make sure that it is on top of all the controls by choosing Order ➤ Bring to front from the right-click context menu.

The following is the XAML code created by doing this exercise:

```
<Image x:Name="imgStage" Grid.Column="1"
    Margin="26.1660003662109,78.1999969482422,41.0110015869141,8" Grid.RowSpan="1"/>
```

Defining a Container for Media

To create a container for media, we select the MediaElement control from the Expression Blend Asset Library, place it on the central area of the application (at the same place and with the same dimensions as the imgStage Image control), and name it vidStage. One thing you need to do in addition to what you did for the Image container is to set the AutoPlay property of the MediaElement control to True. This will allow the selected video to play automatically upon loading the file using the code-behind managed code.

The following is the XAML code for the MediaElement container:

```
<MediaElement x:Name="vidStage" Grid.Column="1" AutoPlay="True"
    Margin="26.1660003662109,78.1999969482422,41.0110015869141,8"
    Grid.RowSpan="1"/>
```

Defining Full-Screen/Normal-Screen Mode

To implement the full-screen/normal-screen functionality, at the top right of the application area draw a TextBlock XAML control using Expression Blend and name it goFullscreen. Set the Cursor property value to Hand and Foreground property to Yellow. The following XAML will be created by Expression Blend:

```
<TextBlock x:Name="goFullscreen"
  Grid.Column="1" Height="25" HorizontalAlignment="Right"
  Margin="0,8,8,0"VerticalAlignment="Top" Width="114"
  Text="Full screen" TextWrapping="Wrap" Foreground="#FFFFFD27" Cursor="Hand"/>
```

Defining the Play/Stop Command

One of the features of our application is to start a slide show of a selected pictures gallery automatically. To implement this, we need to have a toggle symbol that plays and stops the slide show and also changes symbol shape to indicate the current state of the slide show. For the sake of simplicity, we draw two different symbols: one is a triangle (like the typical Play symbol in Windows Media Player), and the second is a rectangle with visibility set to Collapsed.

As shown in Figure 2-21, we draw a simple Ellipse (while holding Shift down so it creates a perfectly round shape). Now we make it more attractive by setting Fill and Stroke properties.

Figure 2-21. *DrawingEllipse control for the Play/Stop symbols*

We set Fill using the Gradient Brush and Stroke to Yellow as shown in Figure 2-22.

Figure 2-22. *Defining brushes for the Ellipse control*

We name it roundBack. The following is the XAML that is generated as we design in Expression Blend:

```
<Ellipse x:Name="roundBack"
    ToolTipService.ToolTip="Start automatic presentation" Height="47"
    HorizontalAlignment="Left" Margin="24.9810009002686,380,0,42.5369987487793"
    VerticalAlignment="Top" Width="47" Stroke="#FFFDFF44" >
    <Ellipse.Fill>
        <LinearGradientBrush EndPoint="0.5,1" StartPoint="0.5,0">
            <GradientStop Color="#FF1A1A19" />
            <GradientStop Color="#FFBDC15A" Offset="1"/>
        </LinearGradientBrush>
    </Ellipse.Fill>
</Ellipse>
```

In the center of the Ellipse, we draw a Play and a Stop symbol using the Pen tool and Rectangle, respectively, and change the Cursor property to Hand. Here we also have populated the ToolTip to display the tooltip when the symbol has the focus. The following is the XAML code for the Play symbol, which is named Play:

```
<Path x:Name="Play"
    ToolTipService.ToolTip="Start automatic presentation" Height="28.235"
    Width="20" HorizontalAlignment="Left" Margin="41.9809989929199,392,0,51"
    VerticalAlignment="Top" Fill="#FFFFFFFF" Stretch="Fill" Stroke="#FF000000"
    Data="M120,362 L120,385 L136,373.99991" Cursor="Hand" />
```

Then we set the Visibility of the Stop symbol to Collapsed in the Appearance category under the Properties tab, as highlighted in Figure 2-23.

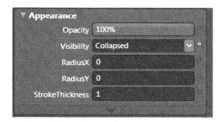

Figure 2-23. *Defining the appearance of the Stop symbol*

We name this symbol Stop. The following is the equivalent XAML code for the Stop symbol:

```
<Rectangle x:Name="Stop" ToolTipService.ToolTip="Stop automatic presentation"
    HorizontalAlignment="Left" Margin="38,396,0,54" VerticalAlignment="Top"
    Fill="#FFFFFFFF"  Visibility="Collapsed" Width="21" Height="20"
    Stroke="#FF000000"/>
```

Figure 2-24 shows the Play/Stop symbol we just created.

Figure 2-24. *Play/Stop symbol for the My Album RIA*

Later in the code-behind step, we will bind an event handler to the Play and Stop symbols to implement the slide show feature.

Defining Animations Using a Storyboard

We'll create four animations: two for a fade-in effect for pictures and thumbnails and two for mouse over and out animations for each category's TextBlock XAML control. Here we define each animation as a Storyboard in Page.xaml using a ContentControl as a Resources item.

The grow and shrink storyboards are initiated for the various categories' MouseEnter and MouseLeave events. You will see in the "Defining Application Behavior Through the Code-Behind" section that we will develop some event handlers that will use both of these animations for the TextBlock XAML controls. Note that for the grow, shrink, and fadeThumb storyboards, we will set the Storyboard.TargetName property dynamically in the Page.xaml.cs code-behind within MouseEnter and MouseLeave event handlers. We assign single storyboard animations for every category and thumbnail by providing the TargetName property dynamically.

The following is the animation implementation using Storyboard elements:

```
<ContentControl Grid.RowSpan="1" Content="">
   <ContentControl.Resources>

      <Storyboard x:Name="grow">
         <DoubleAnimation
            Storyboard.TargetProperty ="FontSize"
            From="14.667"
            To="19"
            SpeedRatio="5"/>
      </Storyboard>

      <Storyboard x:Name="shrink">
         <DoubleAnimation
            Storyboard.TargetProperty ="FontSize"
            From="19"
            To="14.667"
            SpeedRatio="5"/>
      </Storyboard>

      <Storyboard x:Name="fadeIn">
         <DoubleAnimation
            Storyboard.TargetName = "imgStage"
            Storyboard.TargetProperty ="Opacity"
            From="0"
            To="1"/>
      </Storyboard>

      <Storyboard x:Name="fadeThumb">
         <DoubleAnimation
            Storyboard.TargetProperty ="Opacity"
            From="0.4"
            To="1"
            SpeedRatio="5"/>
      </Storyboard>

   </ContentControl.Resources>
</ContentControl>
```

Preparing Thumbnails for the Preview Pane Using Microsoft Expression Encoder

We'll use Expression Encoder to create thumbnails of the pictures and videos of different categories for the preview pane. The following steps explain how to create thumbnails of a video using Expression Encoder:

1. Start Microsoft Expression Encoder.

2. In the File menu, click New Job.

3. In the Media Content section, click Import (see Figure 2-25). This will bring up the Import Media Files dialog box.

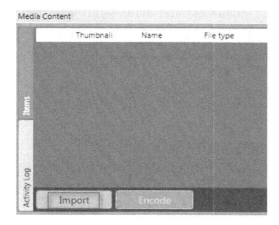

Figure 2-25. *Importing media files using Expression Encoder*

4. Select a video file and then click Open. The Media Content section displays the selected video in the vertical Item tab, as shown in Figure 2-26.

Figure 2-26. *The Item tab displaying imported media files*

5. Add additional videos by repeating steps 3 and 4.

6. On the right side of the application window, click the Output tab (see Figure 2-27).

Figure 2-27. *The Output tab defining encoding properties of imported media files*

7. You are now presented with three options to extract thumbnails from a selected video file: Best Frame, 1st Frame, and Custom (see Figure 2-28). You can choose any one of these you like. When choosing Custom, Expression Encoder will ask for a specified instance of time from which the frame is extracted. If you select None, the thumbnails will not be extracted.

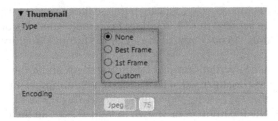

Figure 2-28. *Setting up the Thumbnail section within the Output tab*

8. In the Encoding category, jpeg is the default. Leave this as is for now.

9. In the Job Output category, set Template to None (see Figure 2-29). This will just create video and thumbnail.

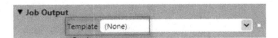

Figure 2-29. *Setting up the Job Output section within the Output tab*

10. In the Media Content section, click Encode to encode the video and generate the thumbnail.

11. Note the directory location that is displayed in the Job Output section of the Media Content section. This directory contains the encoded videos and the thumbnail images. To simplify development efforts, we will keep the original name for the video and related thumbnail by renaming the thumbnail appropriately.

Adding Image and Video Files

Let's add image files to the myAlbum Silverlight project at root level. We will organize image files using the directory structure <CategoryName>/O#.jpg, where # will be the file number (in our case, it will be from 1 to 6 for each category) as shown in Figure 2-30. So the first image in the Cartoon category would be cartoon/01.jpg.

Figure 2-30. *Adding image files to the Silverlight Project*

Since image files will be small compared to video files, we will keep image files as part of the `myAlbum` deployment package (XAP file). You can achieve this by keeping the default value, Resource, of the Build Action property and the default value, Do not copy, of the Copy to Output Directory property.

Now let's reference video files to the `myAlbum` Silverlight project by adding them under the `ClientBin` folder of the `myAlbum.Web` project. We will organize video files and related thumbnail image files using the directory structure `v<CategoryName>/0#.wmv` for video files and `v<CategoryName>/0#.jpg` for related thumbnail files, where # will be the file number as shown in Figure 2-31. So the first video in the Cartoon category would be `vcartoon/01.wmv`, and the related thumbnail image would be `vcartoon/01.jpg`.

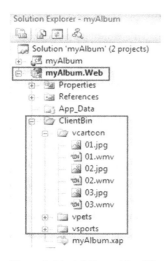

Figure 2-31. *Adding video files to the Silverlight project*

To keep the `myAlbum` deployment package (XAP file) at the minimum size and thus reduce the initial application loading time, we will not include video files as part of the deployment package. You can achieve this by accessing the advance properties of each video file in the Solution Explorer window. Set the Build Action property to None and Copy to Output Directory property to Do not copy (the default value) for each video file.

So when we deploy the My Album application, we need to copy all of these video files to the `ClientBin` folder manually. For debugging purposes, we need to copy them from the `myAlbum` project to the `ClientBin` folder under the `myAlbum.Web` project as shown in Figure 2-31.

The build action topic will be covered in detail in the "Packaging the My Album Silverlight Application" section of this chapter.

Defining Application Behavior Through the Code-Behind

So far we have created a very rich user interface for the My Album application without writing a single line of code. As you have seen, we have used Expression Blend to define the look and feel of the My Album application. Now we will use Visual Studio 2008 SP1 to define the behavior of the application by implementing different event integrations using managed code-behind.

Figure 2-32 demonstrates the different types of required event integration to implement the required functionalities.

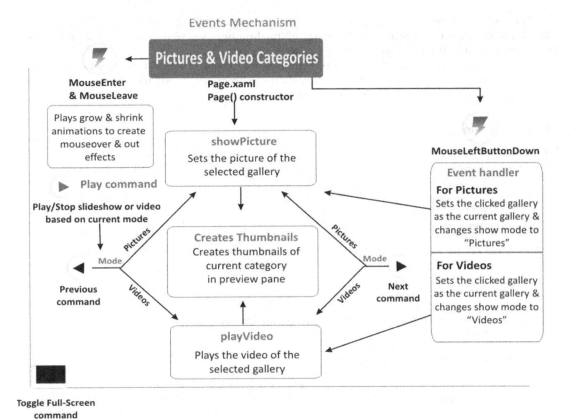

Figure 2-32. *My Album application code-behind events integration*

Now let's write a few lines of code to implement the functionality that allows the user to surf through the various picture and video categories of the My Album application.

Namespace Declarations

When we create a new Silverlight application project using Visual Studio 2008, the following namespaces are added by default:

```
using System;
using System.Collections.Generic;
using System.Linq;
using System.Net;
using System.Windows;
using System.Windows.Controls;
using System.Windows.Documents;
using System.Windows.Input;
using System.Windows.Media;
using System.Windows.Media.Animation;
using System.Windows.Shapes;
```

In addition to the preceding namespaces, we need to add the following two namespaces in order to support the My Album functionality:

```
using System.Windows.Media.Imaging;
using System.Windows.Threading;
```

The `System.Windows.Media.Imaging` namespace allows us to access the `BitmapImage` object. We will use this object to dynamically set the source of the thumbnails as well as to set the source of the Image container (i.e., the imgStage XAML user control).

The `System.Windows.Threading` namespace allows us to access the `DispatcherTimer` object that will enable the My Album application's autoplay slide show feature. We will use a fixed time interval for changing pictures of the currently selected gallery.

Other Declarations

We need to declare a strongly typed list of `Uri` objects to represent the picture path, video path, and thumbnails. The following global class-level variables are defined for the My Album application:

```
//Different Uri for each category of pictures
List<Uri> natureUri;
List<Uri> cartoonUri;
List<Uri> beachUri;

//Different Uri for each category of videos
List<Uri> vcartoonUri;
List<Uri> vpetsUri;
List<Uri> vsportsUri;

//Different Uri for each category of video thumbnails
List<Uri> vthumbcartoonUri;
List<Uri> vthumbpetsUri;
List<Uri> vthumbsportsUri;

//Uri list for storing reference for active picture category
List<Uri> currentPicCategory;

//Uri list for storing reference for active video category
List<Uri> currentVidCategory;
List<Uri> currentVidThumbCategory;
```

Also add two more global class-level variables to iterate through the preceding defined collections and determine the mode of play (i.e., videos or pictures).

```
//Int variable to iterate through Uri collection
int playIndex;

//String to determine current show mode i.e., videos or pictures
string showMode;
```

Next, create a `DispatcherTimer` object called `timer` to enable the automatic slide show.

```
//Timer for automatic slide show
DispatcherTimer timer = new DispatcherTimer();
```

Defining the Constructor

Now let's define the constructor of the `Page` class.

First we need to initialize the list of earlier declared `Uri` objects using the following code snippet:

```
//Initializing the Uri collections
currentPicCategory = new List<Uri>();
currentVidCategory = new List<Uri>();
currentVidThumbCategory = new List<Uri>();
```

Now assign the hard-coded relative path for images, videos, and thumbnails to the Uri object using the Add() method. The following is the sample code snippet.

```
//Different picture category intialization
//Any number of images can be added to the album category.
//Nature pictures
natureUri = new List<Uri>();
natureUri.Add(new Uri("nature/01.jpg", UriKind.Relative));
natureUri.Add(new Uri("nature/02.jpg", UriKind.Relative));
...

//Beach Pictures
beachUri = new List<Uri>();
beachUri.Add(new Uri("beach/01.jpg", UriKind.Relative));
beachUri.Add(new Uri("beach/02.jpg", UriKind.Relative));
...

//Cartoon pictures
cartoonUri = new List<Uri>();
cartoonUri.Add(new Uri("cartoon/01.jpg", UriKind.Relative));
cartoonUri.Add(new Uri("cartoon/02.jpg", UriKind.Relative));
...

//Different video category intialization
//Any number of videos can be added to the album category.
//Cartoon videos
vcartoonUri = new List<Uri>();
vcartoonUri.Add(new Uri("vcartoon/01.wmv", UriKind.Relative));
...

//Pets videos
vpetsUri = new List<Uri>();
vpetsUri.Add(new Uri("vpets/01.wmv", UriKind.Relative));
...

//Sports videos
vsportsUri = new List<Uri>();
...

//Sports thumbnails
vthumbsportsUri = new List<Uri>();
vthumbsportsUri.Add(new Uri("vsports/01.jpg", UriKind.Relative));
```

Our application starts with the pictures gallery, so we need to set the showMode to picture and also specify the name of the initial gallery that should be displayed when the application loads. So add the following lines of code immediately after InitializeComponent():

```
//Default mode is picture
showMode = "picture";
```

```
//Default picture category
currentPicCategory = natureUri;
```

Finally, we call the showPicture() method so it can create thumbnails and set the first picture in the imgStage picture container. You'll see this method in the section "The showPicture Method" later in this chapter.

```
//Set startup picture and thumbnails
showPicture ();
```

Category MouseEnter, MouseLeave, and MouseLeftButtonDown Events

Now we need to use Expression Blend to define the MouseEnter, MouseLeave, and MouseLeftButtonDown events for the Pictures (see Figure 2-33) and Videos (see Figure 2-34) categories.

Figure 2-33. *Defining events for the Pictures category using Microsoft Expression Blend*

Figure 2-34. *Defining events for the Videos category using Microsoft Expression Blend*

Common MouseEnter Event for the Picture and Video Categories

To make things simple and quick, we created the simple grow animation that targets the FontSize property of a TextBlock in the "Defining Animations Using a Storyboard" section. This animation increases the FontSize on MouseEnter, thus highlighting the user's choice. Here we use that animation in the code-behind:

```
//Categories MouseEnter animations
private void categories_MouseEnter(object sender, MouseEventArgs e)
{
      //Stop running "grow" storyboard
      grow.Stop();
      //Get the reference of TextBlock that raises this event by casting
      //sender object to TextBlock
      TextBlock txtRef = (TextBlock)sender;
      //Set TargetNameProperty value of grow storyboard using cast
      //sender object
      grow.SetValue(Storyboard.TargetNameProperty, txtRef.Name);
      //Begin the storyboard
      grow.Begin();
}
```

Common MouseLeave Event for the Picture and Video Categories

We also created the simple shrink animation that decreases the value of the FontSize property of a TextBlock. Here we use that animation in the code-behind:

```
//Categories MouseLeave animations
private void categories_MouseLeave(object sender, MouseEventArgs e)
{
      //Stop running "shrink" storyboard
      shrink.Stop();
      //Get the reference of TextBlock that raises this event by casting
      //sender object to TextBlock
      TextBlock txtRef = (TextBlock)sender;
      //Set TargetNameProperty value of shrink storyboard using cast sender object
      shrink.SetValue(Storyboard.TargetNameProperty, txtRef.Name);
      //Begin the storyboard
      shrink.Begin();
}
```

MouseLeftButtonDown Event for the Pictures Categories

We use one central event handler named picCategories_MouseLeftButtonDown for all three Pictures categories. Here we need to cast the sender object to a TextBlock object so at runtime the event handler can determine which category has raised this event. For that, we use the Name property of the cast catRef TextBlock. Based on the Name property value, we set the currentPicCategory to point to the appropriate category. We also set the showMode variable to picture, make the proper presentation play mode visible, and display the first picture within the container by calling the showPicture() method. The following is the appropriate code snippet:

```
//Picture categories MouseLeftButtonDown
 private void
    picCategories_MouseLeftButtonDown(object sender, MouseButtonEventArgs e)
        {
            TextBlock catRef = (TextBlock)sender;
            switch (catRef.Name.ToUpper())
            {
                case "CATNATURE":
                    currentPicCategory = natureUri;
                    currentView.Text = "Nature";
                    break;

                case "CATBEACH":
                    currentPicCategory = beachUri;
                    currentView.Text = "Beach";
                    break;

                case "CATCARTOON":
                    currentPicCategory = cartoonUri;
                    currentView.Text = "Cartoon";
                    break;
            }
            //Set mode to "picture"
            showMode = "picture";

            //Changing visibility of round play button according to play mode
            Play.Visibility = Visibility.Visible;
            Stop.Visibility = Visibility.Collapsed;

            //Changing visibility of imgStage & vidStage according to mode
            vidStage.Visibility = Visibility.Collapsed;
            imgStage.Visibility = Visibility.Visible;
```

```
            //Reset index so it now points to first picture in the selected category
            playIndex = 0;

            //Show the picture and create thumbnails of selected category
            showPicture ();
        }
```

MouseLeftButtonDown event for the Video Categories

As implemented for the picture categories, we also will use one central event handler named vidCategories_MouseLeftButtonDown for all three video categories. We will cast sender to TextBlock, so the event handler can determine which category has raised this event at runtime. Again, we use the Name property of the cast TextBlock object. Based on the Name property value, we set currentVidCategory to point to the right category. We also set the showMode variable to video, make the proper presentation play mode visible, and play the first video within the container by calling the playVideo() method. The following is the appropriate code snippet:

```
//Video categories MouseLeftButtonDown
private void
  vidCategories_MouseLeftButtonDown(object sender, MouseButtonEventArgs e)
      {

            TextBlock catRef = (TextBlock)sender;
            switch (catRef.Name.ToUpper())
            {
                case "VCATSPORTS":
                    currentVidCategory = vsportsUri;
                    currentVidThumbCategory = vthumbsportsUri;
                    currentView.Text = "Sports";
                    break;

                case "VCATPETS":
                    currentVidCategory = vpetsUri;
                    currentVidThumbCategory = vthumbpetsUri;
                    currentView.Text = "Pets";
                    break;

                case "VCATCARTOON":
                    currentVidCategory = vcartoonUri;
                    currentVidThumbCategory = vthumbcartoonUri;
                    currentView.Text = "Cartoon";
                    break;
            }

            //Set mode to "video"
            showMode = "video";

            //Changing visibility of round play button according to play mode
            Play.Visibility = Visibility.Collapsed;
            Stop.Visibility = Visibility.Visible;

            //Changing visibility of imgStage & vidStage according to mode
            imgStage.Visibility = Visibility.Collapsed;
            vidStage.Visibility = Visibility.Visible;
```

```
        //Reset index so it now points to first video in the selected category
        playIndex = 0;

        //Plays the video and creates thumbnails of selected category
        playVideo ();
    }
```

The showPicture Method

The showPicture() method creates thumbnails by calling the createThumbnails() method and sets up pictures of the selected category. The following is a self-explanatory code-snippet of this method:

```
//Central method for showing picture of current gallery
private void showPicture()
{
  //Shows the image
  imgStage.SetValue(Image.SourceProperty,
      new BitmapImage(currentPicCategory[playIndex]));

  //Creates thumbnails of current category in preview pane
  createThumbnails();

  //Synchronizes the thumbnail with active picture in imgStage image control
  fadeThumb.SetValue(Storyboard.TargetNameProperty, "thumb" + imgIndex);
  fadeThumb.Begin();
  fadeIn.Begin();
}
```

The playVideo Method

Similarly, the playVideo() method creates thumbnails by calling the createThumbnails() method and plays a video of the selected category.

```
//Central method for playing video of current gallery
private void playVideo()
{
  //Plays the video
  vidStage.SetValue(MediaElement.SourceProperty, currentVidCategory[imgIndex]);
  vidStage.AutoPlay = true;

  //Creates thumbnails of current category in preview pane
  createThumbnails();

  //Synchronizes the thumbnail with active video in vidStage media element
  fadeThumb.SetValue(Storyboard.TargetNameProperty, "thumb" + imgIndex);
  fadeThumb.Begin();
  fadeIn.Begin();
}
```

The createThumbnails Method

We use one method to create thumbnails for both picture and video categories based on the value of the showMode string variable. We will use an Image object to create a series of thumbnail objects with proper events (see the following steps) to enable selection of the thumbnail and view/play relative pictures/videos upon selection.

1. Set the Margin property using the Thickness object so each thumbnail will have a slight amount of space at the right.

2. For unique naming of each thumbnail, we will use the idx integer type variable and will increment its value and use the SetValue property to name each thumbnail as we create it.

3. Set Opacity to 0.4 to make thumbnails slightly fade out as default behavior while they are not selected.

4. Set the Cursor property to change from Arrow to Hand on MouseEnter.

5. We also need to dynamically bind two event handlers—MouseLeftButtonDown and MouseEnter—to thumbnails.

6. Finally, we will add each thumbnail Image object to the thumbBar StackPanel preview pane. See the following code snippet for more details:

```
//Central method for creating thumbnails of current gallery
private void createThumbnails()
{
  //Clear thumbnails before displaying the currently selected one
  thumbBar.Children.Clear();
  int idx = 0;

  if (showMode.ToUpper() == "PICTURE")
  {
    foreach (Uri item in currentPicCategory)
    {

      Image thumbnails = new Image();
      //Right margin for each thumbnail
      thumbnails.Margin = new Thickness(0, 0, 10, 0);
      //Unique naming for each thumbnail to reference it later in codeBehind
      thumbnails.SetValue(NameProperty, "thumb" + idx);
      //Set thumbnail image control source property
      thumbnails.Source = new BitmapImage(item);
      //On mouseOver, cursor will be changed to Hand from Arrow
      thumbnails.Cursor = Cursors.Hand;
      //Opacity decreased
      thumbnails.Opacity = 0.4;
      //Add thumbnail image controls to stackpanel thumbBar
      thumbBar.Children.Add(thumbnails);
      //Dynamically attaching event handlers MouseLeftButtonDown & MouseEnter to
      //each thumbnail
      thumbnails.MouseLeftButtonDown += new
          MouseButtonEventHandler(thumbnails_MouseLeftButtonDown);
      thumbnails.MouseEnter += new MouseEventHandler(thumbnails_MouseEnter);
      //Increment in index that will be used in naming of each thumbnail
      idx++;
    }
  }

  else //The mode is video.

  {
    foreach (Uri item in currentVidThumbCategory)
    {

      Image vthumbnails = new Image();
```

```
            //Right margin for each thumbnail
            vthumbnails.Margin = new Thickness(0, 0, 10, 0);
            //Unique naming for each thumbnail to reference it later in codeBehind
            vthumbnails.SetValue(NameProperty, "thumb" + idx);
            //Set thumbnail image control source property
            vthumbnails.Source = new BitmapImage(item);
            //On mouseOver, cursor will be changed to Hand from Arrow
            vthumbnails.Cursor = Cursors.Hand;
            //Opacity decreased
            vthumbnails.Opacity = 0.4;
            //Add thumbnail image controls to stackpanel thumbBar
            thumbBar.Children.Add(vthumbnails);
            //Dynamically attaching event handlers MouseLeftButtonDown & MouseEnter to
            //each thumbnail
            vthumbnails.MouseLeftButtonDown += new
                MouseButtonEventHandler(thumbnails_MouseLeftButtonDown);
            vthumbnails.MouseEnter += new MouseEventHandler(thumbnails_MouseEnter);
            //Increment in index that will be used in naming of each thumbnail
            idx++;
        }
    }

}
```

Thumbnails MouseEnter and MouseLeftButtonDown Events

As shown in the showPicture() and playVideo() methods, we dynamically assign event handlers for MouseEnter and MouseLeftButtonDown for each thumbnail when we create them. The following sections show implementation of both these methods.

thumbnails_MouseEnter Event Implementation

When users mouse over a thumbnail, the MouseEnter event is raised. As we set Opacity to 0.5 when creating thumbnails in the createThumbnails() method, we will increase this Opacity value to 1 using the fadeThumb storyboard by setting the TargetNameProperty property of this storyboard dynamically. This is a similar approach to the one we used for the categories' MouseLeftButtonDown event (i.e., casting the sender object to an Image object named imgRef in this case). The following is the code snippet:

```
//This event is raised when user mouses over a thumbnail and
//changes Opacity to 1
public void thumbnails_MouseEnter(object sender, MouseEventArgs e)
{
    //Stop animation
    fadeThumb.Stop();

    //Cast reference from sender object to Image control
    Image imgRef = (Image)sender;

    //Using name property of cast image, dynamically set
    //TargetNameProperty of fadeThumb storyboard
    fadeThumb.SetValue(Storyboard.TargetNameProperty, imgRef.Name);

    //Start animation
    fadeThumb.Begin();

}
```

thumbnails_MouseLeftButtonDown Event Implementation

When a user clicks a thumbnail, the picture or video gets displayed in the appropriate container. To achieve this function, we bind the `MouseLeftButtonDown` event for thumbnails as shown in the following code snippet. Note that to set the `vidStage` Media element's `Source` property, we have to perform string manipulation to keep it simplified.

```
vidStage.Source = new
    Uri(bmi.UriSource.ToString().Replace(".jpg",".wmv"),UriKind.Relative );
```

In the preceding code, we simply get the `Uri` for the video file by replacing `.jpg` with `.wmv`, and we keep the same name for the video and related thumbnail image. So by just changing the file extension, we can refer to the related video file. As explained earlier, for the enterprise application we should come up with a more generic approach.

```
//This event is raised when user clicks thumbnail to display image/video
//in imgStage/vidStage control
public void
    thumbnails_MouseLeftButtonDown(object sender, MouseButtonEventArgs e)
{
    //Cast reference from sender object to Image control
    Image img = (Image)sender;
    //Using source property of cast image, dynamically create
    //bitmapImage to display in imgStage image control
    BitmapImage bmi = (BitmapImage)img.Source;
    if (showMode == "picture")
        imgStage.Source = new BitmapImage(bmi.UriSource);
    else
    //Getting video source from thumbnail by some string manipulation
    vidStage.Source = new
        Uri(bmi.UriSource.ToString().Replace(".jpg",".wmv"),UriKind.Relative );
    fadeIn.Begin();

}
```

Implementing Full-Screen/Normal-Screen Mode Using the MouseLeftButtonDown Event

As shown in Figure 2-35, Expression Blend allows integration with the XAML control event through its IDE.

Figure 2-35. *Defining XAML control properties using Expression Blend*

Click the Event section of the Full-Screen button within the IDE (the highlighted command in Figure 2-35). This will bring up the section shown in Figure 2-36 to automatically create and bind the code-behind event handler for the `goFullscreen` TextBlock control's `MouseLeftButtonDown` event.

Figure 2-36. *XAML controls event integration using Expression Blend*

As soon as we type **goFullscreen_MouseLeftButtonDown** in the MouseLeftButtonDown event text box and press Enter, Visual Studio will open the Page.xaml.cs code-behind file and create an empty event handler.

The next step is to write simple custom code to control the behavior of the image/video content control mode.

```
//Toggle button for changing view between full and normal screen
private void
    goFullscreen_MouseLeftButtonDown(object sender, MouseButtonEventArgs e)
{
    Application.Current.Host.Content.IsFullScreen =
        !Application.Current.Host.Content.IsFullScreen;
    if (goFullscreen.Text.ToUpper() == "FULL SCREEN")
        goFullscreen.Text = "Normal Screen";
    else
        goFullscreen.Text = "Full Screen";
}
```

As shown, we toggle the content control to full-screen or normal-screen mode based on the current value of the goFullscreen XAML control Text value.

Previous and Next Symbol MouseLeftButtonDown Events

Implement the MouseLeftButtonDown event for the prev and next symbols using Expression Blend as explained in the previous section to move to the previous or next picture or video based on the selected category. The following is the prev version:

```
//Previous button
private void prev_MouseLeftButtonDown(object sender, MouseButtonEventArgs e)
{
    if (showMode == "picture")
    {
        if (playIndex == 0)
            playIndex = currentPicCategory.Count - 1;
        else
            playIndex--;

        showPicture();
    }
    else
    {
        if (playIndex == 0)
            playIndex = currentVidCategory.Count - 1;
        else
            playIndex--;

        playVideo();

    }
}
```

Similarly, you can implement the next symbol event to display the next picture or video.

```
//Next command
private void next_MouseLeftButtonDown(object sender, MouseButtonEventArgs e)
{
    if (showMode == "picture")
    {
```

```
            if (playIndex == currentPicCategory.Count - 1)
                playIndex = 0;
            else
                playIndex++;

            showPicture();
    }
    else
    {
            if (playIndex == currentVidCategory.Count - 1)
                playIndex = 0;
            else
                playIndex++;

            playVideo();

    }
}
```

Play and Stop Picture Slide Show or Video

To play or stop the picture slide show of the selected category or the selected video, we need to bind an event handler to the previously created Play, Stop, and roundBack symbols. We'll use Expression Blend to quickly set up an event handler for play, as shown in Figure 2-37.

Figure 2-37. *Binding event handlers to the object using Expression Blend*

Next we'll discuss the code-behind.

Play/Stop Picture Slide Show or Video

As our application has the play presentation feature for the picture category and play/stop video feature for the video category, we need to implement behavior for the command based on the user selection of media type. The showMode variable defines the selected category. With the value picture for the showMode variable, we implement the play presentation feature for the picture category. Here we use the DispatcherTimer object named timer with the Interval property set to 4 seconds.

For the video category, the same event handler performs the play/stop function on the vidStage media element object. As shown in the following code, we stop the timer object and thus stop the automatic slide show of pictures or currently playing video based on the selected media type category:

```
private void playStopToggle(object sender, MouseButtonEventArgs e)
{
    //Start slide show of pictures and start video

    if (Play.Visibility == Visibility.Visible)
    {
        Play.Visibility = Visibility.Collapsed;
        Stop.Visibility = Visibility.Visible;

        if (showMode == "picture")
        {
            timer.Interval = new TimeSpan(0, 0, 4);
```

```
            timer.Start();
            timer.Tick += new EventHandler(timer_Tick);
        }
        else
        {
            vidStage.Play();
        }
    }
    else
    {

        //Stop the current presentation or video

        Play.Visibility = Visibility.Visible ;
        Stop.Visibility = Visibility.Collapsed ;

        if (showMode == "picture")
        {
            timer.Stop();
        }
        else
        {
            vidStage.Pause();
        }
    }
```

The slide show has a 4-second interval, which is implemented using the `DispatcherTimer` named `timer`. We need to implement the `timer_Tick` event to raise the event every 4 seconds as shown in the following code snippet. Every 4 seconds, we move to the next picture, or if it is the last picture, we move to the first picture.

```
//In picture gallery presentation mode, this event is raised every 4 secs
    void timer_Tick(object sender, EventArgs e)
    {
        if (imgIndex == currentPicCategory.Count - 1)
            imgIndex = 0;
        else
            imgIndex++;

        showPicture();
    }
```

Finishing the Development of the My Album Application

We've now finished the development of the My Album application. If you revisit the preceding sections, you will notice that Silverlight, Visual Studio, and Expression Blend provide a promising agile RIA development platform. I believe this application can easily be developed in 60 minutes, once you know what you are going to develop and have designed it.

If you compile and build the application and run it, it should function properly, meeting our objectives.

Packaging the My Album Silverlight Application

When you compile any Silverlight project, the associated files such as images, videos, text files, and XML files get added into one package with the file extension .xap along with the compiled DLL of Page.xaml.cs, Page.xaml, and any other referenced assemblies. We will deploy the compiled My Album XAP package to the Silverlight hosting server on Microsoft Silverlight Streaming service provided by Windows Live. When a user requests the page, which has Silverlight content embedded, the XAP package is downloaded on the client machine. To reduce the initial download time and improve the overall application startup performance, it is crucial to keep the size of the XAP package as small as possible.

Note The XAP package is nothing but a standard ZIP archive, and you can view its contents using any standard files compression software like WinZip (http://www.winzip.com) or WinRAR (http://www.rarlab.com).

We need to consider the XAP package definition when we work with an application that has a large number of video or image files in order to provide better performance and user experience. If all the files are compiled into the XAP package, it would be a large XAP package that can take significant time to download on the client machine.

The build actions describe how a file relates to the build and deployment processes. You can set the Build Action property of any file that is part of your project through the Properties window of that file as shown in Figure 2-38.

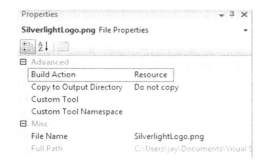

Figure 2-38. *Defining individual file deployment behavior using the Build Action property*

Now let's take a look at the different possible values of the Build Action property and its impact on the compilation of the Silverlight project as an XAP file.

Figure 2-39 shows the different values of the Build Action property.

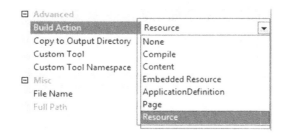

Figure 2-39. *Different options for the Build Action property*

In the following text, we will discuss the Build Action values that are applicable within the scope of our application.

Build Action As Content

Usually you use the Content option to add small web or media files to your Silverlight application within the package file without impacting the application startup performance. In this case the file is

- Added to the XAP package at the application root level.
- Accessible using a URI relative to the application root. You must precede the URI with a leading slash (/)—for example, `<Image Source="/SilverlightLogo.png" />`.

Build Action As None with the Copy to Output Directory Property Set Relatively

The None option is a good one when you are working with large video or image files and want to keep them out of the XAP package. By default, a video file's Build Action property is set to None with the Copy to Output Directory property set to Do not copy. As mentioned earlier for this project, we have set the Build Action property to None for our video files. So upon deployment, you must upload the referenced video files alongside the XAP package. You can also use streaming or progressive download to access them efficiently, as well as employ an absolute URI here.

In this case the file

- Is not added to the XAP package, but the Copy to Output Directory property will ensure it gets copied to the directory where the XAP file is.
- Is accessible using a URI relative to the application root. You must precede the URI with a leading slash (/)—for example, `<Image Source="/SilverlightLogo.png" />`.

Build Action As Resource

By default, the XAP package is created in the `...\PrecompiledWeb\<your project name>\Client-Bin` directory as the `<your Project name>.xap` file. If you set the file's Build Action property to Resource, it gets embedded into the project DLL file. In this case it will not be straightforward to access the resource file. You can retrieve the resource file by decompiling the DLL file using third party tools. There is no need for a leading slash (/) before the URI—for example, `<Image Source="SilverlightLogo.png" />`.

Deploying the My Album Silverlight Application on Microsoft Silverlight Streaming by Windows Live

Once an application has been fully tested and is ensured to be stable, the application can be deployed. The simplest deployment option is to copy the application files and resources to a server. In most cases, Silverlight applications just need to be copied to a web server where users can access them over the Web using a web browser.

To support and accelerate the use of Silverlight among developers and designers, Microsoft created a space online to host Silverlight applications under the Windows Live suite and services. The Microsoft Silverlight Streaming Service, which is free to use (as of the time of writing), can be found at http://silverlight.live.com/.

As described on the Microsoft Silverlight Streaming web site:

Microsoft® Silverlight™ Streaming by Windows Live™ is a companion service for Silverlight that makes it easier for developers and designers to deliver and scale rich media as part of their Silverlight applications. The service offers web designers and developers a free and convenient solution for hosting and streaming cross-platform, cross-browser media experiences and rich interactive applications that run on Windows™ and Mac. Combined with the ability to create content with Microsoft® Expression and other 3rd party tools, web designers and content publishers wishing to integrate Silverlight applications into their online properties can enjoy complete control of the end user experience.

To start with the Microsoft Silverlight Streaming Service, you need to obtain an account ID and account key. To obtain an account, you will need a Windows Live ID. If you have one, you can simply log in to the Microsoft Silverlight Streaming Service and generate your account ID and key. If you do not have a Windows Live ID, you can sign up for one at the streaming service web site.

Once you have an account ID and account key, you are ready to upload the application to the service. The following step-by-step explanation details how to deploy the My Album Silverlight application using the Microsoft Silverlight Streaming Service:

1. Sign up for a Silverlight Live service.

2. Create a Silverlight application.

3. Create valid ZIP package of necessary files.

4. Upload this ZIP archive to Microsoft Silverlight Streaming Server.

5. Create a web page to share the application.

I will assume that you have successfully logged in to the Windows Silverlight Streaming Service using your Windows Live ID.

For deploying the My Album application on the Microsoft Silverlight Streaming Server, you need to work with the Manage Applications feature available on the logged-in page, as highlighted in Figure 2-40.

Figure 2-40. *Deploying Silverlight applications on Microsoft Silverlight Streaming Server provided by Windows Live*

The Manage Applications option allows users to upload and manage one or more Silverlight applications on the Microsoft Silverlight Streaming Server. Clicking the Manage Applications option will bring up the page shown in Figure 2-41. Click the Upload an application option.

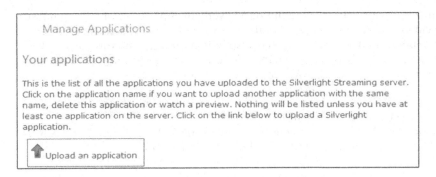

Figure 2-41. *Uploading a Silverlight application XAP package on Microsoft Silverlight Streaming Server*

You will get a screen similar to the one in Figure 2-42. You need to enter your application name, in this case My Album, and click the Create button.

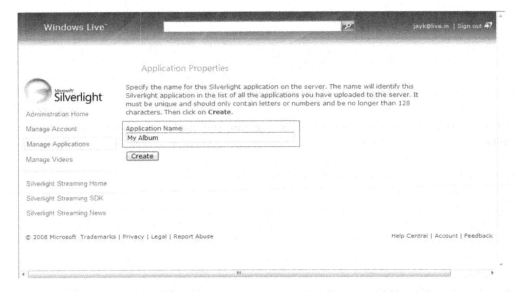

Figure 2-42. *Creating a new Silverlight application on the Microsoft Silverlight Streaming Server*

Once the My Album application is created, you can upload application files using the Browse option.

■Note The size for a single video file must be smaller than 105MB to upload the file successfully on the Microsoft Silverlight Streaming Server.

The selected file must be a valid ZIP archive defining a Silverlight application with its manifest. As our application has videos, you need to copy all of them to the ClientBin folder as described earlier in the "Defining Application Behavior Through the Code-Behind" section. Now you need to create a valid ZIP archive—say, myAlbum.zip—that includes the XAP package and videos: select all the files including myAlbum.xap, right-click myAlbum.xap, and choose Send To ➤ Compressed (zipped) Folder.

Now click the Browse button, and navigate to the ...\PrecompiledWeb\My Album\ClientBin folder. Choose myAlbum.zip, click Open, and then click Upload.

After successfully uploading the myAlbum.zip file, you need to create the manifest for the Silverlight application. Click Create to create the manifest, as shown in Figure 2-43.

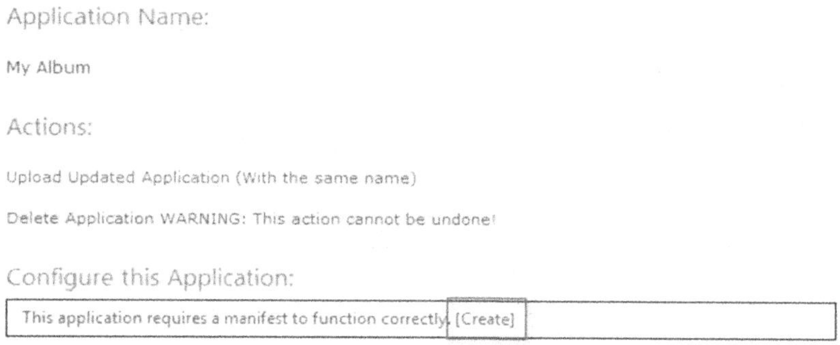

Application Name:

My Album

Actions:

Upload Updated Application (With the same name)

Delete Application WARNING: This action cannot be undone!

Configure this Application:

This application requires a manifest to function correctly [Create]

Figure 2-43. *Creating a manifest for the Silverlight application*

Clicking this button creates a manifest for the application and displays the message box shown in Figure 2-44.

Figure 2-44. *A message indicating the successful creation of your Silverlight application manifest*

When you click OK, you will see the form where you can set different properties that will control the appearance of your Silverlight application. Here we will set three properties, Display name, Height, and Width, as shown in Figure 2-45.

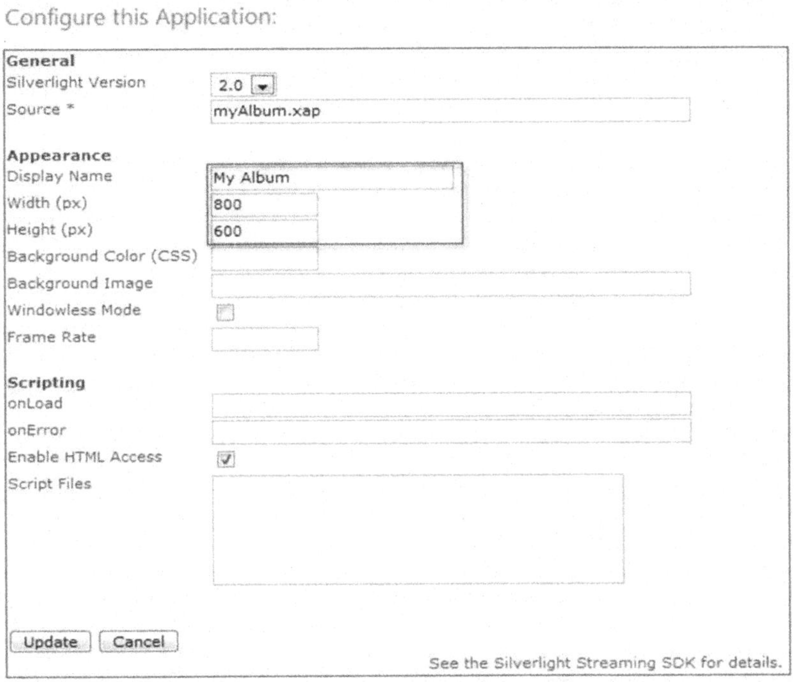

Configure this Application:

General
Silverlight Version   2.0 ▾
Source *   myAlbum.xap

Appearance
Display Name   My Album
Width (px)   800
Height (px)   600
Background Color (CSS)
Background Image
Windowless Mode   ☐
Frame Rate

Scripting
onLoad
onError
Enable HTML Access   ☑
Script Files

[Update] [Cancel]

See the Silverlight Streaming SDK for details.

Figure 2-45. *Configuring the Silverlight application*

After filling up the required values, click Update. Now you can visit the Microsoft Silverlight Streaming site to check your deployed application. The application URL will be based on your account ID and the application name. In this case, the account ID is 60973 and the application name is My Album. As a result, the My Album application can be accessed on the Microsoft Silverlight Streaming Server using the following URL for testing purposes:

```
http://silverlight.services.live.com/invoke/60973/My%20Album/iframe.html
```

■**Note** When you deploy your Silverlight application on the Microsoft Silverlight Streaming Server using your account, you will get a different unique account ID from the one mentioned in the preceding text. The deployed application can be accessed using the proper account ID only.

The next step is to include this deployed application within your page. Microsoft Silverlight Streaming Service provides two options to add the deployed Silverlight application to a web page, as shown in Figure 2-46.

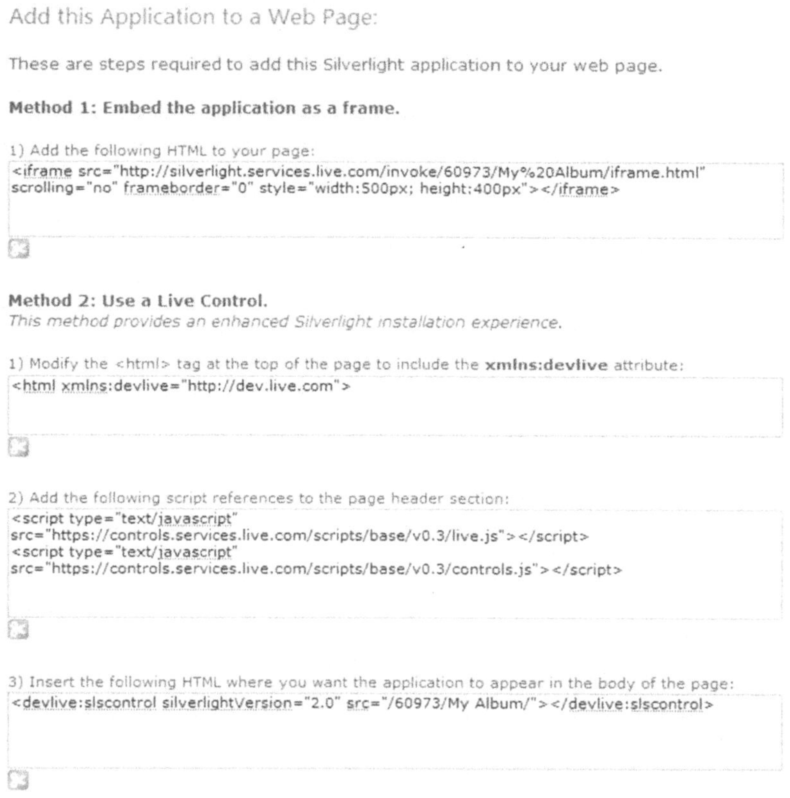

Add this Application to a Web Page:

These are steps required to add this Silverlight application to your web page.

Method 1: Embed the application as a frame.

1) Add the following HTML to your page:

```
<iframe src="http://silverlight.services.live.com/invoke/60973/My%20Album/iframe.html"
scrolling="no" frameborder="0" style="width:500px; height:400px"></iframe>
```

Method 2: Use a Live Control.
This method provides an enhanced Silverlight installation experience.

1) Modify the <html> tag at the top of the page to include the **xmlns:devlive** attribute:

```
<html xmlns:devlive="http://dev.live.com">
```

2) Add the following script references to the page header section:

```
<script type="text/javascript"
src="https://controls.services.live.com/scripts/base/v0.3/live.js"></script>
<script type="text/javascript"
src="https://controls.services.live.com/scripts/base/v0.3/controls.js"></script>
```

3) Insert the following HTML where you want the application to appear in the body of the page:

```
<devlive:slscontrol silverlightVersion="2.0" src="/60973/My Album/"></devlive:slscontrol>
```

Figure 2-46. *Different options for adding the deployed Silverlight application (on the Microsoft Silverlight Streaming Server) to your web page/application*

Let's look at both approaches in detail.

Method 1: Embed the Application As a Frame

Embedding the Silverlight application as a frame is the simplest approach to adding the Silverlight application to your page. You need to copy the provided code (see Figure 2-46) and paste it into your HTML or ASPX page within the <td> or <div> section to embed the application as a frame. This approach has some common IFRAME limitations from the browser support point of view.

Method 2: Using a Live Control

Adding the Silverlight application as a Live Control is an enhancement that provides a better Silverlight installer experience than using an IFRAME. Follow the steps provided in Figure 2-46 to add your application as a Live Control to your page.

You can use one of these approaches to add the My Album application to your main web site as well. I have used Method 1 and embedded the My Album application as a frame to my web site, TechnologyOpinion.com. You can visit http://www.technologyopinion.com/myalbum.aspx to access the application.

Summary

This chapter provided a kick-start on introducing the development of a Silverlight-based RIA. The developed My Album application is a base application for this book, and later I will refer to it again and show you how to transform it into the Enterprise Training Portal RIA by explaining how to develop Silverlight-based enterprise RIAs.

There are two project templates available to develop Silverlight-based projects using Microsoft Visual Studio 2008 SP1. The Application project template helps to create a Silverlight-based RIA, whereas with the Class Library project template we can create reusable Silverlight library components.

We developed the My Album RIA with categorized presentation of images and video files supported. During the development of the application, I covered various aspects of the Silverlight technology capabilities:

- Integration of Silverlight with Visual Studio IDE and development environment
- Seamless integration with Microsoft Expression Blend for rich user interface definition and event integration
- Use of WPF and XAML for the user interface definition
- Managed code-behind integration to develop an interactive application
- Rich .NET class library integration
- Animation capabilities
- Rich media integration
- Use of Expression Encoder

With the development of the My Album application, it can be easily concluded that the combination of Microsoft .NET Framework 3.5, WPF-based Silverlight technology, Microsoft Visual Studio, and Expression Blend provides a promising agile RIA development platform.

The chapter evaluated different approaches to packaging Silverlight applications and the use of Microsoft Silverlight Streaming Service provided by Windows Live to deploy Silverlight applications. We deployed the developed My Album application on the Microsoft Silverlight Streaming Server to understand how you can use the free Microsoft Silverlight Streaming Service to host your media files and Silverlight application.

Use the following link to access the developed Microsoft Silverlight–based My Album RIA: http://www.technologyopinion.com/myalbum.aspx.

As you saw during the development of the My Album RIA, there is a lot we can improve (e.g., hard-coded content) to make it a properly designed enterprise-level application. Silverlight has all the features and capabilities to support the development and deployment of enterprise-level applications and services.

The next chapter uncovers the real meaning of the term "enterprise-ready technology platform" in the era of Enterprise 2.0 and Web 2.0. We will focus on what features and capabilities are required of an enterprise-ready technology platform. The chapter then maps these features and capabilities to those of Microsoft Silverlight to confirm that Silverlight is an enterprise-ready technology platform.

Additional References

Links from the Microsoft Web Site

- ASP .NET Controls for Silverlight, `http://quickstarts.asp.net/3-5-extensions/silverlight/default.aspx`
- Developing Silverlight Library Assembly, `http://msdn.microsoft.com/en-us/library/cc296243(VS.95).aspx`
- Animations in Silverlight Projects, `http://www.silverlight.net/quickstarts/silverlight10/animations.aspx`
- Microsoft Expression home page, `http://expression.microsoft.com/en-us/default.aspx` (click the Products tab and either Expression Blend or Expression Encoder to go to product-specific pages)
- ScottGu's Blog, "First Look at Using Expression Blend with Silverlight 2," `http://weblogs.asp.net/scottgu/archive/2008/02/28/first-look-at-using-expression-blend-with-silverlight-2.aspx`

PART 2

■ ■ ■

Enterprise Application Development with Silverlight

CHAPTER 3

∎∎∎

Silverlight: An Enterprise-Ready Technology Platform

In Chapter 2, we developed a desktop application-like Rich Internet Application (RIA) called My Album using Silverlight. Now the key question is, can it be an enterprise application? I believe we are pretty close.

Chapter 1 provided a good exploration of the Web 2.0 concept. This chapter will start with outlining the concepts behind another buzz word, "Enterprise 2.0." The text then redefines the question, "What is an enterprise-ready technology platform?" in terms of Enterprise 2.0. Later, you'll learn why Silverlight is an enterprise-ready technology that enables Enterprise 2.0 and Web 2.0 applications. At the end of the chapter, I'll discuss why we are pretty close to transforming the My Album application developed in Chapter 2 into an enterprise application.

What Is an Enterprise-Ready Technology Platform?

The impact of globalization, advancements in technology platforms and components, and increased customer expectations led to Web 2.0 and challenged enterprises to think innovatively. This change ultimately altered the implementation of enterprise systems in comparison to the traditional monolithic enterprise information systems. The changes in implementation models also raised the need for radical structural and behavioral changes within organizations. As a result, the Web 2.0 concept also drove the Enterprise 2.0 concept.

Defining Enterprise 2.0

Figure 3-1 shows the "big picture" of the Enterprise 2.0 concept.

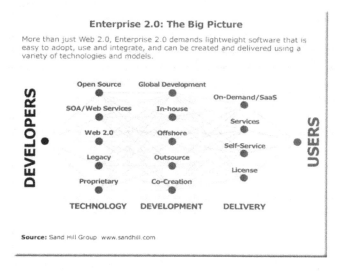

Figure 3-1. *Enterprise 2.0: the big picture*[1]

The term "Enterprise 2.0" is originally defined as the following by Professor Andrew McAfee of the Harvard Business School:[2]

> ***Enterprise 2.0*** *is the use of* ***emergent social software platforms*** *within companies, or between companies and their partners or customers.*

> ***Social software*** *enables people to rendezvous, connect, or collaborate through computer-mediated communication and to form online communities.*

> ***Platforms*** *are digital environments in which contributions and interactions are globally visible and persistent over time.*

> ***Emergent*** *means that the software is* ***freeform***, *and that it contains mechanisms to let the patterns and structure inherent in people's interactions become visible over time.*

> ***Freeform*** *means that the software is most or all of the following:*

> - *Optional*
> - *Free of up-front workflow*
> - *Egalitarian, or indifferent to formal organizational identities*
> - *Accepting of many types of data*

---

1. M. R. Rangaswami, "Enterprise 2.0: The Big Picture," http://sandhill.com/opinion/editorial.php?id=98&page=1, 2006
2. Professor Andrew McAfee, "Enterprise 2.0, version 2.0," http://blog.hbs.edu/faculty/amcafee/index.php/faculty_amcafee_v3/enterprise_20_version_20/, 2006

Professor McAfee also defined the terminology *SLATES* (search, links, authoring, tags, extensions, and signals), demonstrating key elements of Enterprise 2.0 (shown in Figure 3-2).

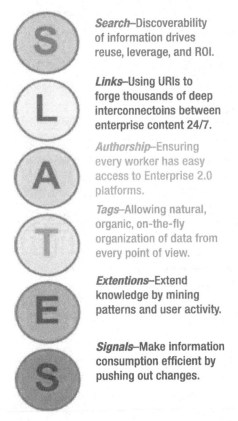

Search–Discoverability of information drives reuse, leverage, and ROI.

Links–Using URIs to forge thousands of deep interconnectoins between enterprise content 24/7.

Authorship–Ensuring every worker has easy access to Enterprise 2.0 platforms.

Tags–Allowing natural, organic, on-the-fly organization of data from every point of view.

Extentions–Extend knowledge by mining patterns and user activity.

Signals–Make information consumption efficient by pushing out changes.

Figure 3-2. *Key elements of Enterprise 2.0*[3]

Further, Dion Hinchcliffe of ZDNet refined the Enterprise 2.0 elements and introduced the term *FLATNESSES* (Freedom, Links, Authorship, Tagging, Network-oriented, Extensions, Search, Social, Emergence, Signals). Figure 3-3 presents the refined elements of Enterprise 2.0.

---

3. Dion Hinchcliff, "The state of Enterprise 2.0," `http://blogs.zdnet.com/Hinchcliffe/?p=143`, 2007

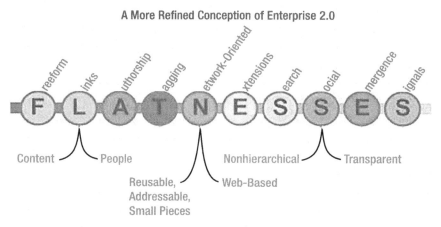

Figure 3-3. *Refined elements of Enterprise 2.0* [4]

Table 3-1 summarizes the key differences between Enterprise 1.0 and Enterprise 2.0.

Table 3-1. *Enterprise 1.0 vs. Enterprise 2.0* [5]

Enterprise 1.0	Enterprise 2.0
Hierarchy	Flat organization
Friction	Ease of organization flow
Bureaucracy	Agility
Inflexibility	Flexibility
IT-driven technology/Lack of user control	User-driven technology
Top down	Bottom up
Centralized	Distributed
Teams are in one building/one time zone	Teams are global
Silos and boundaries	Fuzzy boundaries, open borders
Need to know	Transparency
Information systems are structured and dictated	Information systems are emergent
Taxonomies	Folksonomies
Overly complex	Simple
Closed/proprietary standards	Open
Scheduled	On demand
Long time-to-market cycles	Short time-to-market cycles

It is apparent that the Enterprise 2.0 concept is associated not only with IT, but also with people and organizations. Organizations have to implement an optimized, diversified, simplified, agile, and

---

4. Ibid.
5. Enterprise 2.0 Conference, "What Is Enterprise 2.0?" http://www.enterprise2conf.com/about/what-is-enterprise2.0.php

cohesive IT organization model, as well as a workforce that can support the Enterprise 2.0 concept and can develop, deploy, and maintain Web 2.0–based RIAs.

This chapter will cover only the IT capabilities that are required to move the enterprise toward the Enterprise 2.0 concept and develop and deploy RIAs.

Goals for the Enterprise-Ready Technology Platform

In the era of Enterprise 2.0 and Web 2.0, we need to revisit the definition of an enterprise-ready technology platform. I believe that the technology platforms and components that help enterprises to achieve the following three goals supporting Enterprise 2.0 and Web 2.0 concepts can be defined as enterprise ready:

- Enabling the development and deployment of collaborative business-enabled applications (BEAs) empowering end users and achieving business values

- Supporting seven key principles (flexibility, usability, simplification, reusability, scalability, maintainability, security) for building RIAs as services

- Enabling development of platform-independent RIAs as services to support all types of devices and platforms

Let's take a closer look at these three goals.

Business-Enabled Applications

Enterprise 2.0– and Web 2.0–based technology platforms enable organizations to develop BEAs that drive business value and customer satisfaction. BEAs[6] are IT-driven RIAs, which implies a *balanced approach* for application requirements based on customers' requirements, organization strategies, business value, and quality standards. Development of BEAs usually follows the agile software development life cycle (SDLC) to deliver applications on time and with a controlled cost model meeting customer expectations and the organization's IT budget.

Based on the preceding explanation, a simple formula can be defined for BEAs:

BEAs =

Balanced (requirement implementation + quality standards) + in-time delivery + controlled cost

Today, most organizations look at their IT division as a spending division rather than a profit-making division. Business-enabled RIAs usually strive to deliver maximum customer satisfaction and stakeholder expectations. Due to this reason, in the long term, proper alignment of business-enabled RIAs with an organization's strategies ultimately helps the organization to transform its IT department from a *cost center* to a *profit-making center* by returning maximum return on investment (ROI).

BEAs mainly focus on both angles of the business—customers and organization strategies (i.e., stakeholders). Figure 3-4 demonstrates the user-centric and business-driven key features of BEAs.

---

6. Ashish Ghoda, "'Business Enabled' Applications—Part One," http://advice.cio.com/ashish_ghoda/business_enabled_applications_part_one

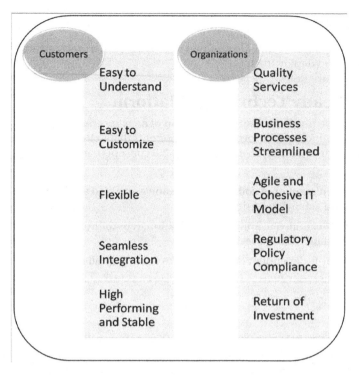

Figure 3-4. *Features of BEAs*

As shown in Figure 3-4, user-centric features of BEAs are focused on three main factors—users, users, and users. Users are empowered to customize services and features (such as user-based and user role–based customized views and subscription-based services) of BEAs easily based on their needs. The following are key user-centric features of BEAs that improve the overall usability of applications and empower end users:

- Richness
- Flexibility
- Consistency
- High performance
- High stability

Business-driven features of BEAs are focused on mainly three factors—*organization strategies*, *quality*, and *cost*. The following are key business-driven features of BEAs that enable organizations to support Enterprise 2.0 and Web 2.0 concepts and help organizations gain maximum ROI in the long term.

- Proper quality standards and quality control process
- Controlled cost
- Remodeled IT organization model and strategies
- Enhanced team integrity and ethical rules to support globalized cross-cultured virtual teams
- Support for global and country-specific regulatory policies
- Streamlined and integrated business processes

The balanced approach mentioned previously represents a balancing act among the four dimensions of BEAs (see Figure 3-5) in order to achieve the maximum ROI:

- Controlled cost

- Adjustment and alignment to requirements and strategies

- Quality maintenance of organizations and applications

- Time to deliver products and time to handle change management

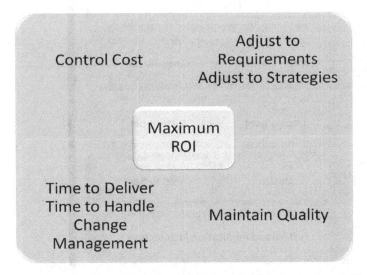

Figure 3-5. *The four dimensions of BEAs to achieve maximum ROI*

Seven Key Principles for Building RIAs As a Service

Abstracted, loosely coupled, and collaborative RIAs based on service-oriented architecture (SOA) help enterprises to develop, deploy, and distribute RIAs as software as a service (SaaS) to the end users.

The SOA-based SaaS helps to achieve several critical success factors, the following of which are but a few, for software applications supporting the Enterprise 2.0 and Web 2.0 concepts:

- Reducing the overhead of software application development and deployment

- Seamless integration among internal and external systems

- Rich and collaborative lightweight RIAs

- Ability to deliver applications on time

Figure 3-6 shows seven principles—usability, flexibility, simplicity, reusability, scalability, maintainability, and security—for building SOA-based RIAs and deploying them as SaaS. I will explain these seven key principles in detail in the next chapter.

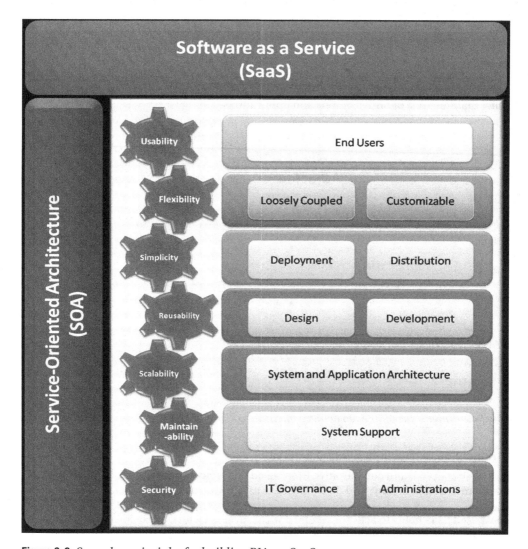

Figure 3-6. *Seven key principles for building RIAs as SaaS*

Device- and Platform-Independent RIAs

The last, but not least important, attribute of an enterprise-ready technology platform is the capability of developing worry-free device- and platform-independent RIAs supporting Enterprise 2.0 and Web 2.0 concepts.

Figure 3-7 demonstrates Enterprise 2.0 platform integration. As shown in the figure, the Enterprise 2.0 and Web 2.0 environment cloud is information (content and metadata) and media rich and contains lightweight services, enabling desktop applications like RIAs on the following:

- Devices such as computers and mobile devices
- Browser platforms such as Internet Explorer, Firefox, and Safari
- Operating systems such as Windows, Mac, and mobile operating systems

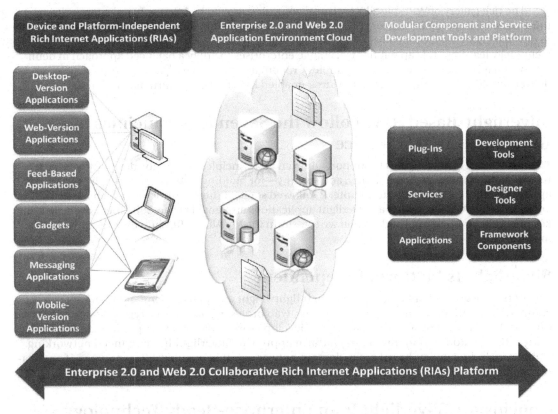

Figure 3-7. *Device- and platform-independent Enterprise 2.0 and Web 2.0 applications*

Is Silverlight an Enterprise-Ready Technology Platform?

It's time to validate that Silverlight is an enterprise-ready technology platform for developing RIAs supporting Enterprise 2.0 and Web 2.0 concepts, and thus are

- BEAs
- SaaS applications supporting the seven principles
- Device and platform independent

Silverlight-Based Applications Are Business-Enabled RIAs

Silverlight has all the potential to empower end users by providing a very rich and personalized user interface. It is also able to drive business with the capability to seamlessly integrate and process all types of digital information (media and nonmedia) in a secure environment, and thus providing a competitive edge in the market.

The powerful integration of Silverlight with key Microsoft development and design platforms such as the .NET Framework, Visual Studio, and Expression Studio enable IT organizations to develop and deliver lightweight, high-quality, Silverlight-based RIAs on time and under budget, returning maximum ROI.

The rich gallery of WPF-based XAML user controls supplied by Microsoft and support from third-party Microsoft partners for enhanced rich XAML user controls provide further opportunities to develop highly usable and loosely coupled Silverlight services and applications. These Silverlight technology features and capabilities will enable enterprises to apply a balanced approach in defining the organization's IT vision and technology roadmap. They allow organizations to develop and deliver simplified, Silverlight-based, business-enabled RIAs that can return maximum ROI.

Silverlight-Based RIAs Follow the Seven Key Principles of Building RIAs As a Service

The main vision of Silverlight is to support all seven key principles—usability, flexibility, simplicity, reusability, scalability, maintainability, and security—for building RIAs as a service. The My Album application that we developed in Chapter 2 followed some of the key principles, such as usability and simplicity. We will prove that Silverlight applications also enable us to implement the remaining key principles in Chapters 4 and 5 when we transform the My Album RIA into the Enterprise Training Portal RIA.

Silverlight Is Platform Independent

One of the key goals of Silverlight is to keep it lightweight and platform independent in terms of compatibility with different operating systems, web browsers, and device types. As described in Chapter 1, Silverlight provides a platform to develop cross-browser, cross-platform, and cross-device RIAs. In addition to this cross-platform approach, Silverlight has enhanced networking support including policy-based cross-domain networking that enables different types of application deployment.

Conclusion: Silverlight Is an Enterprise-Ready Technology Platform

It is crystal clear from the preceding discussion (and from the creation of the My Album application in Chapter 2) that Silverlight is an enterprise-ready technology platform that supports Enterprise 2.0. Using Silverlight, we can develop platform-independent, service-oriented, business-enabled RIAs and deploy them as SaaS.

Design Concepts for Silverlight-Based Enterprise RIAs

Silverlight is clearly an enterprise-ready technology platform that supports the Enterprise 2.0 and Web 2.0 concepts. In this section, we will mainly focus on the design concepts for Silverlight-based Enterprise 2.0 RIAs. We will revisit the My Album application from Chapter 2 so you can understand these design concepts.

Architecture Components for Enterprise RIAs

As shown in Figure 3-8, from the architecture perspective, IT executives, architects, developers, and IT professionals need to focus on the following six key architecture components for enterprise RIAs:

1. System architecture
2. Information architecture
3. Application architecture

4. Services architecture

5. User interface framework design

6. Deployment and distribution

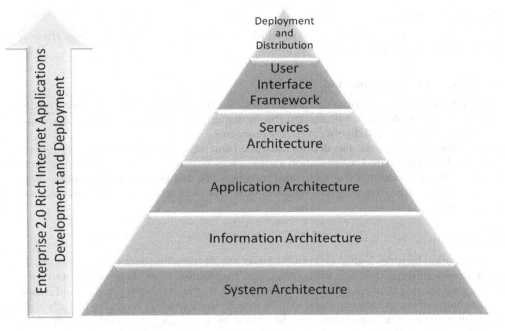

Figure 3-8. *Architecture components for enterprise RIAs*

System Architecture

The system architecture mainly defines the infrastructure environment in which the RIA will be deployed. The system architecture definition supports and aligns with the organization's vision, product landscape, and technology roadmap. During the definition of the system architecture, we should consider and define application environment and deployment-specific aspects such as

- Server and network architecture
- Network impact analysis
- Application software components and their setup and installation process
- Fault tolerance, monitoring, and instrumentation
- Information architecture including metadata definition and implementation
- Database platform definition with high availability, backup, archive, retention, discovery, and digester recovery process implementation
- Domain definition and security
- User provisioning: authentication, authorization, and subscription services
- IT governance and regulatory policy implementation
- Services integration and deployment
- Standardization of administration and maintenance processes

As you can see from the preceding explanation, more than just defining the infrastructure environment, the system architecture defines the enterprise architecture of the RIA and considers and covers the information architecture, application architecture, services architecture, user interface framework, and deployment and distribution strategies at a high level.

Information Architecture

The information architecture of the RIA mainly includes the definition of the data storage environment and the definition of the content.

Data Storage Environment Definition

The data storage environment provides architecture with details and design on how a secured data storage environment is deployed. It will support the implementation of high availability, backup, archive, retention, discovery, and digester recovery processes.

The data storage environment also defines the design and implementation of the data storage platform as a platform for secured collaboration among users. If there is a need for a data warehouse implementation, the information architecture also considers and defines different warehouse implementation approaches (e.g., information data warehouse, operational data warehouse, and data directory warehouse).

Content Definition

The content definition includes logical and physical data models detailing data type definitions, data structures, data relationships, data processing rules, data distribution rules, data security and governance rules, data sharing policies, and data discovery rules. The content definition should clearly define the taxonomy of the metadata related to the content. This metadata is used to identify and categorize different types of data and represent the right data at the right time as information to the end users, reducing the problem of information overload.

It is important to consider the use of industry-standard and open-standard metadata definitions (e.g., Dublin Core Online Metadata Standards—http://dublincore.org) in order to ease and standardize information integration and collaborative information among different interorganization and intraorganization systems. The use of industry-standard and open-standard metadata also helps build and maintain information-rich RIAs.

Application Architecture

The application architecture of RIAs mainly provides the application framework definition, determining the technologies and services that will be used in the development of the application. The application architecture also covers the design and definition of the application's services and components.

Application Framework Definition

The application framework defines the integration of different application layers—the presentation (user interface) layer, the services layer, the business components layer, the data access layer, and the data storage platform layer. The proper definition of the framework defining loosely coupled integration of different layers is critical in order to support the lightweight and service-oriented RIA development model and deploy RIAs as SaaS.

The application framework also defines the use of the following:

- Patterns and best practices. As an example of the use of Microsoft patterns and best practices, consider the Composite Application Guidance for WPF, which helps you implement service-oriented, loosely coupled, enterprise-level WPF-based applications. (In the future, the Composite Application Guidance for WPF is going to support Silverlight-based applications also. Visit the MSDN web site for more details–http://msdn.microsoft.com/en-us/library/cc707819.aspx.)

- An organization's reusable components and services from the components/service library.

- Services and interfaces to integrate different internal and external systems and business processes.

Technology Platform and Components Definition

The definition of the use of technologies and technology platform is critical in order to make sure that the developed RIA is aligned with the organization's long-term vision, product landscape, and technology roadmap. The architecture should be flexible for migrating one version of the technology to the other. Along with the definition of which key technologies and technology platform to use, during the definition of the application architecture, one of the key things you will evaluate is the buy vs. build of services and components.

Buy vs. build is one of the critical and strategic decisions you need to consider before choosing to custom-develop all the components and services. There are numerous strategic advantages (including getting maximum ROI) in buying existing components and services rather than building and maintaining them. You should consider building custom components and services that are unique in terms of features.

Services Architecture

The SOA concept has brought this additional layer into the architecture definition and is now playing a vital role in any enterprise-level application. The deployment of applications as SaaS brought a revolution in the way enterprise architects design applications, enterprises develop and deploy applications as lightweight services, and end users utilize them in a collaborative way.

It is necessary to understand business requirements, requirements for integration between different internal and external systems, organization's product and technology roadmap, and the available open standards in order to define and architect loosely coupled services.

Application services feature integration between the following:

- The abstracted application presentation layer and the business components that perform business logic

- The data storage platform to access the data and feed data to business objects and the presentation layer, and to make the application a data platform–independent application

- Internal and external systems for seamless business process integration and automation

While defining the application architecture, architects should consider implementing business process execution using services that can in the long term be used as reusable services across different applications. The services interface and contract definitions should be generic enough (not tightly coupled) to allow building a generic services library for the organization. This would help to reduce overall development and maintenance efforts and aid organizations in delivering effective and efficient applications just in time.

Developing and deploying applications as SaaS brings simplification, but also brings a number of different challenges such as these:

- The loosely coupled and abstracted SOA approach can bring overhead when integrating different layers of the application to execute business processes. This can have an impact on the overall response time, and thus can degrade the performance of the application. The degraded performance can significantly reduce the usability of the application, making end-user acceptance questionable.

- The system infrastructure architecture plays a critical role in the successful execution of service-based applications. Enterprise architects must consider the network latency and network bandwidth during the network impact analysis in order to achieve acceptable performance for end users accessing services from any part of the world and on any type of network (based on the defined enterprise application scope).

- Security is one of the major concerns of SaaS. The distributed nature of services, web-based access to services, and XML-based, message-oriented digital information exchange using web-based protocols bring numerous types of vulnerabilities such as identity management, cross-domain information exchange, message integrity and confidentiality, and information hacking.

Architects must consider the preceding challenges during the definition, design, implementation, and deployment of services.

User Interface Framework Design

An efficient, interactive, customizable, and rich user interface is one of the key features for any successful enterprise RIA. As described in earlier chapters, Silverlight and Microsoft's tightly coupled designer and developer tools enable professionals to develop a desktop application–like user interface. However, it is not easy to develop an enterprise RIA that can support a user interface that caters to a very wide, cross-border, diversified, and cross-cultural group of end users.

Before implementing the presentation layer, we should consider finalizing the user interface framework of the application. In order to finalize the user interface framework, designers should identify key objectives of the application and different common navigation patterns; they can then align these patterns with formal navigation patterns. In Chapter 2, we followed the same approach: we identified navigation patterns and defined the user interface framework.

The identification of repeatable navigation patterns will help you to develop reusable user controls/components libraries that can be referenced from multiple applications. As described earlier, you should develop the presentation layer using patterns and best practices such as Microsoft's Composite Application Guidance for WPF to develop loosely coupled user interface.

Deployment and Distribution

The SOA and SaaS application development and deployment concepts have led organizations to consider deployment and distribution as key IT strategies. Including package definition and deployment strategies as part of the architecture definition helps organizations to provide secure, high-performing services and improve end-user experience.

For Silverlight-based RIAs, you need to make a decision on what to include within the package and what to include as a reference. The application then downloads the references on demand in order to maintain a minimal package size for distribution. This approach thus reduces download and startup time for the application and improves overall performance and end-user experience.

Silverlight also provides implementation of cross-domain policies in order to supply secured communication and access to cross-domain services and information. It is important to consider and define the cross-domain deployment strategy (if needed) and include the appropriate cross-domain policies as part of your application's system architecture. Chapter 6 will cover in more detail cross-domain policies for Silverlight applications.

Current Design for the My Album RIA

The main focus of Chapter 2 was to develop a fully functional RIA quickly—the My Album RIA—using Silverlight. As a result, from the design point of view, we just concentrated on the application navigation (i.e., user interface).

We were pretty successful in achieving that goal, but the My Album RIA is not flexible and scalable enough to accommodate the dynamic nature of an enterprise-level application and customer requirements. Figure 3-9 presents the application architecture of the Silverlight-based My Album application developed in Chapter 2.

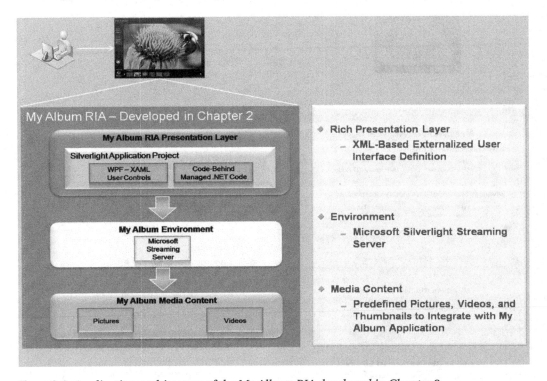

Figure 3-9. *Application architecture of the My Album RIA developed in Chapter 2*

As shown in Figure 3-9, we really did not focus on the enterprise aspects when building the My Album RIA, even though it has a rich desktop application–like user interface and user interactivity functionality.

We used the Silverlight Application project template to create the My Album application project. The presentation layer of the application consists of the XAML-based externalized user interface that we defined based on the user interface framework definition. We provided user interaction by implementing event handlers in the code-behind C# managed code.

The My Album media content (picture images, thumbnail images, and videos) file names and location information was hard-coded within the managed code and included as part of the package. This is not the best way to reference and deploy the media content.

Using the default Silverlight application package mechanism, we developed the application deployment package, included all images and video files as part of the package, and uploaded the application deployment package to the Microsoft Silverlight Streaming Server using the free Microsoft Silverlight Streaming Service. The uploaded application can be accessed directly from your account on the Microsoft Silverlight Streaming Server or can be attached as a plug-in to your web application.

Designing the My Album Application As an Enterprise RIA

In order to understand the design concepts of SOA-based, enterprise-level RIAs deployed as SaaS, we will take a first shot at revising the architecture of the My Album application. We will transform the application architecture so that My Album can be developed as an enterprise-level RIA. Figure 3-10 demonstrates the revised enterprise-level application architecture for the My Album application that will help to transform it into an enterprise RIA.

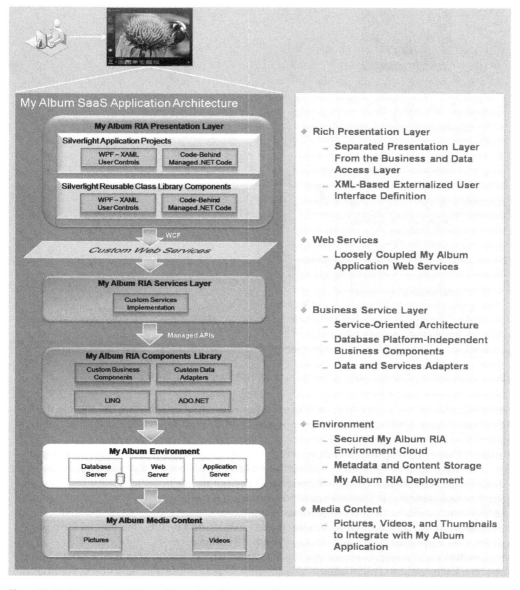

Figure 3-10. *Enterprise RIA architecture of the My Album RIA*

During the process of reevaluating the application architecture of the My Album RIA, we will consider all aspects of the Enterprise 2.0 architecture that we discussed in the preceding sections of the chapter.

Defining a Modular Presentation Layer

We will use the same Silverlight Application project template to create the My Album enterprise RIA project, as well as the same user interface framework design we defined in Chapter 2. The presentation layer of the application consists of the XAML-based externalized user interface framework definition.

The key difference between the initial My Album application and the proposed enterprise-level version is the use of a modular user interface design approach. During the definition of the user interface framework, we need to identify repeatable navigation pattern(s) that can be reused across more than one application. We can implement identified reusable navigation patterns (e.g., preview pane, left-side navigation pane, content container) as custom Silverlight XAML user controls using the Silverlight Class Library project and make them part of the Silverlight custom user controls library.

Again, we'll provide user interaction in code-behind event handlers. However, we need to identify possible reusable functionality (e.g., identifying left navigation pane categories and building tabs dynamically) and make it part of the reusable components library using the Silverlight Class Library project type.

In addition to the XAML-based presentation layer definition, the application presentation layer's modular approach will simplify the process of maintaining a consistent look and feel and functionality across enterprise-level, Silverlight-based RIAs.

Defining Loosely Coupled Custom Web Services

Web Services play a vital role in implementing SOA-based enterprise applications and integrating different internal and external systems. Silverlight-based RIAs are capable of integrating with Web Services because of their code-behind managed code. An XAML user control's code-behind or a referenced class library component can call Web Services to integrate with different database components or different systems, or to perform business logic.

As an example, for the My Album application, we can utilize Web Services to retrieve the definition of the left-side navigation from a centralized location to create the categorized tab dynamically.

Using code-behind managed code, Silverlight can also integrate with Windows Communication Foundation (WCF)—a service-oriented programming model incorporating ASP.NET Web Services, .NET Framework remoting, and enterprise services. I will demonstrate the integration of WCF with Silverlight in Chapter 5.

Defining the Business Components Layer

The enterprise-level RIA business components layer is separated from the presentation layer and abstracted from the data storage platform.

As shown earlier in Figure 3-10, the business components layer comprises

- Abstracted business components to execute business logic.

- A set of data adapters that help us to integrate and access different types of data storage platforms. They allow us to transform data into the standard format required by our business components.

- A set of service adapters that help us to transform the information into the format that is required by various Web Service interfaces to integrate with the application presentation layer.

Setting Up the Application Environment

Defining the infrastructure is critical for high performance and secure execution of enterprise applications. For the My Album application, the infrastructure architecture and database server–based user provisioning can provide effective user management and identity management. The database server can also be used for the metadata management. Based on your enterprise strategy, you need to decide the storage platform for image and video media files.

In addition to the database servers and media storage servers, you need application and web servers at minimum to deploy RIAs. Based on your organization's policy, you need to decide where to deploy the application—in the same domain or cross-domain, on the Internet or intranet zone— and whether to use a demilitarized zone (DMZ) to provide additional security to the organization's network.

Summary

After discussing the concept of Web 2.0 in Chapter 1 and developing the My Album RIA to demonstrate Silverlight's capabilities and supporting development environment in Chapter 2, this chapter defined the following:

- The Enterprise 2.0 concept

- The features of a technology that can make it an Enterprise 2.0–ready technology platform

- The aspects of Silverlight that make it an Enterprise 2.0–ready technology platform

- A new version of the My Album RIA architecture to develop and deploy it as an enterprise-level RIA

The Web 2.0 concept brings revolution to web-based application development and encourages enterprises to reevaluate their organization strategies, organization structure, and information system implementation approach. This new approach to develop and deploy RIAs is what Enterprise 2.0 is all about.

Capabilities to develop and deploy collaborative BEAs, support for the seven key principles (flexibility, usability, simplification, reusability, scalability, maintainability, security) of RIAs, and support for developing RIAs as platform-independent services are key features of Enterprise 2.0 and Web 2.0. Technology platforms and components that support these features are defined as enterprise-ready technology platforms and technology components.

Silverlight is an Enterprise 2.0–ready technology platform that supports all three goals and enables us to develop SOA-based, enterprise-level RIAs and to deploy them as SaaS.

At the end of the chapter, we redefined the My Album application architecture by incorporating SOA-based application development and SaaS deployment principles.

In the next chapter, we will dive into the details of SOA. We will also see details of the seven key principles for building Silverlight-based RIAs as services.

Additional References

Links from the Microsoft Web Site

- ASP .NET Controls for Silverlight, `http://quickstarts.asp.net/3-5-extensions/silverlight/default.aspx`

- Developing Silverlight Library Assembly, `http://msdn.microsoft.com/en-us/library/cc296243(VS.95).aspx`

CHAPTER 4

■ ■ ■

Silverlight and Service-Oriented Architecture

Chapters 3 and 4 of this book are dedicated to new enterprise architecture concepts. These concepts provide new challenges to enterprises that want to accommodate Enterprise 2.0 and enable development and deployment of Web 2.0–based RIAs.

Chapter 3 discussed the definition of an Enterprise 2.0–ready technology platform and how Silverlight fits that definition. The chapter also defined the possible enterprise-level architecture of the My Album Silverlight RIA, which was originally developed in Chapter 2.

This chapter will mainly focus on defining the service-oriented architecture (SOA) concept in detail. We will make a deep dive into the seven key principles of the SOA concept to deploy Silverlight-based RIAs as software as a service (SaaS). The chapter will end by looking at Silverlight's capability to integrate with Web Services and Language-Integrated Query (LINQ). We will develop a service-oriented sample Silverlight application demonstrating dynamic user interface (UI) creation and dynamic content population using enterprise features such as externalization, LINQ, Web Services, and custom user controls.

Defining Service-Oriented Architecture

No single definition can explain or define the SOA concept. The basic definition of SOA is as follows:[1]

> *Service-oriented architecture (SOA) is a method for systems development and integration where functionality is grouped around business processes and packaged as interoperable services.*

SOA supports the Enterprise 2.0 concept by aligning three organizational strategic components—product roadmap, technology roadmap, and IT governance model—by enabling implementation of loosely coupled RIAs and deploying them as SaaS. Thus SOA helps organizations migrate from building monolithic, heavyweight, traditional software applications to building distributed, collaborative, loosely coupled SaaS. This explanation leads us to a detailed definition of SOA:

> *SOA is an architectural concept on how to implement loosely coupled, distributed and lightweight shared services that can be consumed by internal and external applications for systems integration and executing different business processes.*

---

1. Wikipedia, http://en.wikipedia.org/wiki/Service-oriented_architecture

Key Objectives of SOA-Based Applications

Organizations can achieve three basic objectives by developing SOA-based applications:

1. **Meet expectations**: Understanding users' needs and market expectations is essential for the implementation of successful SOA-based systems. This basic concept ultimately drives organizations to define a business values–driven organizational IT model and develop an integrated IT and product roadmap.

2. **Keep it simple**: It is important to keep the organization's IT model simple, flexible, light-weight, and sustainable. This basic goal will help to identify key technologies that can enable simplified, lightweight SOA-based systems. The "keep it simple" principle will help IT departments transform from maintenance organizations (i.e., a cost center) to business-enabled organizations (i.e., a profit-making center).

3. **Follow the rules**: To remain competitive and successful in the digital, diversified global market and achieve maximum user satisfaction, it is critical to provide a secured environment to end users and to consider and comply with government and regulatory body rules, standards, and policies. The proper implementation and monitoring of the organizational-level IT governance model to implement secured and high-performing SOA-based systems is one of the key strategic components of the organization model.

Before getting a technical overview of the SOA concept, I think it is important to understand how SOA-based application objectives can help organizations to achieve their strategic goals in terms of implementing the defined product, technology roadmaps, and effective IT governance.

Figure 4-1 demonstrates the relationship between the three basic objectives of an SOA-based application and the three key strategic components of organizations.

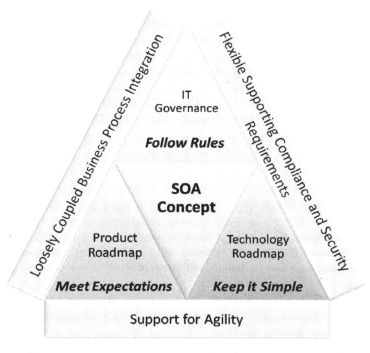

Figure 4-1. *SOA concept: relationship between SOA-based application objectives and organizational strategic components*

Now let's take a brief look at the three strategic components of organizations.

The *product roadmap* usually provides a path (mostly with a phased approach) to achieve the stakeholders' short- to long-term business goals in the form of a series of product releases that is very much aligned with the overall organization vision. The product roadmap clearly defines milestones of product releases with a high-level definition of the scope of each release that drives organizations to achieve the "meet expectations" and "keep it simple" basic objectives.

The *technology roadmap* usually provides strategic technical directions to the organization on the usage of different technology platforms and technology components. The technology roadmap is usually aligned with the organization vision and key vendors' technology roadmap (e.g., if Microsoft Office is one the key technology platforms, the organization technology roadmap should be aligned with the Microsoft Office roadmap). The technology roadmap facilitates directions on the usage of the technology components that drive organizations to achieve the "meet expectations," "keep it simple," and "follow the rules" basic objectives.

As organizations become more and more dependent on IT systems and the markets become more globalized, virtual, and digital, governments place a more controlled, measurable, and governed environment (including IT-related efforts) around organizations. This environment introduces more accountability, performs adequate risk assessment, and facilitates a well-secured and standard organization environment. The *IT governance* model within the organization is the answer for achieving the mentioned objectives. IT governance is defined as the following:[2]

> ***Information Technology Governance***, *IT Governance, or ICT (Information & Communications Technology) Governance is a subset discipline of Corporate Governance focused on information technology (IT) systems and their performance and risk management.*

Table 4-1 summarizes the SOA-driven organizations key components—product roadmap, technology roadmap, and IT governance—in terms of "what," "why," "how," and "when" factors that can support the implementation of loosely coupled business process integration services flexible to accommodate changing requirements and policies in the agile mode.

Table 4-1. *SOA-Driven Organizations Key Components Matrix*

	Product Roadmap	**Technology Roadmap**	**IT Governance**
What	• Understand user needs and market and stakeholders' expectations to identify core business values. • Define measurable key deliverables and milestones for each product. • Validate deliverables to achieve the "meet expectations" objective.	• Define short-term and long-term technology platform, technology components, and services. • Define migration path to transform legacy systems to Web 2.0–based service-oriented RIAs. • Identify high-level loosely coupled, shared, and generic application services aligning with the product roadmap.	• Identify and document requirements to comply with regulations and policies defined by government and regulatory bodies. • Define organization-level security and performance management model. Validate defined IT governance model against the "follow the rules" objective.

Continued

---

2. Wikipedia, http://en.wikipedia.org/wiki/IT_governance

Table 4-1. *Continued*

	Product Roadmap	**Technology Roadmap**	**IT Governance**
Why	• Justify defined items scope in terms of the business values. • Perform different types of analysis for each milestone to predict short-term and long-term return of investment (ROI).	• Justify identified technology platform, technology components, and application services. • Perform different types of technical analysis to predict the short-term and long-term ROI. • Validate the technology roadmap and product roadmap to achieve the strategic mission of moving from cost center to profit-making center.	• Define and document benefits of the implementation of the IT governance model including the security model and performance model. • Identify and measure the success factor of implementation of the IT governance model to emphasize the importance of implementing the model.
How	• Define interdependencies and integration points among business processes. • Identify unique behavioral patterns. Identify a shared and reusable list of simplified, distributed, secured, reusable, and loosely coupled product services. • Validate identified product services against the "keep it simple" objective.	• Identify application service needs to be developed, the high-level IT governance model to implement proper security for user management and information exchange, and the infrastructure environment by defining the high-level enterprise architecture. • Validate enterprise architecture against the "keep it simple," "meet expectations," and "follow the rules" objectives.	• Define the integration approach to integrate the IT governance model with the regular organization software development life cycle (SDLC) • Define the approach of incorporating policies, the security model, and the performance model within your applications. • Validate identified policies, the security model, and the performance model against the "follow the rules" objective.
When	• Prioritize the business process implementation plan. • Based on the priority, define time-sensitive key milestones to finalize the product roadmap. • Consider the user acceptance phase and plan for incorporation of customer feedback as part of the product roadmap.	• Define a timeline and milestones for technology components, product service implementation, and the deployment plan. • Consider different proof of concepts (POCs) and technical analysis on different advance technology components in the isolated technology lab environment before implementing in the production environment.	• Define timeline and major milestones to incorporate regulatory policies plan and integrate with the product roadmap and the technology roadmap.

Technical Overview of SOA

Most of the time, there is a general misconception that SOA equals Web Services. However, as described earlier, SOA is an architectural concept that covers how to implement loosely coupled, distributed, lightweight shared services that can be consumed by internal and external applications for systems integration and executing different business processes. The Web Service is one of the vital components for implementing lightweight and loosely coupled services following the SOA model.

It is apparent that services are the main component of SOA-based applications. Now let's start with examining the service concept in the simplest way. Services with public interfaces are typically developed by organizations (service providers) and deployed on the network cloud to allow access to other applications/services (service consumers) as shown in Figure 4-2. Service integration can be performed asynchronously or synchronously.

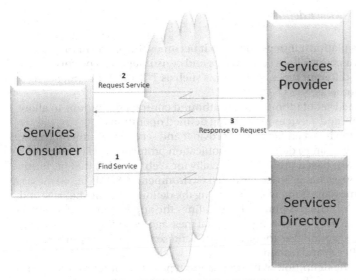

Figure 4-2. *Service integration based on SOA*

Key Components of Services

Now let's take a look at the implementation of services and their behavior in detail by focusing on their key features and key components. You need to follow these steps during the implementation of any qualified self-contained service that can maintain its own context and state:

1. Define public interfaces and contracts to enable integration with other applications and services.

2. Based on its scope, the service must be interoperable and support different protocols.

3. Use XML as the description of the service contract to make the service platform independent. The service can then be found using dynamic service discovery.

Figure 4-3 defines a service and demonstrates its key components. It also maps the service with a Web Service definition, since the Web Service is one of the most common ways of implementing SOA-based applications.

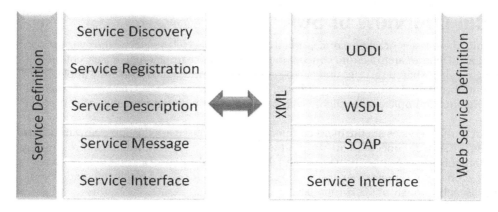

Figure 4-3. *Service definition and Web Service definition*

XML is an open standard and is platform independent, so it becomes the platform to describe interoperable services, establish connections between services and consumers, and perform operations defined as XML messages over different types of protocols such as TCP/IP, HTTP(S), SOAP, SMTP, and any other proprietary protocols.

A *service interface* is a well-defined set of inbound and outbound contract definitions to allow integration by consumer applications and services performing defined operations.

A *service message* allows interaction between the service provider and service consumer by passing the required parameters of the interface using a defined communication protocol based on the service description. SOAP is a widely used XML-based protocol (especially for Web Services) that performs structured message-based information exchange in a distributed environment. A SOAP-based message consists of an *envelope* detailing the message framework describing the definition of the message and how to interact and process it; a *header*, which is optional and defines the application-specific information related to the SOAP message; a *body* containing the actual message; *encoding rules* defining application-defined data types and how to serialize them; and RPC representation, a convention that represents Remote Procedure Calls (RPCs) and responses.

A *service description* consists of the definition of the messages, types of parameters, and policies in a standardized format that can provide understanding of the service and how to invoke it. The Web Services Description Language (WSDL) facilitates the Web Service definition in a standard XML structured format that is available to the consumer. The WSDL file contains the interface definition that will be used to invoke and integrate with the Web Service and the binding information defining the Web Service URI.

Service registration and discovery is a platform for publishing/registering the definition of your services that is publicly available as a services repository. Consumers can then search for those services and invoke them. As the name suggests, Universal Description, Discovery, and Integration (UDDI) is a platform-independent, XML-based public and private registry on the Internet for Web Services available for consumers for the discovery.

Silverlight and SOA

I think you now are prepared to learn about the high-level SOA for the development of Silverlight-based RIAs. This section revisits some capabilities of Silverlight discussed earlier in the book that make it possible to architect, develop, and deploy service-oriented enterprise RIAs using Silverlight.

In general, to present the SOA concept for Silverlight RIAs, I refined the diagram depicting device- and platform-independent Enterprise 2.0 and Web 2.0 applications (Figure 3-7) as shown in Figure 4-4.

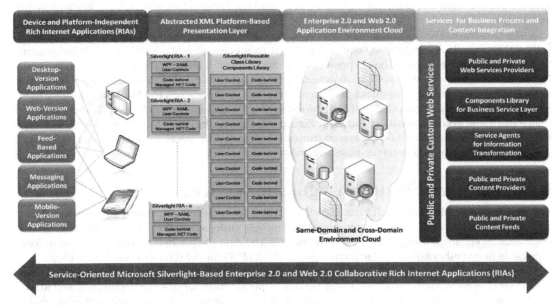

Figure 4-4. *SOA concept for Microsoft Silverlight–based RIAs*

Figure 4-4 presents the high-level general architecture diagram for service-oriented, Silverlight-based Enterprise 2.0 and Web 2.0 collaborative RIAs.

Let's see how suitable Silverlight is for implementing such applications. The following four factors are key characteristics of SOA-based RIAs:

- Device and platform-independent applications
- Abstracted presentation layer (separated from the business service and data access layers)
- Integration with platform-agnostic services
- Modular and reusable

Device and Platform-Independent Applications

One of the key features of SOA is to architect device- and platform-agnostic, service-based applications. Silverlight allows us to develop browser-independent and operating system–independent RIAs and integrate platform-agnostic services to perform different business processes.

The "Device and Platform-Independent Rich Internet Applications (RIAs)" section of the diagram represents different types of RIAs that can be developed and deployed using Silverlight. As discussed earlier, Silverlight is a platform-agnostic technology and is compatible with all well-known web browsers and operating systems, which makes it a perfect match to implement the SOA concept for the development of RIAs.

Abstracted Presentation Layer

Silverlight is a subset of WPF that enables us to create an XML-based externalized and abstracted definition of the user interface. This Silverlight XAML-based user interface design allows us to separate the presentation layer and the business service and data access layers, which is a key feature for any SOA.

The "Abstracted XML Platform–Based Presentation Layer" section of the diagram represents WPF XAML–based Silverlight RIAs (containing XAML user controls and related code-behind assemblies). The XAML user control–based presentation layer does not include any kind of business logic. However, depending on the application design approach, the immediate managed code-behind file can include business logic and direct data access (the way we developed the My Album application in Chapter 2). It is recommended that SOA-based RIAs keep only validation logic within the immediate code-behind component. As shown in Figure 4-4, for SOA-based RIAs, the main business logic and data access code should be separated from the presentation layer by placing it in a reusable code library component or a server-based managed code assembly.

Integration with Platform-Agnostic Services

The integration of Silverlight with Visual Studio and thus integration with code-behind managed code makes it possible to implement modular and loosely coupled service components. Managed code enables seamless integration with Web Services and data feeds (such as RSS feeds) and makes it possible to use other cutting-edge technology such as LINQ for the data/content integration.

The "Enterprise 2.0 and Web 2.0 Application Environment Cloud" section of the diagram contains a set of Web Services published in the private or public Internet space. Silverlight-based RIAs can perform any business-related functionality or access to the available content in the secured environment within the same domain or cross-domain in a secured way via Web Services.

As represented in the "Services for Business Process and Content Integration" section of the diagram, public and private Web Services form the platform-agnostic gateway for secured business logic execution and content access, making them completely separated from consumer applications and services.

Modularity and Reusability

Silverlight Visual Studio integration allows easy development of modular and reusable class library components for the presentation layer, business service layer, and data access layer. These components can be reused across one or more Silverlight-based applications, making the Silverlight application architecture more flexible.

The "Abstracted XML Platform–Based Presentation Layer" section of the diagram represents reusable user controls in a code-behind class library. One or more Silverlight-based RIAs can reference these class libraries and decide between the in-package or on-demand deployment approach based on the application's need. During your application design time, it is important to break out your user interface design and functional components to adopt the modular design concept and introduce reusability and abstraction using the Silverlight class library concept and server-based application service development concept.

The "Services for Business Process and Content Integration" section of the diagram depicts the Public and Private Web Services interface serving as the "gateway." These services can leverage business process integration and content access using the library of service providers, custom business components, service agents for information transformation, data adapters, and different types of XML platform–based feeds.

SOA-Based RIAs: Seven Key Principles

Chapter 3 briefly discussed the seven key principles—usability, flexibility, simplicity, reusability, scalability, maintainability, and security—to develop, deploy, and distribute SOA-based abstracted, loosely coupled, collaborative RIAs as SaaS to the end users (see Figure 4-5).

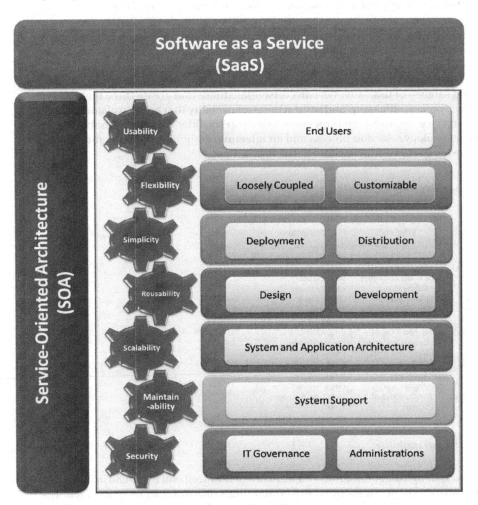

Figure 4-5. *Seven key principles for building RIAs as SaaS*

The main vision of the Silverlight technology is to support all seven key principles for building RIAs as services.

Usability

The ISO 9241-11 guidelines define usability as follows:[3]

> **Usability** *is the extent to which a product can be used by specified users to achieve specified goals with effectiveness, efficiency, and satisfaction in a specified context of use.*

Business-enabled RIAs, being very user-centric, are focused on mainly three factors—users, users, and users—enabling Web 2.0 and Enterprise 2.0 concepts. As a result, in my list, *usability* is the first principle of any SOA-based RIAs empowering end users/customers.

In Chapter 1, we identified the five key detailed dimensions—availability, responsiveness, clarity, utility, and safety—of usability. We can consolidate these and create three higher-level dimensions—effectiveness, efficiency, and satisfaction—of usability that are also aligned with the preceding definition (see Figure 4-6). It is recommended you consider these three usability dimensions during the technology selection process and architecting/designing and implementing your application to provide the maximum customer satisfaction.

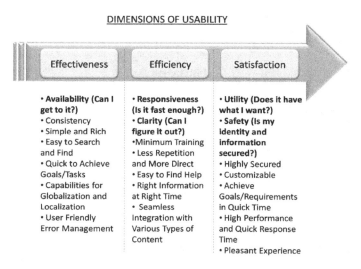

Figure 4-6. *Dimensions of usability*

The *effectiveness* dimension of usability is a measure of how well end users can achieve the vision and goals through the services-based RIA containing a user-friendly user interface. The implementation of highly available ("Can I get to it?"), high-quality, and consistent service-based RIA makes it a highly effective application. The designers can bring consistency across the application by finding repeatable, usable patterns and implementing a common and consistent theme across the application. To improve effectiveness, it is also important to provide an easy search functionality and make it easy to navigate to a help feature to finish different functionalities.

The *efficient* dimension of usability is a measure of how fast you can achieve, perform, or execute an action by using the provided serviced-based, simplified RIA with its intuitive user interface. Highly responsive ("Is it fast enough?"), simplified, and high-clarity ("Can I figure it out?") RIAs are more efficient. It should not matter if end users are familiar (experienced) with the application or not. New end users should be in a position to learn the application with no or very little training.

---

3. ISO 9241-11, http://www.iso.org/iso/iso_catalogue/catalogue_tc/catalogue_detail. htm?csnumber=16883, 1998

For quick execution, it is important to consider the total number of clicks and overall response time (factoring in different types of connectivity and different levels of users) to complete a particular task.

The *satisfaction* dimension of usability is a measure of how happy and satisfied end users are at the end of their interaction with the application in terms of achieving goals comfortably. Utility ("Does it have what I want?") and safety ("Is my identity and information secured?") are key factors to achieve maximum satisfaction. It is important to consider and analyze the audience of the application, learn the culture and expectations of potential customers, and provide a secured application platform to achieve their trust.

Flexibility

IEEE Standard 610.12 provides the following definition for flexibility:[4]

> *Flexibility is the ease with which a system or component can be modified for use in applications or environments other than those for which it was specifically designed.*

After usability, flexibility is the next key principle for IT solutions, a requirement that allows those solutions to remain competent in a continuously changing global market. Implementing and giving flexibility in IT solutions empowers end users and enables organizations to cope with the changes in different dimensions of the market, end user expectation, and governance rules and regulations.

Figure 4-7 presents the main characteristics—platform independent, loosely coupled and customizable, and support for agility—of the flexibility principle that mainly cover all SOA aspects to provide a platform to implement decoupled IT solutions that can adopt the dynamic nature of the business easily. The characteristics of flexibility can drive achievement of other principles of SOA-based RIAs.

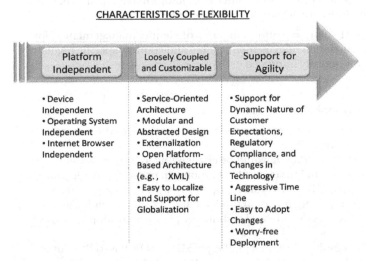

Figure 4-7. *Characteristics of flexibility*

---

4. IEEE Standard 610.12, http://standards.ieee.org/reading/ieee/std_public/description/ se/610.12-1990_desc.html, 1990

The platform-independent characteristic of IT solutions provides a flexible IT solution that can support all types of devices, browsers, and operating systems and helps to achieve the goal of "one solution for all." It is important to consider designing the user interface components to resize automatically based on the different device screen sizes and screen resolutions. By achieving this goal, the overall usability of the application and reusability of the user interface components will be improved.

The loosely coupled and customizable characteristics of the IT solutions helps organizations to develop distributed RIAs supporting a global and diversified community and the dynamic nature of the business. The following are key service-based application architecture principles that help to implement flexible, loosely coupled, customizable RIA solutions; they also can help to introduce "plug-in" functionality, which enables adding or detaching different services to or from the application and upgrading from the current version to a newer version of the service.

- Modular and abstracted component design to develop decoupled presentation, business service, and data access layers

- Externalization of resource definition and configuration to support globalization, localization, and integration with different environment setups

- Open platform–based (e.g., XML-based) architecture to support unified communication and integration among different services and application layers

The support for agility characteristic of IT solutions defines the capabilities to cope with the continuously changing global marketplace. In the era of the Web 2.0

- IT came within reach of most people across the world and became a part of their day-to-day lives in one form or another. The diversified global community in terms of geographic locations, culture, expectations, and abilities brings challenges to IT executives, who need to support the continuous increase of customer expectations and ever-changing requirements.

- Globalization, digitization of information, and advance technology make the market very competitive and agile and also raise the issue of information overload.

- In order to facilitate a secured IT solution platform in terms of identity management, information management, and organization management, global and country-specific regulatory rules and policies must be continuously improved.

Agile Software Development Life Cycle Model

The topic of the Agile SDLC model is vast enough for an entire book. However, for the purposes of this book, a summary of the Agile SDLC will suffice.

To support the dynamic nature of the market, it would be challenging for organizations to follow the traditional waterfall SDLC model to implement IT solutions. In order to provide *faster*, *cheaper*, and *better* products delivering high business value, organizations have to implement an optimized, diversified, agile, and cohesive IT organization model that can facilitate global and virtual environments and provide a flexible service-oriented technology platform to adopt changes in the technology and customer requirements.

The Enterprise 2.0 concept embraces the new concept of Agile SDLC. SOA-based RIAs, at the heart of which are lightweight, externalized, distributed, and loosely coupled application services, are flexible enough to support the Agile SDLC and thus the dynamic nature of the market and "time to market" principle. Figure 4-8 provides a high-level overview of the Agile SDLC.

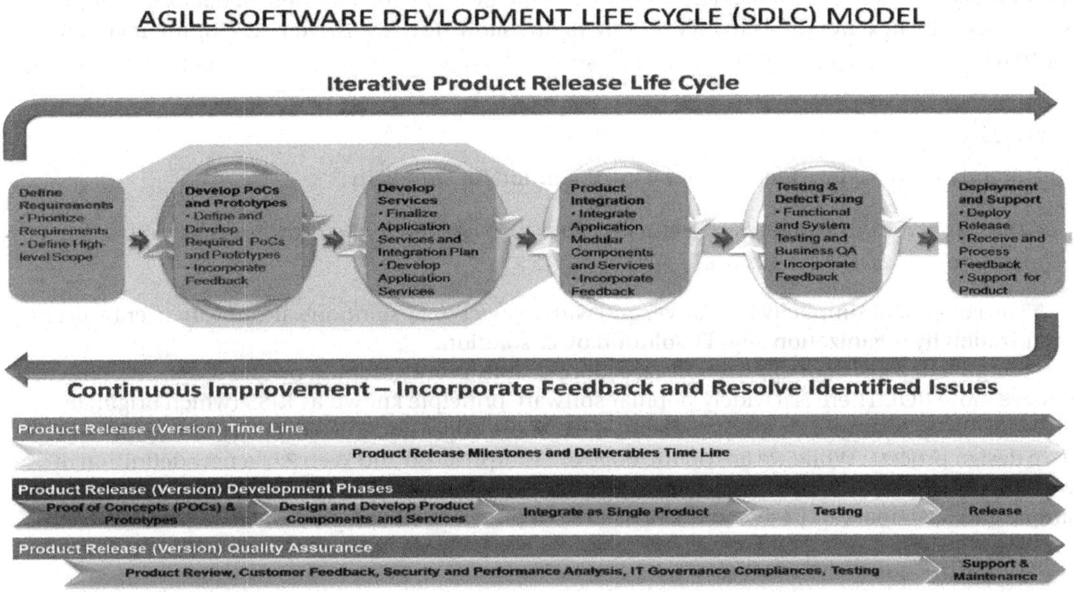

AGILE SOFTWARE DEVLOPMENT LIFE CYCLE (SDLC) MODEL

Iterative Product Release Life Cycle

Figure 4-8. *Agile SDLC Model*

Agile software development is defined as follows:[5]

Agile Software Development methodologies generally promote a project management process that encourages frequent inspection and adaptation; a leadership philosophy that encourages team work, self-organization, and accountability; a set of engineering best practices that allow for rapid delivery of high-quality software; and a business approach that aligns development with customer needs and company goals.

As shown in the Figure 4-8, the Agile SDLC mainly follows an incremental and iterative-phased approach for software development. In the diagram, moving from left to right, the level of uncertainty and unknowns decreases. As you progress, say, from the "Proof of Concepts (PoCs) and Prototypes" phase to the "Testing" phase, the level of uncertainty and unknowns will be reduced, and the product release will be more stable and deployable.

The Agile SDLC implies working very closely and strategically with stakeholders and customers, and balancing expectations against the time line and business values to create a road map for the development of business-enabled RIAs. It is not necessary for the first release of the product to feature all requirements and meet all expectations. Instead, requirements and expectations are prioritized and delivered incrementally in a phased approach to deliver maximum business values and ROI.

Once the high-level scope of a particular release, based on prioritized requirements, is defined, the agile development model allows you to determine different iterations. Based on the quality of the requirements and understanding of those requirements and technology, the release life cycle may start with the development of different POCs and prototypes to finalize the scope of the release.

From the beginning of the product-specific release life cycle, customers, stakeholders, and quality assurance and IT governance teams are continuously involved to review product output and business process implementation and provide constructive feedback to the project team. At the

---

5. Wikipedia, http://en.wikipedia.org/wiki/Agile_software_development

end of every iteration, the project team will revisit and evaluate the received feedback and adjust the scope of the next iterations to incorporate them following a test-driven development (TDD) approach.

Simplicity

IEEE Standard 610.12 provides the following definition for simplicity:[6]

> *The degree to which a system or component has a design and implementation that is straightforward and easy to understand.*

The concept of simplicity is relative, and with respect to IT solutions, it can vary user by user, organization by organization, and IT solution by IT solution.

Simplified, consistent applications are more usable, more accepted by end users, and tend to achieve more ROI. There is a widely popular software principle known as KISS (which originally stood for "Keep It Simple, Stupid") that emphasizes the importance of simplicity during the software design process. While we are on the edge of Enterprise 2.0 and Web 2.0, a new definition of the KISS principle is emerging that applies to both end users (customers) and enterprises: "Keep it Simple and Sustainable." Based on the revised KISS principle, simplicity can be defined as follows:

Simplicity *is the level of easiness for*

- *Targeted customers to understand and use the IT solution and services without or minimum training by providing* **consistency** *in the user interface design*

- *Enterprises to design IT solutions and services, which are* **consistent** *and* **sustainable** *by facilitating easy development, deployment, distribution, support, and maintenance*

In order to achieve simplicity in IT solutions, during technology selection and architecting/designing and implementing your application, you need to consider two dimensions of the simplicity principle—consistency and sustainability—as shown in Figure 4-9.

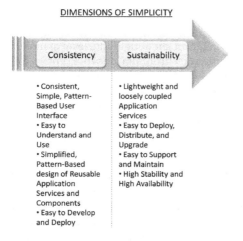

Figure 4-9. *Dimensions of simplicity*

---

6. IEEE Standard 610.12, `http://standards.ieee.org/reading/ieee/std_public/description/se/610.12-1990_desc.html`, 1990

The *consistency* dimension of simplicity brings unification in terms of user interface, application service, and component design for implementation and integration among different business processes. Pattern identification is a key factor to define consistent user interface components and provide simplified component and service definitions.

A consistent user interface within various modules of the same application or across applications makes them easy to understand and use, which improves the user experience and thus improves the usability of applications. Identification of commonality in different business processes by defining key patterns enables enterprises to define and develop a common library of lightweight application services, which makes them easy to support and maintain.

The *sustainability* dimension of simplicity presents ease of end-user training, maintenance, supportability, and upgradability of application services. The common library of lightweight and loosely coupled application services is easy to deploy, distribute, support, and upgrade.

Reusability

IEEE Standard 610.12 provides the following definition for reusability:[7]

> *The degree to which a software module or other work product can be used in more than one computing program or software system.*

Based on the identified patterns and common functionalities among business processes, reusability can be introduced by following the modular and abstracted component design and with the development of lightweight, decoupled application services. The product team can also develop a set of templates and standards as well as follow best practices from industry experts as a part of the core framework to enable easy development, testing, and deployment.

If an IT solution is planned, documented, and implemented correctly, and built upon the right set of technology platforms and components, an organization can capitalize on a reusable, common set of lightweight, loosely coupled application services and components. In the long term, it can achieve maximum ROI in terms of improved productivity, efficiency, and maintainability as shown in Figure 4-10.

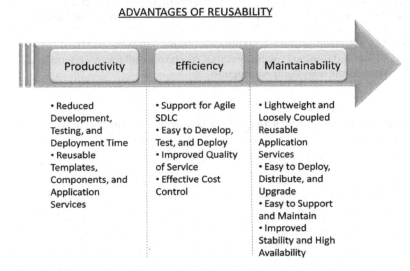

Figure 4-10. *Advantages of reusability*

7. Ibid.

In the long term, with the development of reusable templates, reusable components, and reusable application services comes a significant improvement in *productivity*. With the available common set of template, component, and service libraries, the development and testing teams do not need to retest these existing components and services again and again. Eventually, this will allow development, testing, and deployment of new IT solutions based on the existing component and service libraries with less effort and in less time. This helps organizations to achieve the goal of "faster, better, and cheaper."

Reusability will also improve organization *efficiency* in terms of development, testing, and deployment of new IT solutions based on the component and service library by improving overall organization execution and IT solution quality, controlling cost, simplifying support and maintenance processes, and supporting the Agile SDLC.

The reusability of software components and services also eases the *maintenance and support* processes of organizations. With the development of reusable, lightweight, loosely coupled application services using a component library, it would be easy to deploy, distribute, and support such services. Version management and upgrades of reusable components and services would be easier in terms of testing, deployment, and distribution.

Scalability

Scalability is one of the most critical factors you need to consider when you plan for the development and deployment of Silverlight-based RIAs, because such applications usually deal with rich, large content and media files.

Scalability is a very broad subject with various definitions. Following is one such definition:[8]

> ***Scalability*** *represents the capability of increasing the computing capacity of a service provider's computer system and system's ability to process more user requests, operations, or transactions in a given time interval.*

Scalability also deals with the performance criteria of IT solutions in executing different actions. Scalability represents the capabilities of application services (software) and deployed environments (hardware) to cope with increased user requests and data volume to provide the same or better performance.

Figure 4-11 shows the three key dimensions of the scalability—volume, software, and hardware—that need to be considered to develop and deploy IT solutions that can handle all types of demands and loads without having any impact on networks and connections.

---

8. Shuping Ran, "A Model for Web Services Discovery with QoS" (ACM SIGecom Exchanges, 2003)

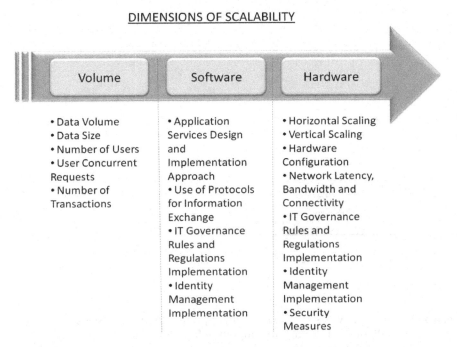

Figure 4-11. *Dimensions of scalability*

The *volume* dimension of scalability mainly focuses on various end users and data-related parameters. Application scalability and performance is highly dependable and measurable upon different user- and data-related factors such as data size, data volume, number of users, number of concurrent requests, number of transactions, and types of user requests.

The *software* dimension of scalability mainly focuses on the application design and implementation approach. If you have all types of required hardware, but the application and application services are not well designed and well implemented, the application may not be scalable enough to handle large-size data, high-data volume, a large number of users, many user requests, and a large number of transactions. It is important to consider various areas of software engineering such as memory management (including caching and object management), definition of data types, determination on the use of protocols for information exchange, client-side vs. server-side processing, data connection management, and security measure implementation based on IT governance and identity management standards.

The first dimension that most people think of when talking about the scalability is *hardware*. It is important for hardware configuration and implementation to align with the other two dimensions—volume and software—of scalability. Once enterprise architects determine the volume factor (including customer-related information, scope of the customers—internal or external customers—availability, and types of connectivity) and the software factor, the next thing to determine is the environment setup, which is done by defining the system architecture. During the process of defining the system architecture, you need to consider the organization's long-term vision in terms of future usage of systems, geographically diversified customers, identity management, IT governance rules and regulations, and security measures.

Figure 4-12 compares the horizontal scaling (scale out) and vertical scaling (scale up) approaches to improve the scalability of an application environment.

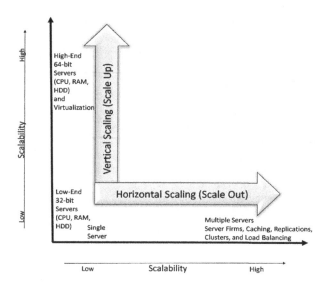

Figure 4-12. *Vertical and horizontal scaling to improve scalability*

Vertical scaling, which is also known as *scaling up*, is an approach to improve scalability by improving an existing server configuration through the migration from low-end servers to high-end servers with multiple processors (CPU), high RAM, and more HDD space. In today's market, the virtualization concept is becoming more acceptable and popular. Virtual server technology makes the vertical scaling approach more practical, and thus it has become a part of the strategic technology direction for many organizations. At the same time, upgrading from 32-bit to 64-bit servers also scales up the environment and can provide significant improvement in application performance. The vertical scaling approach may end up in a single-point failure and is not a good approach for the applications that need to have high availability.

Horizontal scaling, which is also known as *scaling out*, is an approach to improve scalability by adding multiple servers for the same applications and applying the concept of server firms, caching, replication, server clustering, and load balancing. The horizontal scaling approach is also considered to provide high availability; since more than one environment is holding the application, it is possible to switch from one to another in terms of the failure of a specific environment.

Now the next logical question is, what is the best approach to achieve maximum scalability? Looking at the nature of Silverlight-based RIAs, a *balanced approach* is required to provide the right environment for highly scalable RIAs. It would not be acceptable for any organization to deploy enterprise solutions with high-end servers but single-point failure by implementing only the vertical scaling approach. At the same time, the low-end servers required to implement the horizontal scaling approach will not be appropriate for deploying high-performing and highly scalable RIAs, as such an environment doesn't enable integration of very large rich media files. The best approach is a balanced one: having high-end multiple servers facilitating high availability. The server configuration and number of servers required would be dependent on the overall application requirements.

Maintainability

IEEE Standard 610.12 provides the following definition of maintainability:[9]

(1) The ease with which a software system or component can be modified to correct faults, improve performance or other attributes, or adapt to a changed environment.

(2) The ease with which a hardware system or component can be retained in, or restored to, a state in which it can perform its required functions.

In other words, IT solutions that are easy to monitor and support are called maintainable IT solutions. Figure 4-13 shows two key dimensions of maintainability—supportability and monitoring—that need to be considered and predicated during the process of the development and deployment of RIAs.

DIMENSIONS OF MAINTAINABILITY

Supportability	Monitoring
• Technical and Nontechnical Customer Support • Training and User Guide Documentation • Defined Process to Identify, Analyze, Debug, and Isolate Problem and Resolve it • Easy to Maintain and Upgrade • Availability of Support Tools • Develop Awareness and Expertise	• Implementation of Instrumentation for Monitoring • Regular Review of Usage and Status Report • Continuous Monitoring of Environment Health • Security Measurements • Processing Feedback • Status Reporting • Preventive Maintenance • Security and Application Updates

Figure 4-13. *Dimensions of maintainability*

Offshore outsourcing is becoming a critical cost-saving strategy for many organizations, and maintainability plays a critical role in the success of this strategy. It is important to consider the maintainability principle during the requirement analysis, design, and development phases, and processes to assist postdeployment support, maintenance, administration, and monitoring should be implemented.

---

9. IEEE Standard 610.12, http://standards.ieee.org/reading/ieee/std_public/description/se/610.12-1990_desc.html, 1990

The *supportability* dimension of maintainability is a measure of IT system quality and an organization's capabilities to provide postdeployment user support. An early consideration of supportability in the SDLC helps organizations to

- Implement a proper level of error handling and instrumentation within the application. Proper error handling facilitates a user-friendly notification approach in case of any application errors. Instrumentation provides the capabilities of monitoring, tracing, and debugging applications postdeployment by implementing logging and reporting mechanisms integrated with enterprise applications.

  Use components created using best practices and patterns provided by industry leaders to standardize the enterprise-wide application implementation process. As an example, Microsoft Enterprise Library provides different types of application blocks (components) that can be used as core framework components to build enterprise application features. To facilitate standardized error management and instrumentation, enterprises can use the Microsoft Exception Handling Application Block, Logging Application Block, Policy Injection Application Block, and Validation Application Block, which are all part of the Microsoft Enterprise Library.

- Define and develop required support tools and support processes that help the organization support team to identify, analyze, debug, and isolate problems and resolve them.

- Develop required documentation such as user guides, training materials, technical documentation, FAQs, and instruction documents that are used to develop awareness and expertise among end users and organization support teams.

The *monitoring* dimension is all about being proactive in terms of predicting future problems and future end user needs, taking preventive actions to resolve problems before they actually appear, and enhancing applications to improve customer satisfaction. Thus the monitoring dimension helps organizations to maintain and improve the quality of their products. Instrumentation techniques for end-user application usage and the infrastructure environment are key for providing critical reports and implementing an effective monitoring process. End-user reports such as error reports, application usage statistics, application event management reports, and application performance analysis reports (performance counters, etc.) are helpful for understanding the application and user behavior during application execution, and assisting in problem resolution and future application quality improvements. Infrastructure environment reports such as CPU usage reports, memory usage reports, workload reports, user request reports, and response time reports can assist support teams in keeping the environment up and running; they also provide key information to enterprise architects on environment resource usage to help them determine how to improve scalability and availability.

Security

As markets become more digital and application services become more loosely coupled, the chances of vulnerability in every aspect of IT management increases. Organizations have to implement an IT governance model and security measures as part of their IT system implementation and maintenance life cycle.

Organizations can consider five dimensions—information security, identity management, software security, infrastructure security, and regulatory compliances—of IT security (see Figure 4-14) in implementing a security model as part of IT governance.

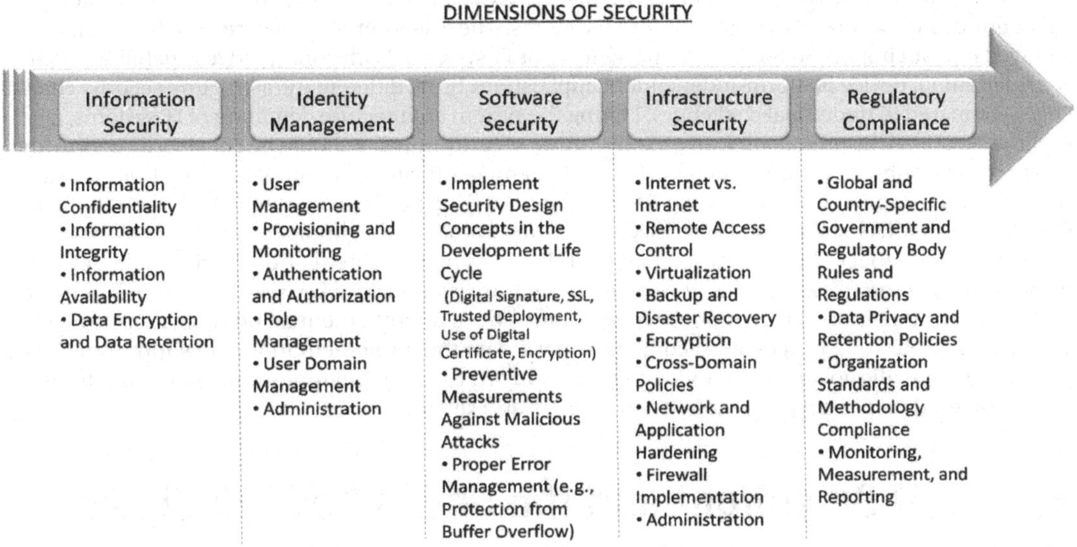

DIMENSIONS OF SECURITY

Information Security	Identity Management	Software Security	Infrastructure Security	Regulatory Compliance
• Information Confidentiality • Information Integrity • Information Availability • Data Encryption and Data Retention	• User Management • Provisioning and Monitoring • Authentication and Authorization • Role Management • User Domain Management • Administration	• Implement Security Design Concepts in the Development Life Cycle (Digital Signature, SSL, Trusted Deployment, Use of Digital Certificate, Encryption) • Preventive Measures Against Malicious Attacks • Proper Error Management (e.g., Protection from Buffer Overflow)	• Internet vs. Intranet • Remote Access Control • Virtualization • Backup and Disaster Recovery • Encryption • Cross-Domain Policies • Network and Application Hardening • Firewall Implementation • Administration	• Global and Country-Specific Government and Regulatory Body Rules and Regulations • Data Privacy and Retention Policies • Organization Standards and Methodology Compliance • Monitoring, Measurement, and Reporting

Figure 4-14. *Dimensions of security*

The *information security* dimension of security plays a critical role since most interorganization and cross-organization business process execution has become electronic, and thus most information is available in digital format. Information security is mainly focused on the processes, standards, and implementation of information security measures to achieve confidentiality, integrity, and availability. The ISO/IEC Standard 27002 defines information security as the following:[10]

> **Information Security** *is described as the preservation of* **confidentiality** *(ensuring that information is accessible only to those authorized to have access),* **integrity** *(safeguarding the accuracy and completeness of information and processing methods), and* **availability** *(ensuring that authorized users have access to information and associated assets when required).*

The identity management dimension of security mainly deals with user management; it defines standard processes, policies, and administration tools to provide simplified user provisioning, domain management, role management, and subscription services to implement secured (possibly single sign-on), authorized, and role-based access to applications and services. Advance Enterprise 2.0 concepts, such as virtualization, remote access, and multiple device platforms for information access, and advanced Web 2.0 concepts, such as social-networking and RIAs, bring about different types of challenges to implement and maintain efficient and effective identity management systems. To support Enterprise 2.0 and Web 2.0 concepts, identity management also involves some innovative concepts such as *federated identity management* and *OpenID* (http://openid.net/foundation/) to simplify enterprise-level identity management processes and provide better user experience. These concepts support a common user-provisioning and access mechanism that enables users to access more than one cross-enterprise application and web site using the same user identification.

The *software security* dimension of security drives organizations to define security standards, policies, and measures to incorporate during the design, development, and quality assurance phases of IT system implementation. These measures are taken during the IT system implementation process to prevent postdeployment vulnerabilities.

---

10. ISO/IEC Standard 27002, http://www.iso.org/iso/catalogue_detail?csnumber=50297, 2007

The *infrastructure security* dimension of security is a key factor in providing a scalable, high-performing, secured environment for IT systems. The selection of hardware and the way it is deployed have an impact on the security provisions for IT systems. With cutting-edge capabilities such as virtualization, device platform-independent applications bring different infrastructure security challenges compared to traditional challenges. During the system architecture definition of IT systems, all required security measures along with possible future security impacts should be considered to provide a secured environment. Proper testing of the implemented infrastructure mimics the real world in an isolated lab environment to test real-world scenarios involving performance, network impact analysis, data capacity analysis, stress testing, and security testing to validate the implemented security measures.

Due to the impact of globalization and overall efforts to implement effective risk management policies, the *regulatory compliance* dimension of security is one of the key strategic components of the organization IT governance model. Organizations have to implement all possible measures, validation, and monitoring processes to confirm and validate the implementation and support of global and country-specific government and regulatory body rules and regulations that are related to risk management, data privacy, IT system performance, and security.

Microsoft Silverlight and the Seven Key Principles

You already know what makes Silverlight an enterprise-ready technology platform. Table 4-2 maps Silverlight's capabilities to the seven principles of SOA to prove that we can develop SOA-based Silverlight RIAs.

Table 4-2. *Microsoft Silverlight and the Seven Key Principles of SOA-Based RIAs*

Seven Principles of SOA	Silverlight Capabilities
Usability (effectiveness, efficiency, satisfaction)	• Silverlight allows easy development of simplified, rich user interface with the use of Visual Studio and Expression Blend.
	• .NET Framework 3.5 and WPF XAML–based user interface definition help the Silverlight platform to render 2D vector graphics, multimedia, animation, text, and rich data-bound user interface controls seamlessly and in an interactive and integrated fashion.
	• The Silverlight Deep Zoom feature provides the ability to smoothly present and navigate large amounts of visual information. The Silverlight framework and code-behind .NET enable design of decoupled presentation layer.
	• Support is provided for single and multibyte characters to accommodate localization.
	• Applications are lightweight (minimum client footprint), providing high-performance.
Flexibility (platform independent, loosely coupled and customizable, support for agility)	• Silverlight provides a device-, browser-, and operating system–independent platform. XML-based user interface design makes it easy to customize.
	• .NET platform–based application development supports designing externalized and loosely coupled services.
	• The Silverlight application development platform supports WCF and Web Service integration via REST, WS*/SOAP, POX, RSS, and standard HTTP protocols.
	• Silverlight enables loosely coupled data-integration capabilities in asynchronous mode with the rich presentation layer.
	• Silverlight makes it easy to adopt changes.

Table 4-2. *Continued*

Seven Principles of SOA	Silverlight Capabilities
Simplicity (consistency, sustainability)	• Pattern-based, reusable Silverlight XAML–based user control library enables consistent simplified user interface development. • Applications are easy to deploy, support, and maintain.
Reusability (productivity, efficiency, maintainability)	• Silverlight Application and Class Library templates allow creation of reusable user controls and managed code-based components, which can be stored in a common library. • Applications are easy to support and maintain due to common component library. • Support for Agile SDLC is enabled by rapid application development with the use of common components and services.
Scalability (volume, software, hardware)	• The Silverlight platform supports data volume and hardware scaling to provide high performance with high workload. • Support for adaptive media streaming helps to improve the synchronization of media, providing high-performing media integration. • Silverlight supports object animation and embedded code-based animation to provide high-performing graphics and animation support. • Silverlight applications can be developed to include background threading and asynchronous communication.
Maintainability (supportability, monitoring)	• Managed code-based Silverlight applications are easy to support. • Rich user interface development is easy to understand and support. • The .NET platform enables regular instrumentation and other monitoring services to integrate with Silverlight applications.
Security (information security, software security, infrastructure security, regulatory compliance)	• Support for digital rights management (DRM) for media streaming encourages enterprises to distribute digital media using Silverlight RIAs. • Silverlight supports policy-based application development and secured cross-domain deployment. • .NET-based service and data access layer implementation enables organizations to provide required information security and software security, and comply with regulatory policies.

Now let's briefly examine the key .NET enterprise features such as LINQ and externalization. To understand how to integrate these features and Web Services with Silverlight, we will create a small, dynamic Silverlight application in the section "Building a Dynamic Service-Oriented Silverlight Application." Later in Chapter 5, we will capitalize on these design and implementation concepts while building the Enterprise Training Portal RIA using Silverlight.

LINQ

LINQ, which is part of .NET Framework 3.5, is a way to query data natively. In other words, the data is held as an object and that object is queried, and it doesn't matter what the source of that data is. Figure 4-15 defines the high-level LINQ architecture.

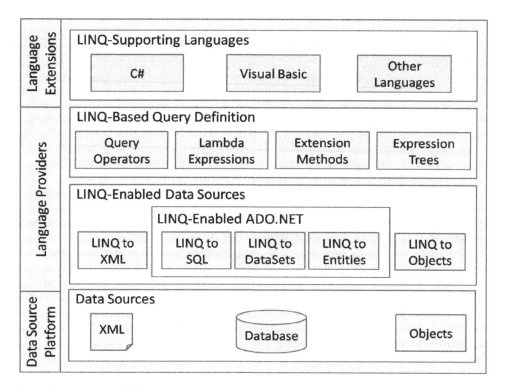

Figure 4-15. *LINQ architecture*

As shown in Figure 4-15, LINQ mainly consists of LINQ language extensions and LINQ query providers. With the release of Visual Studio 2008 and .NET Framework 3.5, programming languages such as Visual Basic and C# support *LINQ language extensions*. Programming languages that support LINQ language extensions enable developers to implement standard query definitions using different *LINQ query providers* such as standard query operators, lambda expressions, expression trees, expression methods, object initializers, and anonymous typed and implicitly typed local variables. LINQ query providers manage application LINQ queries and resulting data marshalling between the native data source and in-memory enumerable types. You can write LINQ query expressions to query different types of data source platforms that support implementations of IEnumerable or IEnumerable<T>.

- LINQ to XML allows you to query XML using SQL-like queries and add/remove/modify XML document nodes in memory. For detailed information, visit http://msdn.microsoft.com/ en-us/library/bb387098.aspx.

- LINQ to SQL enables you to manage a relational database as an object model to build effective query expressions. This is achieved with an object-relational mapping that translates the query into a SQL query. LINQ to SQL defines two core parameterized attributes, [Table] (to associate with the SQL table and view) and [Column] (to associate with the SQL column), which indicate which CLR types and properties correspond to external SQL data. For detailed information, visit http://msdn.microsoft.com/en-us/library/bb386976.aspx.

- LINQ to Entities allows you to develop strongly typed queries against the Entity Data Model (EDM) object using the object services infrastructure. The `ObjectContext` class is the primary class for interacting with an EDM. You can construct `ObjectQuery` instances through the `ObjectContext`. Entity objects returned by `ObjectQuery` are tracked by the `ObjectContext` and can be updated by using the `SaveChanges()` method. For detailed information, visit `http://msdn.microsoft.com/en-us/library/bb386964.aspx`.

- LINQ to DataSet enables you to query the data cached in a `DataSet` object. You can build LINQ to DataSet–based query expressions using the `DataRowExtensions` and `DataTableExtensions` classes of ADO.NET. For detailed information, visit `http://msdn.microsoft.com/en-us/library/bb386977.aspx`.

- LINQ to Objects enables you to define query expressions to retrieve data from any `IEnumerable` or `IEnumerable<T>` collection. For detailed information, visit `http://msdn.microsoft.com/en-us/library/bb397919.aspx`.

There are numerous concerns related to the implementation of enterprise-level security and traditional layered enterprise architecture with the use of LINQ for enterprise applications, since you can directly query the data source from your application. However, when used with a properly architected multilayered (presentation, business service, data access layers) enterprise solution, LINQ can help you to build a secured, SOA-based enterprise application.

Externalization

Implementation of the externalization design concept plays a critical role for providing modularity and flexibility in your service-oriented applications. Externalization can be implemented in all three layers—presentation, business service, and data access —of your SOA-based applications. Tight integration of an XML-like open platform with .NET enables you to implement loosely coupled presentation and service layers and data-platform-agnostic data access layers.

Silverlight helps to facilitate externalized customization and configuration of user interface styles and definition by enabling WPF XAML–based, XML platform–based user interface definition with support for localization and globalization features. You can change the XAML-based user interface definition without recompiling. The Silverlight project can then be redeployed with the new user interface definition. You need to recompile the application only when you have to change the code-behind .NET managed code portion. Integration with the .NET managed code-behind makes it possible to create dynamic user interface definitions based on repeatable user interface patterns such as horizontal or vertical tabs. In our sample application, we will create a number of tabs and the title of the tabs dynamically based on an XML configuration file definition.

XML-based configuration files enable externalized configuration of services, data platforms, and infrastructure to allow dynamic runtime integration with other required services and data platforms. This helps to make SOA-based RIAs data-platform and infrastructure-environment agnostic.

Building a Dynamic Service-Oriented Silverlight Application

Now let's build a service-oriented sample Silverlight application with a dynamic user interface and content population to explore different enterprise features (such as externalization, LINQ, Web Services, and custom user controls).

Note The main focus of this simplified UI-based Silverlight application is to demonstrate the enterprise capabilities of Silverlight. In a real implementation, this type of application will have a rich user interface and may use different types of Silverlight WPF user controls.

Design Concepts

As shown in Figure 4-16, we will implement an externalized Silverlight user interface by developing dynamic tabs (horizontal and vertical) based on an XML-based tab definition and will integrate tab-specific content at runtime based on an externalized data storage definition.

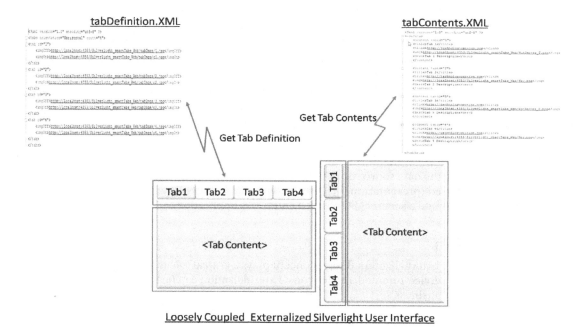

Figure 4-16. *Building loosely coupled Silverlight user interface*

Loosely Coupled Silverlight User Interface

The use of tabs is one of the most common practices in modularizing web sites. Externalized definitions of tabs (defining how many tabs are required and the direction and attributes of each tab) help to introduce reusability of tab control components across different applications and have flexibility within the application to create and configure tabs dynamically.

To understand how to develop a loosely coupled Silverlight user interface, we will develop a Silverlight application called SmartTabs. Required tabs and their behavior are defined in an externalized XML file—tabDefinition.XML. The getTabDefinition Web Service, which uses LINQ, is employed to get the information from the tabDefinition.XML file. Based on the information received from the XML file, we will populate a Grid to create tabs and related content areas with the horizontal or vertical tab orientation at runtime.

Tab Content Integration

The tabDefinition.XML file also contains the data source information for each tab along with the tab's attributes. The getTabContents Web Service with the use of LINQ will connect to the data source (XML file, SQL Server database, or any other data source) and retrieve the content of the particular tab. The retrieved content can be mapped to the Silverlight controls (Image, TextBlock, MediaElement, etc.) for each tab to populate the tab content. The externalization of the data platform definition makes the application data platform independent, and end users always get the latest content.

We will implement the simplest scenario where all tab content is stored within a single XML file—tabContents.XML. In a more complicated and practical scenario, the content of every tab is stored at different data sources with different data types. It is important to convert the contents into the required data types before they get mapped to the Tab Content's Silverlight controls.

Developing the Dynamic User Interface

The SmartTabs Silverlight web site project creates the Application class (app.xaml and app.xaml.cs) and the Page class (page.xaml and page.xaml.cs) by default. The Page class represents the main user interface and is derived from UserControl. We will add only the StackPanel layout user control with the Name masterHolder as the master container (as shown in the following code) to host tabs and tab content as its child elements at runtime.

```
<Grid x:Name="LayoutRoot" Background="White">
    <StackPanel x:Name="masterHolder" Orientation="Vertical"></StackPanel>
</Grid>
```

Adding Custom Silverlight User Controls

Silverlight UserControls are a basic unit for the reuse of the XAML-based user interface and code-behind within the application and across applications. For our SmartTabs project, we need to add two custom Silverlight UserControls: tabDefinition, which defines tabs, and tabContent, which presents tab-specific content.

The tabDefinition UserControl contains two StackPanel layout controls within the Grid layout control. The tabHolder StackPanel control holds a number of tabs based on the tabDefinition.xml file. The default Orientation attribute of the tabHolder StackPanel is set to Vertical. However, it would be changed to Horizontal or Vertical based on the definition in the tabDefinition.xml file at runtime. The contentsHolder StackPanel control holds tab-specific content from the defined data source, which in our case is the tabContents.XML file. Instances of tabContent will be placed for each tab to represent tab-specific content within the contentsHolder StackPanel user control. Following is the resulting code snippet from tabDefinition.xml:

```
<Grid x:Name="LayoutRoot" Background="White">
    <StackPanel x:Name="tabsHolder" Orientation="Vertical"
        HorizontalAlignment="Left">
    </StackPanel>
    <StackPanel x:Name="contentsHolder" Orientation="Vertical"
        HorizontalAlignment="Left">
    </StackPanel>
</Grid>
```

The tabContent user control contains a Grid layout control to display content received from the defined data source, as shown in the following code snippet. The tabContent will include three controls—Image, HyperlinkButton, TextBlock—to display the content.

```
<Grid x:Name="LayoutRoot" Background="White" HorizontalAlignment="Center" >
    <Grid.RowDefinitions>
        <RowDefinition Height="*"/>
        <RowDefinition Height="*"/>
    </Grid.RowDefinitions>
    <Grid.ColumnDefinitions>
        <ColumnDefinition Width="*"/>
        <ColumnDefinition Width="*"/>
    </Grid.ColumnDefinitions>
    <Image Grid.Column="0" Grid.RowSpan="2" x:Name="icon"
```

```
                        HorizontalAlignment="Center" VerticalAlignment="Center" Stretch="None"
                        Margin="10,0,8,0" />
                <HyperlinkButton Grid.Column="1" Grid.Row="0" x:Name="title"
                        HorizontalAlignment="Stretch" VerticalAlignment="Bottom"
                        FontSize="13" FontWeight="SemiBold" FontFamily="Arial"
                        Foreground="#FF0472C7"/>
                <TextBlock  TextWrapping="Wrap" Grid.Column="1" Grid.Row="1"
                        x:Name="details" HorizontalAlignment="Stretch"
                        VerticalAlignment="Stretch"
                        FontSize="13" Foreground="#FF000000" FontFamily="Arial"/>
    </Grid>
```

Code-Behind to Generate Tabs Dynamically

Upon adding the tabDefinition and tabContent UserControls, the corresponding XAML and
code-behind files are automatically generated.

tabDefinition.xaml.cs is the core code-behind class that performs all the required actions to
create tabs dynamically and populate content in each tab using Web Services and LINQ.

Before we get into the details of this core code-behind class, you need to add references to the
following .NET library components:

```
using System;
using System.Collections.Generic;
using System.Linq;
using System.Windows;
using System.Windows.Controls;
using System.Windows.Documents;
using System.Windows.Input;
using System.Windows.Media;
using System.Windows.Media.Animation;
using System.Windows.Shapes;
using System.Xml.Linq;
using System.IO.IsolatedStorage;
using System.IO;
using System.Net;
using System.Windows.Media.Imaging;
```

You also need to declare variables as shown in the following code. The comments are
self-explanatory.

```
namespace Silverlight_smartTabs
{
    public partial class tabDefinition : UserControl
    {
        //String array to hold tab contents
        public string[,] contents = new string[100, 5];
        //In-memory image cache for tab's rollover effect
        BitmapImage[] imgOn = new BitmapImage[11];
        BitmapImage[] imgOff=new BitmapImage[11];
        //Image array for tab creation
        public Image [] tab = new Image [11];
        //String to hold information about tab orientation
        public  string tabOrientation;
        //Int to hold tab count (number of tabs but not more than 10)
        public  int tabCount = new int();
```

Some assumptions were made and a few limitations kept to simplify the development process.
The main assumption is that the number of tabs will not be more than ten. The rest of the variables

are defined so that they can support a maximum of ten tab definitions. Of course, you may like to make it more generic and not tie any limitations to this application.

Web Service Integration to Get Tab Definition XML File

As a part of the constructor of the tabDefinition class, we need to read the tabDefinition.xml file by calling the Web Service getTabDefinition, and then, once we've read it successfully, raise an event, getTab_getTabDefinitionCompleted. The code snippet of the constructor is shown here:

```
public tabDefinition()
{
  InitializeComponent();
  //Here we call getTabDefinition Web Service and set up tab images for
  //mouseOver and normal state.
  getTabDefinition.getTabDefinitionSoapClient getTab = new
     Silverlight_smartTabs.getTabDefinition.getTabDefinitionSoapClient();
  getTab.getTabDefAsync();
  getTab.getTabDefCompleted +=new
    EventHandler<Silverlight_smartTabs.getTabDefinition.
    getTabDefCompletedEventArgs>
  (getTab_getTabDefCompleted);
}
```

The getTab_getTabDefinitionCompleted event will call the processTab() method and pass the retrieved XML file as a string to create tabs based on an XML-based tab definition and then populate the respective content.

```
void getTab_getTabDefCompleted(object sender,
    Silverlight_smartTabs.getTabDefinition.getTabDefCompletedEventArgs e)
{
  //Call to processTab method
  processTab(e.Result.ToString());
}
```

Defining Tabs Using LINQ

With the use of LINQ, the processTab(string sXML) method will process the XML file (the returned tabDefinition.xml file), create the required tabs, and populate the content in the following steps:

1. Load the retrieved XML file to the XDocument object to process later using LINQ:

   ```
   XDocument xDoc = XDocument.Parse(sXML.Remove(0,3));
   ```

   For your reference, the following is the retrieved tabDefinition.xml file:

   ```
   <?xml version="1.0" encoding="utf-8" ?>
   <tabs orientation="Horizontal" count="4">
    <tab id="1">
     <imgOff>http://localhost:4353/Silverlight_smartTabs_Web/tabImgs/1.jpg</imgOff>
     <imgOn>http://localhost:4353/Silverlight_smartTabs_Web/tabImgs/o1.jpg</imgOn>
    </tab>
    <tab id="2">
     <imgOff>http://localhost:4353/Silverlight_smartTabs_Web/tabImgs/2.jpg</imgOff>
     <imgOn>http://localhost:4353/Silverlight_smartTabs_Web/tabImgs/o2.jpg</imgOn>
    </tab>
    <tab id="3">
     <imgOff>http://localhost:4353/Silverlight_smartTabs_Web/tabImgs/3.jpg</imgOff>
     <imgOn>http://localhost:4353/Silverlight_smartTabs_Web/tabImgs/o3.jpg</imgOn>
   ```

```
   </tab>
   <tab id="4">
    <imgOff>http://localhost:4353/Silverlight_smartTabs_Web/tabImgs/4.jpg</imgOff>
    <imgOn>http://localhost:4353/Silverlight_smartTabs_Web/tabImgs/o4.jpg</imgOn>
   </tab>
  </tabs>
```

2. The XML file contains tabs as the root node and orientation and count as attributes defining the required orientation of the tab and total number of tabs to create, respectively. Now
   we use LINQ to XML to get the tab orientation and tab count from the in-memory XML file
   loaded as xDoc and use proper data-type conversion to convert these values into the string
   and integer data types.

```
//Use LINQ to XML to get info about tab orientation and tab count (no. of tabs)
var tabinfo = from t in xDoc.Descendants("tabs")
              select new
              {
                ori = t.Attribute("orientation").Value,
                cnt = t.Attribute("count").Value,
              };
foreach (var itm in tabinfo)
{
    tabOrientation = itm.ori.ToString();
    tabCount= int.Parse(itm.cnt);
}
```

3. The retrieved XML file also defines images to provide some visual impact on MouseEnter and
   MouseOut events on the tabs. We will cache all images to improve performance using LINQ
   to XML, and then store images in a BitmapImage object instead of relying on the browser's
   cache. Here imgOn and imgOff are BitmapImage arrays. The Uri object is used to pass the
   absolute Uri related to the image to locate the image and store it as a BitmapImage object to
   the memory. Following is the code snippet that does all this:

```
//Use of LINQ to XML to store image Uris to BitmapImage arrays for
//mouseEnter and mouseOut images
 var tabinfo = from t in xDoc.Descendants("tab")
 select new
     {
       id = t.Attribute("id").Value,
       imgOff= t.Element("imgOff").Value,
       imgOn = t.Element("imgOn").Value,
     };
foreach (var itm in tabinfo)
  {
  //Image allocation. imagOn is an image for MouseEnter,
    //imgOff is default image
    imgOn[int.Parse(itm.id)] = new BitmapImage(new _Uri(itm.imgOn));
    imgOff[int.Parse (itm.id)] = new BitmapImage(new Uri(itm.imgOff));
  }
```

Creating Tabs at Runtime

Now that we have all the information about the required tabs available, it's time to build the
dynamic tab page. For that, we call the buildTab() method at the end of the processTab() method.
The buildTab() method will set the tab orientation and then create the required tabs dynamically as
shown in the following steps:

1. Set the tab orientation and set up the tabHolder and contentsHolder controls accordingly. Based on the value stored in the tabOrientation variable, we need to set orientation of the tabHolder StackPanel object to either Horizontal or Vertical.

   - If tabs need to be vertical, we need to define two columns in the Grid using the ColumnDefinition object and ColumnProperty of the Grid object; using the ColumnProperty and SetValue properties, the tabHolder StackPanel is placed in Column 0 of the Grid object, and the contentsHolder StackPanel is placed in Column 1 of the Grid object.

   - If tabs need to be horizontal, we need to define two rows in the Grid using the RowDefinition object and RowProperty of the Grid object; using the RowProperty and SetValue properties, the tabHolder StackPanel is placed in Row 0 of the Grid object, and the contentsHolder StackPanel is placed in Row 1 of the Grid object.

   Following is the code snippet for setting tab orientation:

```
//Set orientation of tabholder stackpanel based on tabOrientation value
if (tabOrientation.ToUpper() == "VERTICAL")
{
  tabHolder.Orientation = Orientation.Vertical;

  //Based on orientation, changes are needed in the grid layout
  ColumnDefinition c1 = new ColumnDefinition();
  ColumnDefinition c2 = new ColumnDefinition();
  LayoutRoot.ColumnDefinitions.Add(c1);
  LayoutRoot.ColumnDefinitions.Add(c2);
  //We put the tabHolder stackpanel in column0 and the contentsHolder
  //in column1
  tabHolder.SetValue(Grid.ColumnProperty, 0);
  contentsHolder.SetValue(Grid.ColumnProperty, 1);
}
else
{
  tabHolder.Orientation = Orientation.Horizontal;
  //Based on orientation, changes are needed in the grid layout
  RowDefinition r1 = new RowDefinition();
  RowDefinition r2 = new RowDefinition();
  LayoutRoot.RowDefinitions.Add(r1);
  LayoutRoot.RowDefinitions.Add(r2);
  //We put the tabHolder stackpanel in row 0 and the contentsHolder
  //in row 1.
  tabHolder.SetValue(Grid.RowProperty, 0);
  contentsHolder.SetValue(Grid.RowProperty,1);
}
```

2. Now that the tabHolder and contentsHolder StackPanel controls are properly laid out, we are all set to create the number of tabs based on the value of the tabCount variable (earlier populated from the tabDefinition.xml file). As shown in the following code snippet, first you assign the default image, and then add it as part of the child collection of the tabHolder StackPanel control:

```
//Create tabs in the tabHolder Stackpanel
for (int count = 1; count < tabCount + 1; count++)
{
  //Image allocation
  tab[count] = new Image();
  tab[count].Stretch = Stretch.None;
  tab[count].Source = imgOff[count];
```

```
    //Add to the tabholder stackpanel
    tabHolder.Children.Add(tab[count]);
}
```

3. Now let's set up the MouseEnter event for each tab to provide a visual effect. The following code example assigns the MouseEnter event handler for tab1:

```
//Assigning eventhandler for mouseEnter event,
//using try catch block if tabs are less than 10
int index = 1;
try
{
  for(index=1;index<11;index++)
    if (index==11)
      break;
    else
    {
      tab[index].MouseEnter += new MouseEventHandler(tab_MouseEnter);
    }
}
catch (NullReferenceException e)
{
  //Be silent, do nothing.
}
```

We want to have a different image appear when the mouse enters a particular tab area. In order to achieve this, we must set the current tab image to the image stored in the imgOn collection. The rest of the tab images should be set back to the corresponding image stored in the imgOff collection, which we will achieve by calling the resetTabs() method. The following code example sets the first tab image from the imgOff type image to the imgOn type image using the Source property:

```
//Method called upon tab_mouseEnter event
void tab_MouseEnter(object sender, MouseEventArgs e)
{
  Image tabRef = (Image)sender;
  int tempId = int.Parse(tabRef.Name);
  resetTabs(tempId);
  buildContents(tempId );
  tab[tempId].Source = imgOn[tempId];
}
```

You need to call the resetTabs() method upon every MouseEnter event to reset all images to the default image type—imgOff—as shown in the following code snippet:

```
//resetTabs method for proper tab mouseOver and out effect
public void resetTabs(int tabId)
{
  for (int index = 1; index < tabCount + 1;index++ )
  {
    //Skip selected tab
    if (index == tabId)
      continue;
    tab[index].Source = imgOff[index];
  }
}
```

Once the selected tab image is properly set up, you need to call the `buildContents()` method to populate the selected tab with the appropriate content. You'll see how to use this method in the section "Populating Tab Content."

Code-Behind to Populate Tab Content

At this point, we have created the required number of tabs dynamically at runtime based on the external XML file definition. We have also set up the proper events to implement the visual impact on the tab selection. Now we can populate the tab content area for each tab with content.

Web Service Integration to Get Tab Definition XML File

At the end of the `buildTab()` method, we will call the `processContents()` method to read the `tabContents.xml` file by calling the `getTabContents` Web Service. The code is very similar to that for reading and processing the `tabDefinition.xml` file for tab creation:

```
//Call Web Service to get tab contents as XML
public void processContents()
{
  //Here we call the getTabContents Web Service and receive XML that will
  //define tab contents.
  getTabContents.getTabContentsSoapClient getContent = new
     Silverlight_smartTabs.getTabContents.getTabContentsSoapClient();
  getContent.getTabConsAsync();
  getContent.getTabConsCompleted += new
     EventHandler<Silverlight_smartTabs.getTabContents.
     getTabConsCompletedEventArgs>(getContent_getTabConsCompleted);
}
```

Defining Tab Content Using LINQ

Once the `tabContents.xml` file is read successfully, we raise an event, `getContent_getTabConsCompleted`, as shown in the following code snippet. Here we are using LINQ to read the XML file and store it in the contents string array for future use to display the appropriate content based on the selected tab.

```
//Parsing XML and assigning its value to diff. object which will be used to
//make up tab contents later
void getContent_getTabConsCompleted(object sender,
   Silverlight_smartTabs.getTabContents.getTabConsCompletedEventArgs e)
{
  int i = 0;
  //Use of LINQ to XML to parse XML string
  XDocument xDoc = XDocument.Parse(e.Result);
  //Parsing of each tab's contents
  var tabcontent = from t in xDoc.Descendants("content")

    select new
    {
id = t.Attribute("tabid").Value,
title = t.Element("title").Value,
hlink = t.Element("hlink").Value,
img = t.Element("img").Value,
    desc = t.Element("desc").Value,
    };
  //Storing above parsed values to contents string array
  foreach (var itm in tabcontent)
  {
```

```
      i++;
      contents[i, 0] = itm.id;
      contents[i, 1] = itm.title;
      contents[i, 2] = itm.hlink;
      contents[i, 3] = itm.img;
      contents[i, 4] = itm.desc;
   }
}
```

The following is a snapshot of the tabContents.xml file for your reference:

```
<?xml version="1.0" encoding="utf-8" ?>
<tabData>
 <content tabid="1">
  <title>Tab 1</title>
  <hlink>http://technologyopinion.com</hlink>
  <img>http://localhost:4353/Silverlight_smartTabs_Web/image1.png</img>
  <desc>Tab 1 Description</desc>
 </content>
 <content tabid="2">
  <title>Tab 2</title>
  <hlink>http://technologyopinion.com</hlink>
  <img>http://localhost:4353/Silverlight_smartTabs_Web/image2.png</img>
  <desc>Tab 2 Description</desc>
 </content>
 <content tabid="3">
  <title>Tab 3</title>
  <hlink>http://technologyopinion.com</hlink>
  <img>http://localhost:4353/Silverlight_smartTabs_Web/image3.png</img>
  <desc>Tab 3 Description</desc>
 </content>
 <content tabid="4">
  <title>Tab 4</title>
  <hlink>http://technologyopinion.com</hlink>
  <img>http://localhost:4353/Silverlight_smartTabs_Web/image4.png</img>
  <desc>Tab 4 Description</desc>
 </content>
</tabData>
```

Populating Tabs with Content

For every MouseEnter event of the tab, we need to populate the appropriate tab with content, which we can achieve by calling the buildContents() method. First we clear existing selected tab content by calling the Clear() method of the contentHolder control. Then based on the selected tab's ID, tabID, we create the tabContent object based on the tabContents.xml file, assign the retrieved image to the Image control (with the name icon), assign retrieved title hyperlink information to the HyperlinkButton control (with the name title), and assign a description to the TextBlock control (with the name details). The following is the code snippet of the buildContents() method:

```
//Based on getContent_getTabConsCompleted, actual implementation of each
//tab's contents
public void buildContents(int tabId)
{
  //Clear any previous contents
  contentsHolder.Children.Clear();
  //Set values based on tabId from contents string array (which we constructed
  //in "getContent_getTabConsCompleted")
  //Need to loop through whole array
```

```
for (int i = 1; i < 101; i++)
{
  if (contents[i, 0] == null)
    break;
  else if (int.Parse(contents[i, 0]) == tabId)
  {
    //Create tabContent object from userControl "tabContent.xaml"
    tabContent tabConts = new tabContent();
    tabConts.title.Content=contents[i,1];
    tabConts.title.NavigateUri = new Uri(contents[i, 2]);
    BitmapImage bmp= new
        BitmapImage (new Uri (contents[i,3],UriKind.RelativeOrAbsolute));
    tabConts.icon.Source = bmp;
    tabConts.details.Text = contents[i, 4];
    contentsHolder.Children.Add(tabConts);
  }
}
}
```

Both Web Services getTabDefinition and getTabContents are very straightforward, so the code is not shown in the book. However, you can download the complete project from the Source Code page on the Apress web site (http://www.apress.com).

Now if you run the project, four tabs (horizontal or vertical) will be created dynamically based on the XML file definition and displayed, as shown in Figure 4-17.

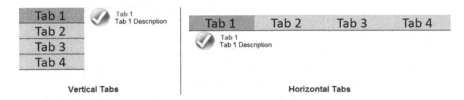

Figure 4-17. *Horizontal and vertical dynamic tabs*

Summary

This chapter is considerably weighty, since it focused mainly on defining the SOA and its key concepts and principles. The enterprise leadership and technology teams need to understand and consider the SOA concept and align their technology and product roadmaps before implementing key IT systems to achieve long-term benefits.

The SOA concept aligns three organizational strategic components—product roadmap, technology roadmap, and IT governance model—to implement externalized, distributed, shared, and loosely coupled service-based RIAs and deploy them as SaaS, enabling Enterprise 2.0 and Web 2.0 concepts in the agile mode. The SOA-based application services will help organizations to achieve three key basic concepts—meet expectations, keep it simple, and follow the rules—vital for developing business-enabled RIAs and transforming IT organizations to move from cost center to profit-making center in the long term.

SOA does not mean just Web Services. SOA is an architectural concept describing how to implement loosely coupled, distributed, lightweight shared services to enable IT systems integration. Usually Web Services become the heart of the SOA implementation for the RIAs. In this chapter, we focused especially on defining the architecture of Web Services.

Since .NET Framework is the core platform for building Silverlight-based RIAs, Silverlight technology can support the seven key principles—usability, flexibility, simplicity, reusability, scalability, maintainability, and security—for building RIAs as services. The following four factors are key characteristics of SOA-based RIAs developed using Silverlight:

- Device- and platform-independent RIAs
- Abstracted presentation layer (separated from the business service and data access layers)
- Integration with platform-agnostic services
- Modular design and reusable component and service libraries

You learned how Silverlight supports enterprise-level features such as integration with Web Services, LINQ, externalization, use of Silverlight custom user controls, and dynamic creation at runtime of the user interface based on an externalized tab definition.

The next chapter will extend the lessons you've learned by taking you through the implementation of an enterprise-level, service-oriented, Silverlight-based RIA. We will take the My Album RIA developed in Chapter 2 as a base and migrate to the Enterprise Training Portal RIA so you can understand how to implement the SOA concept for Silverlight-based RIAs. During this exercise, you will learn in detail how to integrate different key .NET technology components such as LINQ, WCF and Web Services, XML, and SQL Server with Silverlight. The chapter will also highlight some key capabilities of Silverlight such as development of reusable components using Application and Class Library templates and the Deep Zoom functionality to improve usability by improving the user experience.

CHAPTER 5

■ ■ ■

Developing a Service-Oriented Enterprise RIA

Chapters 3 and 4 of this book mainly focused on explaining the need for enterprises to embrace the Enterprise 2.0 concept and enable development and deployment of service-oriented RIAs. Chapter 3 defined the Enterprise 2.0–ready technology platform and explained how Silverlight fits in this category. In Chapter 4, you learned about the SOA concept and the seven key principles of SOA for developing service-oriented RIAs and deploying them as SaaS. I also explained different features and capabilities of Silverlight such as WCF/Web Services, LINQ, and feed integration to implement SOA-based RIAs by developing a sample Silverlight application.

This chapter will transform the My Album RIA developed in Chapter 2 into the Enterprise Training Portal RIA utilizing Silverlight and its service-oriented features and capabilities.

Recapping the My Album RIA

During the development of the My Album RIA, I covered various aspects of the Silverlight's basic technology features and capabilities using Microsoft development tools such as the following:

- Integration of Silverlight with the Visual Studio IDE and development environment
- Seamless integration with Microsoft Expression Blend for rich user interface definition and event integration
- Use of WPF and XAML for the user interface definition
- Managed code-behind integration to develop an interactive application
- Rich .NET class library integration
- Animation capabilities
- Rich media integration
- Use of Expression Encoder

Figure 5-1 shows the My Album RIA.

Figure 5-1. *The My Album RIA developed in Chapter 2 using Silverlight*

Defining the Enterprise Training Portal RIA Project

The Enterprise Training Portal RIA extends the My Album RIA concept, enabling the enterprise to provide different types of interactive training through an enterprise portal to internal and external audiences. The training subjects and material are very dynamic in nature. The enterprise portal must be flexible and should provide dynamic features such as support for multiple languages with rich presentation capabilities to display media, content, and RSS (Really Simple Syndication) feed integration with proper categorization, just as a traditional desktop application would have. Figure 5-2 shows the Enterprise Training Portal RIA compared to the My Album RIA.

"My Album" RIA

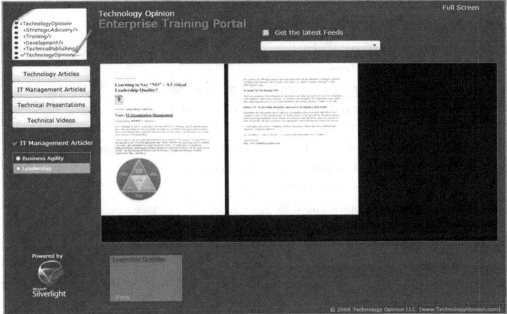

"Enterprise Training Portal" RIA

Figure 5-2. *The Enterprise Training Portal RIA*

We will be building the Enterprise Training Portal RIA for an enterprise named Technology Opinion. Now let's define the Enterprise Training Portal RIA project scope.

Enterprise Strategic Vision

The Enterprise Training Portal RIA will provide interactive training to internal and external users using an online central server or a distributed offline portal. The scope of the training (subject, category, who should get what) and content (media, documents, feeds) of the training is dynamic, supporting different cultures, languages, and user preferences. The RIA should feature subscription- and nonsubscription-based training portal views.

Application Features

The Enterprise Training Portal RIA has the following features:

- Generic and subscription-based portal
- User preference–based views
- Support for internal (organization employees) and external users
- Support of central online portal or distributed offline portal
- Simplified and interactive user interface
- Support for dynamic media files, image files, documents, and RSS integration
- Training content preview functionality using thumbnails
- Play and stop capabilities for video files
- Zoom-in functionality for the image files
- Easy navigation
- RSS feed viewer
- Support for multiple languages
- Full-screen view option
- Easy to customize

Design and Development Considerations

When developing the application, we need to bear the following in mind:

- Support for an agile project life cycle
- Prioritizing requirements and defining development iteration phases
- Service-oriented, externalized, and pluggable architecture
- Development of reusable services and components/custom controls
- RSS 2 reader
- Lightweight application
- Easy to deploy, support, and maintain
- Support for globalization and localization features
- High-performing application

Supported Content Types

The application will support the following types of media:

- *Documents*: Any document type (referenced as a link and can be opened in a native format in a separate new window)
- *Picture file types*: JPG, PNG, BMP, GIF (other file types should be supported but not tested), with minimum 800×600 resolution for better-quality pictures
- *Video file types*: WMV (Compressed Broadband Version)
- *RSS feed*: RSS 2 feed

Technology Platform Used to Develop the Enterprise Training Portal RIA

The application will be based on the following platforms:

- Microsoft Silverlight 2
- Microsoft .NET Framework 3.5 SP1
- WPF and XAML
- LINQ
- WCF/Web Services
- XML/SQL Server
- RSS 2 feed
- C# for the managed code development

Development Tools Used to Develop the Enterprise Training Portal RIA

We'll use the following tools to develop the application:

- Microsoft Visual Studio 2008 SP1
- Microsoft Silverlight Tools for Visual Studio 2008 SP1
- Microsoft Expression Blend 2 SP1
- Microsoft Expression Encoder 2 SP1
- Microsoft Deep Zoom Composer

Designing the Enterprise Training Portal

Along with following enterprise best practices for application architecture and design, a fluent user interface design to provide high application usability is a key design consideration for RIAs. As discussed earlier in this book, the architecture and design teams should define a system and application architecture that is aligned with the enterprise's strategic vision and technology and product roadmaps. However, the implementation of a designed solution may follow a phased approach to provide priority-based features in the Agile SDLC.

In this chapter, the following prioritized application features will be implemented as part of the first phase. The designed application architecture will allow the developed portal to support additional features in future phases.

Application Features to Be Implemented in This Chapter

We will implement the following application features in this chapter:

- Generic portal
- Support for internal (organization employees) and external users
- Support of central online portal or distributed offline portal
- Simplified and interactive user interface
- Two-level categorized content files
- Support for dynamic media files, image files, documents, and RSS integration
- Training content preview functionality using thumbnails
- Play and stop capabilities for video files
- Zoom-in functionality for the image files
- Easy navigation
- RSS feed viewer
- Full-screen view option
- Easy to customize

Application Architecture

Figure 5-3 defines the application architecture of the Enterprise Training Portal RIA.

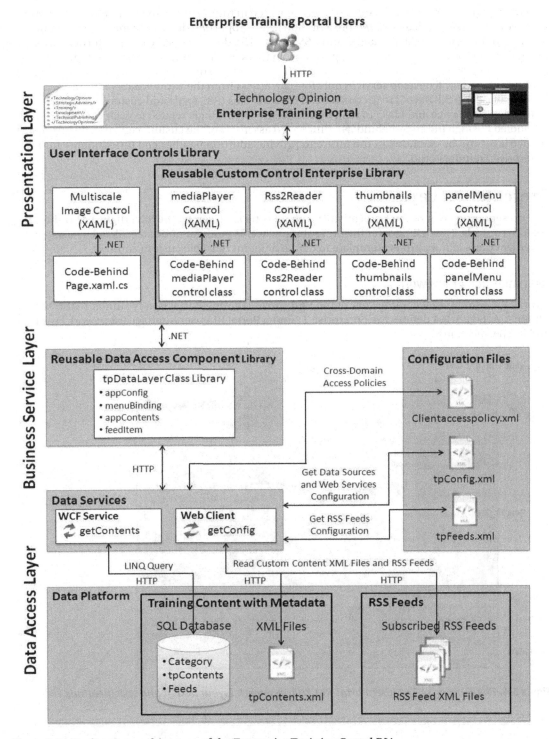

Figure 5-3. *Application architecture of the Enterprise Training Portal RIA*

During the first phase of the development (covered in this chapter), the main focus is to define an interactive, rich, service-oriented presentation layer supporting dynamic content presentation of different file types (media, images, and RSS feeds). The data access layer is platform agnostic, pluggable, and based on external configuration, so the RIA can connect to different types of data platforms such as SQL Server, RSS feeds, and XML files. At present, the business service layer is very lightweight, and we'll develop services only for data access from the various data platforms.

We'll use the .NET WebClient class to read the XML files (RSS feeds and custom XML files) and a custom WCF Service and LINQ to read from SQL Server. The logic related to each custom control is handled through the code-behind .NET managed assembly of the custom control. The business service layer can be extended in the future to provide additional enhanced functionality for the Enterprise Training Portal.

Presentation Layer

The presentation layer of the Enterprise Training Portal is driven by the Silverlight XAML-based custom controls. The definition of the presentation layer is modular and externalized by using the Silverlight Class Library project template to define different reusable custom controls.

User Interface Framework

Overall the user interface framework of the Enterprise Training Portal is very similar to the My Album RIA. Figure 5-4 defines the Enterprise Training Portal RIA user interface framework layout and its specifications.

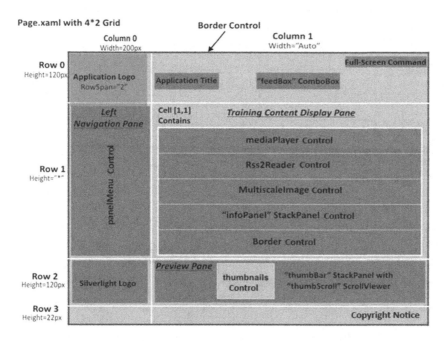

Figure 5-4. *The Enterprise Training Portal RIA UI framework layout design and specifications*

User Interface Navigation Patterns

Consistent to the My Album RIA, the following are the key navigation patterns of the Enterprise Training Portal RIA:

- The *center stage theme* displays the selected content (media, RSS feed, image) in the main StackPanel control as a container.

- The left navigation pane dynamically drives the user to navigate through the available categorized content to receive the appropriate training. We will use the *static multilevel hierarchy* navigation pattern (two-level) to display different categories of training content.

- We will follow the *linear animated slide transition* navigation pattern to preview collections of training content based on the selection of the category using the StackPanel control as a container.

- The RIA window layout will be configured as a *liquid layout* to enable us to resize the application when the user resizes the browser window to match the browser window size.

User Interface Layout Definition

We will expand the grid from 2×2 to 4×2 (compared to the My Album RIA) to accommodate different parts of the RIA, which will ease the work of designing, placing, and maintaining controls.

- We will set Row 1's height to * and Column 1's width to Auto to cover a portion of the window. This allows the content container to keep the width to the size of the content and the application to resize according to the browser window's size, maintaining the original aspect ratio of the different parts of the application.

- The Row 0/Column 0 cell contains the enterprise logo with the height and width configured to 120 px and 200 px. The logo image will have RowSpan set to 2.

- The Row 0/Column 1 cell contains the enterprise name and the RIA name with a drop-down box containing the available RSS feeds to select and view. It also contains the Full Screen/Normal Screen command, enabling users to toggle the content control to full-screen mode or normal screen mode. The cell is configured with height and width set to 120 px and Auto.

- The Row 1/Column 0 cell contains the main navigation pane. It will build the dynamic subject categories of the available training, and upon selection of a particular category, available subjects will be displayed. The cell is configured with the height and width set to * and 200 px.

- The Row 1/Column 1 cell contains the main container to display the selected content (media, image, or RSS feed). Based on the selection from the preview pane, the training will be loaded utilizing the proper custom control (mediaPlayer for media, Rss2Reader for the RSS feed, and MultiscaleImage for image display). The cell is configured with the height and width set to * and Auto.

- The Row 2/Column 0 cell contains the official Silverlight logo. The cell is configured with the height and width set to 120 px and 200 px.

- The Row 2/Column 1 cell contains the preview pane displaying thumbnails of available training programs of the selected subject. You can view the content within the content container upon selection. With Next and Previous functionality, the selected subject thumbnail will be animated and highlighted, and the rest will be dimmed slightly. The preview pane would also allow users to link to the original source from where the training content is made available. The cell is configured with the height and width set to 120 px and Auto.

- We will not have anything in the Row 3/Column 0 cell. The cell is configured with the height and width set to 22 px and 200 px.

- The Row 3/Column 1 cell contains the copyright notice of the enterprise. The cell is configured with the height and width set to 22 px and Auto.

Reusable Key User Interface Components

Based on the application features I've defined and the preceding user interface framework discussion, it is clear that we will need the following key user interface components:

- The *left navigation pane* is a driver of the training portal. It builds the vertical tab-based training menu. As shown in Chapter 4, a dynamic left navigation pane will be created at runtime based on external definitions of the available training categories and subjects.

- The *preview pane* dynamically presents available training as thumbnails based on the selected training category and training subject using the left navigation pane. The preview pane allows a user to get a quick overview of available training and select content to display in the display area of the portal.

- The enterprise training portal supports media (video files), image files, and RSS feed types of content to display. The *training content display pane*, which is at the center of the screen, hosts the selected training content. We will need custom controls that can host the required types of content. The **MultiscaleImage** control will show the selected images with the Deep Zoom functionality. The mediaPlayer custom control enables users to play video files with the default video player. The Rss2Reader custom control will display all RSS feed–related items.

All of the preceding functionality is very common, and usually an enterprise will need these types of functionality repeatedly in more than one application. We can use Silverlight Class Library project templates to build these custom controls individually as user interface components that can be reused across different RIAs.

Figure 5-5 shows the high-level XAML control class diagram of the Enterprise Training Portal. The class diagram demonstrates the use of different Silverlight controls to develop the previously mentioned reusable custom controls.

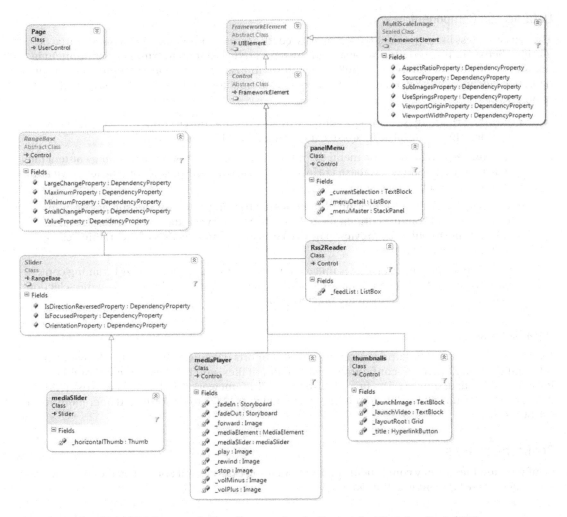

Figure 5-5. *Silverlight XAML control class diagram for the Enterprise Training Portal RIA*

Business Service Layer and Data Access Layer

The loosely coupled business service layer of the Enterprise Training Portal is very lightweight and mainly focused on data management. It supports integration with multiple data platforms, as we discussed previously. The data access layer provides data platform–agnostic services to retrieve the requested information from the business service layer.

Code-Behind Assemblies

The custom control class library project contains the code-behind .NET assembly that performs presentation layer–specific functionality (e.g., for the `mediaPlayer` custom control, the code-behind assembly will perform all media-related functionalities—play, pause, stop, resume, control volume, etc.).

Data Access Component

The reusable class library project tpDataLayer is a data access component .NET assembly that is a bridge between the presentation layer and the data services and platform. This component is mainly responsible for retrieving the following information at runtime from different types of configuration files and data sources. It then provides this information to the presentation layer and related components.

- Read the tpConfig.xml configuration file to get the data source configuration and data service definition and tpFeeds.xml to get the subscribed RSS feed information.

- Get the left navigation pane menu definition from the tpContents.xml training content file or from the SQL Server database trainingPortalDB_Data.mdf file to build the left navigation pane dynamically.

- Get the preview pane definition of the selected training category and subject from the tpContents.xml training content file or from the SQL Server database trainingPortalDB_Data.mdf file to build the preview pane dynamically upon selection of the training category and specific subject.

- Get the training content (HTML, image, or video) from the tpContents.xml training content file or from the SQL Server database trainingPortalDB_Data.mdf file based on the selection of the training program from the preview pane .

Data Services

As discussed earlier, the Enterprise Training Portal supports data integration with SQL Server and different types of XML files—configuration files, content files, and RSS feeds. We will build two loosely coupled data services. The first will use the .NET Framework WebClient class to read XML files, and the second will be a custom WCF service that uses LINQ to perform read operations from the SQL server.

Configuration Files

Configuration files are key components for implementing externalized and pluggable solutions. The portal uses three key configuration files:

- tpConfig.xml

- tpFeeds.xml

- Clientaccesspolicy.xml

tpConfig.xml File

As part of the walkthrough in Chapter 2, we hard-coded/embedded the following items and made them part of the application deployment package:

- Image and video file categories were named Pictures and Videos, respectively. If we want to update (add, modify, or delete) these predefined categories, we need to change the code and recompile and redeploy the project.

- The image and video files were embedded within the project at compile time. This does not allow us to change existing content or add new content types and content without recompiling.

To decouple training content from the Enterprise Training Portal RIA, we will integrate data source definitions, training content types, and training content files dynamically at runtime by externalizing their definition using the tpConfig.xml configuration XML file. This file mainly provides the data source definition (SQL Server and XML) and what type of data source to be used (SQL Server or XML) for the training portal. It also provides the WCF-based service URL to retrieve the content from SQL Server (or any other types of database, if used). This will allow the enterprise to incorporate future content updates without recompiling or redeploying the Enterprise Training Portal RIA.

Note For the central deployment of the application, every resource in the tpConfig.xml configuration file must be provided with an absolute URL, not a relative URL. See the note at the end of the "Centralized Deployment of the Enterprise Training Portal RIA" section of this chapter for more details.

We will use the .NET Framework WebClient class to retrieve the tpConfig.xml XML file and store the retrieved information using the custom appConfig data class.

Since the training content database does not store original training content, only training content–related metadata—training category, training track, and individual training profile with the link to the original training file available for display—it is a best practice to keep all training-related taxonomy information in a single data source (in our example, either SQL Server database or XML file).

For this chapter, all the actual training materials are stored on a file system as files or as RSS feeds, rather than storing them in a database.

tpConfig.xml is an application-level configuration file. During deployment, it must reside alongside the TrainingPortal XAP package within the same folder.

The following is a snapshot of the tpConfig.xml file, where the database is stored locally on the machine and the WCF service is also locally hosted. tpContents.xml is stored on the technologyopinion.com server.

```xml
<?xml version="1.0" encoding="utf-8" ?>
<TrainingPortal Datasource="XML">
  <Datasource>
    <SQL>
        <connectionString>
            "Data Source=VISTA64DT\SQLEXPRESS;
                AttachDbFilename=|DataDirectory|\trainingPortalDB_Data.mdf;
                Initial Catalog=trainingPortalDB;Integrated Security=True"
        </connectionString>
        <Url/>
    </SQL>
    <XML>
        <connectionString/>
        <Url>http://technologyopinion.com/Documents/tp/tpContents.xml</Url>
    </XML>
  </Datasource>
  <webservice>
    <getContents>
        <serviceEndpoint>
            http://localhost:63167/getContents.svc
        </serviceEndpoint>
    </getContents>
  </webservice>
</TrainingPortal>
```

The `Datasource` attribute of the `<TrainingPortal>` root node defines what type of data source is being used to provide the available training profile information. In our example, it is XML, which is the same as the data source node name defined under the `<Datasource>` node. It means that the `tpDatalayer` data access component will read the `<XML>` node and read the XML file (in this case `tpContents.xml`) to build the left navigation pane and the preview pane. If the `Datasource` attribute is set to `SQL`, `tpDatalayer` will connect to the SQL Server database to populate the navigation and preview panes.

■**Note** This version of the Enterprise Training Portal supports only two types of database—SQL Server and XML files. However, it can be enhanced very easily by just adding a database type–specific node under the `<Datasource>` element to support other database types.

---

tpFeeds.xml File

The Enterprise Training Portal also displays predefined RSS feeds. The portal can display any RSS feeds published by either the enterprise itself or third parties. The `tpFeeds.xml` configuration XML file provides the set of feeds available to display on the portal. Each feed configuration contains two nodes—the value of the `<Title>` node will be displayed in the Portal menu, and the `<Url>` node points to the URL where the RSS feed is published.

Like `tpConfig.xml`, `tpFeeds.xml` is also an application-level configuration file. During deployment, it must reside alongside the `TrainingPortal` XAP package within the same folder.

The following is a snapshot of the `tpFeeds.xml` file:

```
<?xml version="1.0" encoding="utf-8" ?>
<TrainingPortal>
<feed>
    <Title>TechnologyOpnion New</Title>
    <Url>http://technologyopinion.com/Documents/technologyopinionRSS</Url>
</feed>
</TrainingPortal>
```

■**Note** The application can access the cross-domain-published RSS feed only if the proper `Clientaccesspolicy.xml` or `Crossdomain.xml` policy file is published, allowing cross-domain access.

Clientaccesspolicy.xml File

To demonstrate a complex scenario, we can deploy the `tpContents.xml` file and/or the WCF service on a different domain from that of the Enterprise Training Portal. In this case, to access the content XML file and service successfully, you need to deploy either a `Crossdomain.xml` or a `Clientaccesspolicy.xml` file.

We will use the `Clientaccesspolicy.xml` file to allow access from the Enterprise Training Portal.

Data Platforms

The training portal mainly presents media-centric training. The training material consists of a collection of media files (audio and visual) and images. To provide proper categorization of the training material, each training item contains a set of predefined metadata (providing a training profile) and physical training files. The Enterprise Training Portal will support the published training content in the same domain and cross-domain (with properly defined security policies).

The enterprise can use any type of document/content management system (e.g., Microsoft Office SharePoint Server) to store the training media files. We can use an XML file or a relational database (e.g., SQL Server) to maintain the available training profiles (with reference to the published training media files) that we will use to feed the presentation layer. Upon selection of the specific training item from the preview pane, the portal will access the physical media file based on the training profile reference and will display the training content in the training content display pane.

In this chapter, I will demonstrate the use of SQL Server and XML file to maintain the training profiles.

SQL Server

Figure 5-6 shows a simple relational schema diagram of the `trainingPortalDB_Data.mdf` database.

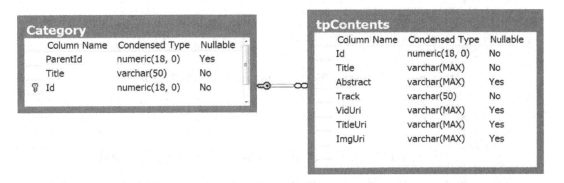

Figure 5-6. *Database schema of the* `trainingPortalDB_Data.mdf` *database containing Enterprise Training Portal training profiles*

The database contains only two tables—`Category` and `tbContents`. The `Category` table contains all the training categories representing the complete training taxonomy. The left navigation pane is built dynamically at runtime based on the `Category` table.

In this chapter, we will populate only one level of category. The developed `Panelmenu` custom control component supports only one level of category. However, the `Category` table definition supports n-levels in the training category taxonomy. The combination of the `ParentId` and `Id` fields can build n-levels of category taxonomy. The first level of the category will have `ParentID` with a `NULL` value.

The `tpContents` table defines the different tracks (with the `Track` field) available in each training category. The tracks will be displayed in the left navigation pane upon selection of a particular category. Each track contains one or more training items. The preview pane will display the available training items of the selected track based on the `Title` field. The type of training and definition of the training file location for each training item is decided based on the populated `VidUri` (for video files) or `ImageUri` (for image files). The `TitleUri` field provides a link to the original source of the training material. The `Abstract` field contains a short description of the training.

■**Note** The current database schema (tpContents table) and Enterprise Training Portal only support image and video file types. You can have additional types of training materials (e.g., PowerPoint presentations, Word documents, XPS documents, and PDF documents). It would be very easy to enhance the database to support additional types of training materials. However, currently Silverlight does not support hosting different types of documents (PowerPoint, PDF, etc.). The alternative is to show the abstract as HTML or as an image file in the training content display pane and provide a link to the original document to open in a native format in a new window. The approach is shown in the Technology Articles and IT Management Articles categories in our example.

Custom Content XML Files

The alternative approach is to use an XML file (in our example it is tpContents.xml) defining training profiles to build the left navigation and preview panes. The structure of the tpContents.xml file is very much aligned with the trainingPortalDB_Data.mdf database.

   The following is a snapshot of the tpContents.xml file containing example information:

```
<?xml version="1.0" encoding="utf-8" ?>
<TrainingPortal>
    <Category Title="Technology Articles" Id="1">
        <Training>
            <Title>Manage Metadata with Document Information Panels</Title>
            <Abstract>This article demonstrates how to enable.... </Abstract>
            <Track>Microsoft Office 2007</Track>
            <ImgUri></ImgUri>
            <TitleUri>
                    http://msdn2.microsoft.com/en-us/magazine/cc500578.aspx
            </TitleUri>
            <VidUri></VidUri>
        </Training>
        <Training>
            <Title>
                Publish a Self-Signed InfoPath Form Template to Local Computer
            </Title>
            <Abstract>To attach an InfoPath form template ...</Abstract>
            <Track>Microsoft Office 2007</Track>
            <ImgUri>
                    http://technologyopinion.com/Documents/tp/content/
                    PublishInfoPathTemplateToLocalComputer/dzc_output.xml
            </ImgUri>
            <TitleUri>http://technologyopinion.com/word2007.aspx#pubinfopath</TitleUri>
            <VidUri></VidUri>
        </Training>
    </Category>
    <Category Title="IT Management Articles" Id="2">....</Category>
</TrainingPortal>
```

■**Note** In this example, the <ImgUri> node is populated with a reference to an XML file rather than any image file (e.g., http://technologyopinion.com/Documents/tp/content/sayNo/dzc_output.xml). This XML file represents the outcome of the image collection using the Deep Zoom composer to enable the Deep Zoom functionality.

RSS Feeds

RSS is a widely used open standard format to feed updated information to end users without their having to actually visit sites. As organizations become virtual and transform their paper-based processes to electronic/digitized processes, they will start utilizing RSS-like open standards in their knowledge management systems and services, enabling effective interorganization information exchange.

The Enterprise Training Portal can display RSS 2 feeds in the training content display pane. The RSS 2 feed drop-down of the portal is populated based on the `tpFeeds.xml` definition. Upon selection of a particular RSS feed, the related feed items will be displayed within the portal.

There is no particular training portal RIA–specific database schema required to display the RSS feeds.

Understanding Silverlight Custom Controls

Silverlight has extensive support for SOA capabilities when defining the presentation layer of an RIA. It provides a reusable custom control library that supports the following SOA features

- Modular design of rich user interfaces and related business logic supporting reusability of custom controls across applications

- Separated user interface definition and business logic

- Style-based control template definition to enable an application-specific look and feel without having an impact on the business logic of the custom control

Before we dive into the development of the Enterprise Training Portal, I think it is fairly important for you to understand Silverlight custom control capabilities and how to develop them, since we are using this feature to define the modular, reusable, and customizable presentation layer of the RIA.

Key Components of Custom Controls

Silverlight custom controls contain a clear separation between the user interface definition and business logic (see Figure 5-7) compared to other reusable GUI custom controls (e.g., Windows Forms or ASP.NET, where there is no clear separation between the visuals and logic). This feature enables the development team to customize an application-specific look and feel without having an impact on the business logic of the custom control.

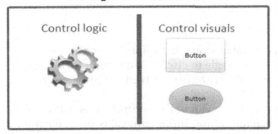

Silverlight Custom Control

Control logic | Control visuals

Button

Button

Figure 5-7. *Microsoft Silverlight custom controls contain a clear separation between visuals and business logic.*

Silverlight custom controls are derived from the `Control` class. To define how custom controls look, we use the `Style` and `ControlTemplates` classes. Microsoft recommends utilizing the Parts and States model with the Visual State Manager (VSM) to define customization scope and behavior of visual of custom controls.

Following is a quick overview on three key components of Silverlight custom controls—the `Style` class, the `ControlTemplates` class, and the Parts and States model.

Style Class

One of the ways to apply a consistent look and feel across an application is to define the style of the application controls. The `Style` class is a part of the .NET Framework class library for Silverlight and is a collection of one or more `Setter` objects. Each `Setter` object has `Property` and `Value` attributes. `Property` defines the name of the property of the element to which the style is applicable, and `Value` is the value that is applied to the defined property.

Figure 5-8 demonstrates how to define a style for the `Button` element and how you can apply it to one or more instances of the `Button` element. `x:key` and `TargetType` are key attributes for defining the style of a control, whereas `Style` is a key attribute for applying the predefined style to a control.

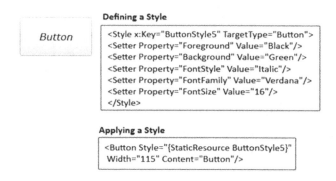

Figure 5-8. *Demonstrating how to define and apply style to the* `Button` *control*

We can define the `Style` in `App.xaml` in the `<Application.Resources>` section to make it visible at the application level. In the custom control, we can define a `Style` in the `<UserControl.Resources>` section of the XAML file where we want to place that particular styled control.

The definition and use of `Style`-based controls across an enterprise-level application is the best way to apply and maintain enterprise-level presentation (user interface) standards.

ControlTemplate Class

The main constraint of the `Style` class is that you cannot customize the appearance of the styled control (e.g., changing the shape of the button from rectangle to circle); you cannot do it using only a styled control. To achieve the visual customization of controls, Silverlight provides the `ControlTemplate` class.

A `ControlTemplate` defines the visual structure and behavior of the control. Thus, with the use of the `ControlTemplate`, you can have different shapes of the `Button` control without having an impact on its functionality. In our example, you can change the appearance of buttons in your application from rectangle to oval, but the behavior of the button is not changed (e.g., there is no impact on the `MouseEnter` and `Click` events). For the same control/functionality, you can have more than one `ControlTemplate` defining different visual structures.

Figure 5-9 demonstrates how to define the `ControlTemplate` for the `Button` control to change its regular shape to oval, and how you can apply it to one or more instances of the `Button` element. `x:key` and `TargetType` are key attributes for defining a template of a control, whereas `Template` is a key attribute for applying a predefined template to a control.

Defining a ControlTemplate

```
<ControlTemplate x:Key="ButtonControlTemplate1" TargetType="Button">
    <Grid>
        <Ellipse Margin="8,0,0,0" Stroke="#FF000000">
            <Ellipse.Fill>
                <LinearGradientBrush EndPoint="0.5,1" StartPoint="0.5,0">
                    <GradientStop Color="#FF4292F2"/>
                    <GradientStop Color="#FFC9EDF7" Offset="1"/>
                </LinearGradientBrush>
            </Ellipse.Fill>
        </Ellipse>
        <TextBlock Margin="48,19,19,14" Text="Button" TextWrapping="Wrap"/>
    </Grid>
</ControlTemplate>
```

Applying a ControlTemplate

```
<Button Height="56" Width="119" Content="Button"
Template="{StaticResource ButtonControlTemplate1}"/>
```

Figure 5-9. *Demonstrating how to define* `ControlTemplate` *to change the* `Button` *control's shape to* `Oval` *and apply the template to the* `Button` *control*

The definition of a `ControlTemplate` library for a set of controls across enterprise-level applications is the best way to apply and maintain enterprise-level presentation standards.

Parts and States Model

As you saw, the `ControlTemplate` class defines the custom visual structure of the control. Now I'll explain how you can manage a control's behavior with different types of look and feel for different states and while the control is transitioning from one state to another (e.g., `MouseEnter` to `Click`). You can achieve this functionality very easily with the help of the Parts and States model and the VSM of Expression Blend.

The main objective of the Parts and States model is to define the control structure and behavior of the control by defining the control contract (associated with the VSM) and separating the control visual appearance and the control logic. Microsoft recommends utilizing the Parts and States model to define and maintain control structure and state management. The Parts and States model and VSM are tightly integrated with Expression Blend for easy definition and development.

There are three main components of the Parts and States model—parts, states, and transitions.

Parts

Many Silverlight controls (though not all controls, such as the `CheckBox` and `Button` controls) consist of distinct visual components (e.g., the `Slider` control) where each component can be named in the `ControlTemplate`. Each distinct component is called a *part*. The behavior and structure of these parts can be controlled by the control logic.

As shown in Figure 5-10, the Slider control consists of four distinct parts—DownRepeatButton, UpRepeatButton, Thumb, and Track. Each part is accessible and can be controlled through the control logic.

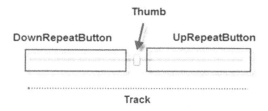

Figure 5-10. *The* Slider *control has four distinct parts.*

States

All Silverlight controls have distinct states. A particular control's specific state defines its visual appearance. As shown in Figure 5-11, the CheckBox has a check mark when in the checked state and is embossed with a gradient fill when in the MouseEnter state.

Figure 5-11. *Different states of the* CheckBox *control*

Each *state group* represents a collection of mutually exclusive states. Silverlight controls can contain more than one state group. State groups are orthogonal, which means that it is possible for a Silverlight control to have more than one state at a time as long as each of those states is in a different state group.

As shown in Figure 5-12, the CheckBox control has two state groups—CommonStates and CheckStates. At any one time, the CheckBox control can be in two different states (e.g., MouseEnter and Checked states), one from each state group.

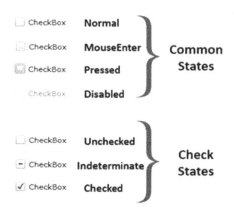

Figure 5-12. *Two different state groups of the* CheckBox *control*

Transitions

Transitions represent the way a control looks visually as it transitions from one state to another. For example, when the CheckBox control goes from the MouseEnter state to the Pressed state, the background changes from light blue to dark blue (see Figure 5-13).

Transition

☐ CheckBox ————————————————→ ☐ CheckBox

MouseEnter State   **Pressed State**

Figure 5-13. *State transition of the CheckBox control*

■**Note** Get more information on the Parts and States model and Visual State Manager by visiting the Scorbs site—Karen Corby's blog— at http://scorbs.com/2008/06/11/parts-states-model-with-visualstatemanager-part-1-of.

Visual State Manager

The Silverlight 2 VSM follows the Parts and States model and features visual states and state transitions within the control templates. Within ControlTemplate, the VisualStateManager class manages states and the logic for transitioning between states defining the control's behavior. The attached property VisualStateManager.VisualStateGroups contains a collection of VisualStateGroup objects. Each VisualStateGroup object contains a collection of mutually exclusive VisualState objects and VisualTransition objects.

As mentioned, Expression Blend makes it very easy to manage control states and to define control state transitions (by defining the duration of a transition to animate). At runtime, Silverlight will dynamically run the appropriate animation storyboards to move the control from one state to another. The key advantage of integration with Expression Blend is that there is no need to write code and create animation storyboards manually.

So that you understand the VSM, try this Button control example. Add a Button control to the Blend design surface. Right-click the Button control and choose the options Edit Control Parts (Template) and Create Empty. You will then be prompted for the name of the Style resource you want to create. Now you will notice that a new States window at the top-left side in the Blend IDE is displayed, as shown in Figure 5-14.

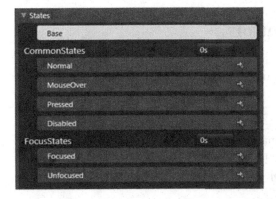

Figure 5-14. *States management window in Microsoft Expression Blend*

As you click any of the states except Base, automatic recording of the design surface starts, and it records all the steps performed and creates animation for the selected state. You can also define the transition value (of the `TimeSpan` type) to transit from one state to another. The following is an example XAML snapshot:

```xml
<Setter Property="Template">
    <Setter.Value>
        <ControlTemplate TargetType="Button">
            <Grid>
                <vsm:VisualStateManager.VisualStateGroups>
                    <vsm:VisualStateGroup x:Name="CommonStates">
                <vsm:VisualStateGroup.Transitions>
                    <vsm:VisualTransition To="MouseOver"
                        GeneratedDuration="0:0:0.6"/>
                </vsm:VisualStateGroup.Transitions>
                        <vsm:VisualState x:Name="Normal"/>
                        <vsm:VisualState x:Name="MouseOver">
                            <Storyboard>
                                <! —Some animation-->
                            </Storyboard>
                        </vsm:VisualState>
                        <vsm:VisualState x:Name="Pressed">
                            <Storyboard>
                                <! —Some animation-->
                            </Storyboard>
                        ......
                    <vsm:VisualStateGroup x:Name="FocusStates">
                    <vsm:VisualState x:Name="Focused">
                        <Storyboard>
                        <! —Some animation-->
                        </Storyboard>
                        ......
                    </vsm:VisualStateGroup>
                </vsm:VisualStateManager.VisualStateGroups>
        ......
</Setter>
```

Note Get more information on the Visual State Manager by visiting the Scorbs site—Karen Corby's blog—at http://scorbs.com/2008/06/11/parts-states-model-with-visualstatemanager-part-1-of/.

Developing a Sample Custom Control

Developing a custom control is a six-step process:

1. Create a Silverlight class library project in Visual Studio 2008 SP1 and name it `SampleCustomControl`.

2. Define `generic.xaml` under the `themes` folder. The `generic.xaml` file defines the default visual appearance of the custom control. This file also contains keyed resources under the `<ResourceDictionary>` element that we will manipulate in `SampleCustomControl.cs`. We can also define custom states for the custom control in this file.

    a. Right-click the `SampleCustomControl` project and choose Add ➤ New Folder to create a new folder with the name themes.

b. Right-click the newly created themes folder and choose Add ➤ New Item. Select the Text File file type and name it generic.xaml.

c. As shown in Figure 5-15, change the Build Action property to Resource to add generic.xaml as a resource file. Also clear the Custom Tool property value.

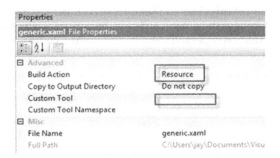

Figure 5-15. *Changing the* generic.xaml *file to a resource file*

d. Add a <ResourceDictionary> element to the generic.xaml file to place all the resources as shown in the following. The ResourceDictionary provides a dictionary that contains key resources that we will manipulate in SampleCustomControl.cs and also in the ControlTemplate defined in the generic.xaml file.

```
<ResourceDictionary
    xmlns="http://schemas.microsoft.com/winfx/2006/xaml/presentation"
    xmlns:x="http://schemas.microsoft.com/winfx/2006/xaml">
</ResourceDictionary>
```

3. Add the default Style for the control under the ResourceDictionary section. Start by including the XML namespace of the assembly, and then add the default Style for the control as shown in the following code snippet:

```
<ResourceDictionary
   xmlns="http://schemas.microsoft.com/winfx/2006/xaml/presentation"
   xmlns:x="http://schemas.microsoft.com/winfx/2006/xaml"
   xmlns:local="clr-namespace:CustomControl;assembly=SampleCustomControl">
    <!-- Default style for CustomControl -->
    <Style TargetType="local: SampleCustomControl ">
        <Setter Property="Template">
            <Setter.Value>
                <ControlTemplate TargetType="local: SampleCustomControl ">
                    <!--Control template for CustomControl -->
                </ControlTemplate>
            </Setter.Value>
        </Setter>
    </Style>
</ResourceDictionary>
```

4. Define the custom control class. Rename the default added class Class1.cs to SampleCustomControl.cs. The custom control class derives from the base Control class. The custom control class contains the metadata that allows it to conform to the Parts and States model enabling integration with VSM and control logic such as properties, dependency properties, event handlers, and methods.

The TemplatePart represents a contract as an attribute that is applied to the class definition to identify the types of the named parts that are used in control template and to place them under the VSM domain (this is an optional step).

You can add the TextBlock control as an attribute to the SampleCustomControl custom control.

You can add the following code snippet within the namespace section or under the class definition:

```
[TemplatePart(Name = panelMenu.CurrentSelection, Type = typeof(TextBlock))]
```

We also need to create a constructor for this class and set the Control.DefaultStyleKey property. The DefaultStyleKey references the default style for the control. To work correctly as part of theme style lookup, this value is expected to be the Type of the control being styled (in our case, SampleCustomControl).

The following is the code snippet of the SampleCustomControl class:

```
//Default Included Namespaces
using System;
using System.Net;
using System.Windows;
using System.Windows.Controls;
using System.Windows.Documents;
using System.Windows.Ink;
using System.Windows.Input;
using System.Windows.Media;
using System.Windows.Media.Animation;
using System.Windows.Shapes;

namespace CustomControl
{
    [TemplatePart(Name = panelMenu.CurrentSelection, Type = typeof(TextBlock))]
    public class SampleCustomControl: Control
    {
        public SampleCustomControl()
        {
            this.DefaultStyleKey=typeof(CustomControl);
            this.Loaded+=new RoutedEventHandler(SampleCustomControl_Loaded);
            OnApplyTemplate();
            ....
        }
    }
}
```

5. Define the template handlers. You need to define the Override OnApplyTemplate method and GetTemplateChildren method as the main template handlers:

```
public override void OnApplyTemplate()
{
    base.OnApplyTemplate();
    GetTemplateChildren();
        ....
}
```

The GetTemplateChildren method is used to retrieve the named element in the instantiated control template visual tree:

```
private void GetTemplateChildren()
{
...
}
```

6. The final step is to define the required custom properties and dependency properties (private and public fields) and methods and event handlers of the custom control.

Figure 5-16 shows the overall generic structured template of a typical Silverlight custom control. We will follow the same structure for developing our required custom controls.

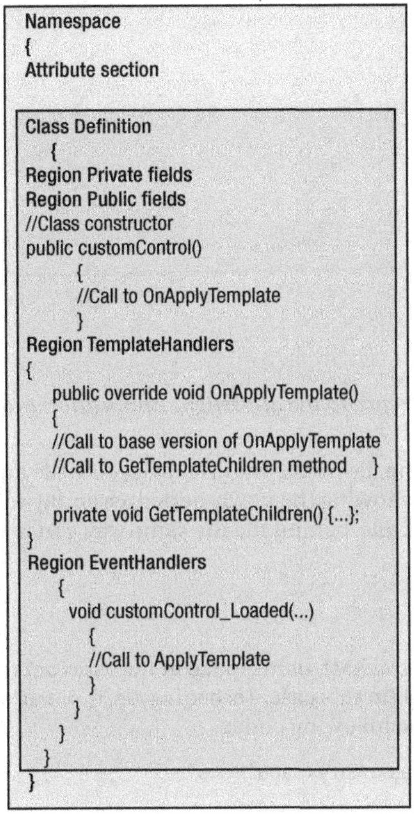

```
Namespace
{
Attribute section

Class Definition
    {
Region Private fields
Region Public fields
//Class constructor
public customControl()
        {
        //Call to OnApplyTemplate
        }
Region TemplateHandlers
{
    public override void OnApplyTemplate()
    {
    //Call to base version of OnApplyTemplate
    //Call to GetTemplateChildren method     }

    private void GetTemplateChildren() {...};
}
Region EventHandlers
    {
        void customControl_Loaded(...)
        {
        //Call to ApplyTemplate
        }
      }
    }
  }
}
```

Figure 5-16. *Generic structured template for a typical Silverlight custom control*

Note Get more information on how to develop custom controls by reading "Digging into Custom Controls," http://silverlight.net/blogs/jesseliberty/archive/2008/09/12/digging-into-custom-controls. aspx. The "Additional References" section at the end of this chapter also lists a couple articles on this topic.

Deploying a Custom Control

There are two ways you can make a custom control visible to Silverlight projects as a reference. Here we will use the panelMenu.dll custom control (which we will develop for the left navigation pane later in the chapter) as an example.

Manually Adding the Control As a Reference

You can add the panelMenu.dll file to the Silverlight application project as a reference using Add Reference option; select it from the context menu that appears when you right-click the project. This will open the dialog box shown in Figure 5-17.

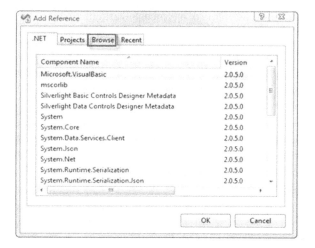

Figure 5-17. *Adding a Silverlight custom control as a reference to the Silverlight Application project*

Click the Browse tab to browse to the location of the file panelMenu.dll. Select the file and click OK. The References section in the project will expand, showing the newly added assembly reference.

Now you can use this control in an XAML file or a code-behind file the same way you use other Silverlight controls.

Adding the Control in XAML

To add your custom control in XAML, you need to add the XML namespace in the UserControl section that will contain the CLR namespace of the control (in this case, TechnologyOpinion) and the assembly name (in this case, panelMenu) as shown in the following code:

```
xmlns:myControl="clr-namespace:TechnologyOpinion;assembly=panelMenu"
```

___

■Note In the case of a Silverlight class library project, you need to add the custom control namespace in the generic.xaml file under the ResourceDictionary section.

___

Now you are all set to use the referenced custom control in XAML by using <xmlns>:<assembly name> as shown here:

```
<myControl:panelMenu ...>
```

Note that as you start typing this line, the Visual Studio IntelliSense feature will help the same way it helps with other Silverlight controls.

Using the Control in the Code-Behind

To use the control in the code-behind, add the generic namespace (TechnologyOpinion in this example) as shown here:

```
using TechnologyOpinion;
```

Note In the case of a Silverlight class library project, you need to add the namespace in the custom control class definition.

Adding a Custom Control in the Visual Studio Toolbox

You can also add Silverlight custom controls to the Visual Studio Toolbox tab pane. Until you remove this item, it will be part of the Visual Studio toolbox for every Silverlight project you create. Follow these steps to do so.

As shown in Figure 5-18, right-click the Visual Studio Toolbox tab to which you would like to add the custom control. In this case, right-click the Custom tab and select the Choose Items option. Now in the opened Choose Toolbox Items dialog box, click the Silverlight Components tab and browse to the panelMenu.dll file. Upon adding the custom control, it will be displayed on the list with the selected check box. Click OK to finish the process. You should see the panelMenu custom control available in the Custom tab.

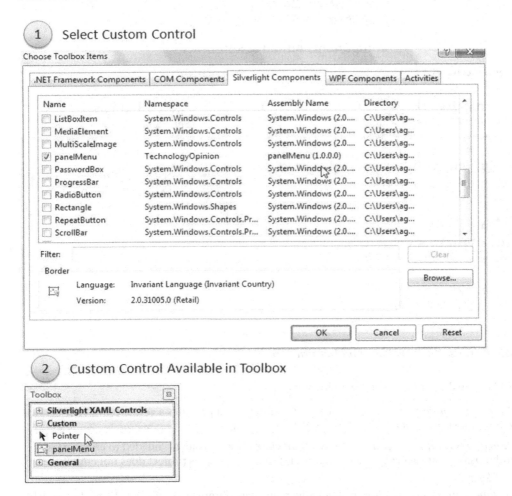

Figure 5-18. *Adding the custom control to the Visual Studio Toolbox*

Now you can just drag and drop this panelMenu item into the XAML view of the page when you want to add this control to your Silverlight application project.

Developing the Enterprise Training Portal

Now that the design of the Enterprise Training Portal has been established, it's time to start developing this application.

Project Structure of the Enterprise Training Portal

The Enterprise Training Portal RIA consists of the project structure shown in Figure 5-19.

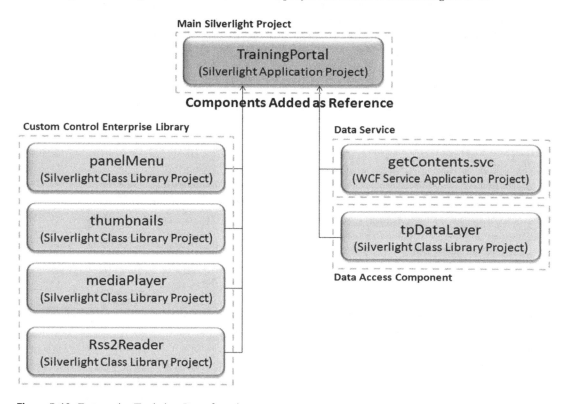

Figure 5-19. *Enterprise Training Portal project structure*

We will create these projects in the following order:

1. *Data service project*: The WCF Service application project provides a getContents WCF service to integrate the application with the SQL Server database.

2. *Data access component project*: A Silverlight class library project is needed to create a core and reusable data access layer component, tpDataLayer. This project does not contain any user control.

3. *Custom control enterprise library*: Four Silverlight class library projects—panelMenu, thumbnails, mediaPlayer, and Rss2Reader—will be used to create a custom control enterprise library. These projects can be added as a reference to any Silverlight projects.

4. *Main training portal project*: The TrainingPortal is the main Silverlight application project for building the Enterprise Training Portal. This project will reference the previously mentioned components to build a complete service-oriented Enterprise Training Portal.

To simplify the development process, we will create one temporary Silverlight application project solution, PortalComponentsLibrary, and add these four projects one by one.

Developing the Data Access WCF Service: getContents

First we need to create a WCF-based data access service to integrate the Enterprise Training Portal with the SQL Server database so it can retrieve the available training information. We'll use the metadata with LINQ to SQL classes bridging between the Web Service class and SQL Server.

Add a new project to the solution by selecting WCF in the Visual Studio project template section, choosing WCF Service Application for the project type, and naming it getContents. The project will contain the default files Service1.svc and iservice.cs, which you need to delete.

Now right-click the project in Solution Explorer, select Add/New Item to add a WCF service, and name it getContents. This will create three new files—getContents.svc, a service file; associated code-behind file getContents.svc.cs; and a service interface file, IgetContents.cs.

Delete all the lines of the dummy DoWork method from IgetContent.cs and getContent.svc.cs. Later, we will implement the service interface and custom methods to query the SQL Server database and parse it using LINQ.

Figure 5-20 shows the class diagram of the getContents WCF service.

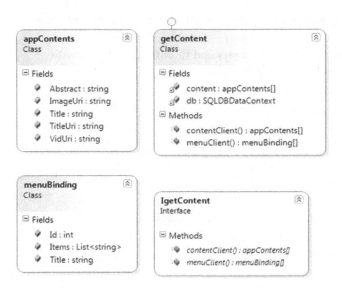

Figure 5-20. *getContents WCF service class diagram*

Creating LINQ to SQL Classes

Before you create LINQ to SQL classes, make sure you have created the TrainingPortalDB_Data.mdf file following the schema shown earlier in Figure 5-6.

1. Right-click the server project, add the LINQ to SQL Classes template as shown in Figure 5-21, name the class SQLDB.dbml, and click the Add button.

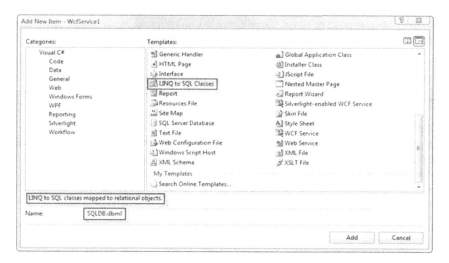

Figure 5-21. *Adding* SQLDB.dbml *LINQ to SQL classes mapped to relational objects*

2. When the Object Relational Designer window opens, open the Server Explorer and navigate to the TrainingPortalDB database.

3. Expand to reveal the tables and drag both the Category and tpContents tables onto the SQLDB.dbml designer workspace as shown in Figure 5-22.

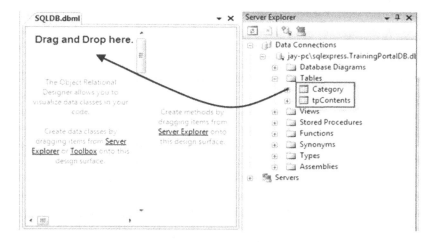

Figure 5-22. *Creating data classes*

4. The generated LINQ class corresponding to both the tables is not Serializable by default. We need to change it to Serializable to integrate with the WCF service. Click the design surface to bring up the properties of the entire class and change the Serialization Mode setting from None to Unidirectional, as shown in Figure 5-23.

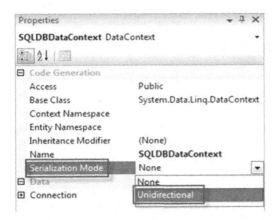

Figure 5-23. *Making the data class* `Serializable`

Defining the Service Interface: IgetContent.cs

Now we are all set to define the contract for the service and write the LINQ query.

Defining the Service Contract

Open `IgetContent.cs` and insert the following line of code to define the `IgetContent` service contract:

```
[ServiceContract]
public interface IgetContent
{
    [OperationContract]
    menuBinding[] menuClient(string connectionString);
    [OperationContract]
    appContents[] contentClient
        (string selectedItem, string selectedMenuId, string connectionString);
}
```

As shown in this code snippet, the `menuClient` method will query the SQL Server database to get the data to generate the left navigation pane. It has a return type of `menuBinding`, which we will define in the `DataContract` of this interface. The `contentClient` method will query the database to get the content of the selected menu item (which is actually the `Track` field value). It has a return type of `appContents`, which we also define in the `DataContract` section.

Defining Data Contracts

Next, we define the `menuBinding` and `appContents` data contract classes:

```
[DataContract]
public class menuBinding
{
    [DataMember]
    public int Id;
    [DataMember]
    public string Title;
    [DataMember]
    public List<string> Items;
}
```

```
[DataContract]
public class appContents
{
    [DataMember]
    public string Title;
    [DataMember]
    public string Abstract;
    [DataMember]
    public string ImageUri;
    [DataMember]
    public string VidUri;
    [DataMember]
    public string TitleUri;
}
```

Defining the Service Class: getContent.svc.cs

Now we jump to the code-behind getContent.svc.cs and declare two class-level variables as shown in the following code snippet:

```
private appContents[] content;
private SQLDBDataContext db;
```

Note that in this code, we declare an instance of the SQLDBDataContext (a LINQ to SQL class) to use with the LINQ query.

```
public menuBinding[] menuClient(string connectionString)
{
    db = new SQLDBDataContext(connectionString);

    menuBinding[] menuData =
        (from cat in db.Categories
         select new menuBinding()
         {
             Id = (int)cat.Id,
             Title = (string)cat.Title,
             Items = (from row in db.tpContents
                         where row.Id == cat.Id
                         select (string)row.Track).Distinct().ToList()
        }).ToArray();

    return menuData;
}
```

As shown in the preceding code snippet, the method signature has a return type of menuBinding and accepts connectionString as a String type parameter. We pass this connectionString to the SQLDBDataContext constructor so it can point to the location that we supplied in tpConfig.xml under the Datasource node for the SQL Server database. This way we override the local connection string created earlier (when we dragged and dropped the SQL database table from the local SQL Server) to the connection string specified in tpConfig.xml.

```
public appContents[]
  contentClient(string selectedItem, string selectedMenuId,string
  connectionString)
{
    db = new SQLDBDataContext(connectionString);
```

```
var rowData =
    (from cat in db.Categories
     where cat.Id == int.Parse(selectedMenuId)
     select new
     {
         trainings = (from training in db.tpContents
                      where training.Track == selectedItem
                      select new appContents()
                      {
                          Title = training.Title,
                          Abstract = training.Abstract,
                          TitleUri = training.TitleUri,
                          ImageUri = training.ImgUri,
                          VidUri = training.VidUri,
                      })
     });

foreach (var item in rowData)
{
    content = item.trainings.ToArray<appContents>();
}

return content;
}
```

Note that the foreach loop converts the System.Linq.IQueryable<AnonymousType#1> to getContents.appContents[] so it is compatible with the return type of the method.

Now getContents is ready to be deployed and consumed by the TrainingPortal application's business layer, tpDataLayer, which we define in the next section.

Deploying the getContents WCF Service

To publish the getContents WCF service, right-click the project from Solution Explorer and select the Publish option. You will get the Publish Web window as shown in Figure 5-24.

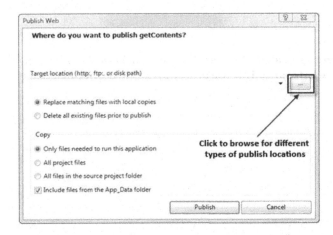

Figure 5-24. *Publishing the* getContents *WCF service*

There are four types of publish locations: file system, local IIS, FTP site, and remote site. Based on your criteria, you can choose the option that best suits you. For example, you can choose the Local IIS option to deploy to your local IIS for testing purposes to take full advantage of IIS features, such as process recycling, idle shutdown, process health monitoring, and message-based activation during development time.

Note As mentioned, this service will be used only if we use the SQL Server database. We are going to develop and explore the WCF service for demonstration purposes only. For this chapter, to simplify the overall deployment process, we are going to use XML as the content database file with our `TrainingPortal` project. As a result, we do not need to deploy and access this service during this chapter.

Since we are not going to utilize the deployed WCF, we are not going to get into the details of publishing WCF services here. A number of sources and books covering this topic are available for your reference. To deploy on the IIS server, you can visit these links from the Microsoft MSDN site: `http://msdn.microsoft.com/en-us/library/ms733766.aspx` and `http://msdn.microsoft.com/en-us/library/aa751792.aspx`.

Developing the Core Data Access Component: tpDataLayer Class Library

Add a new project to the solution by creating a new Silverlight class library project named `tpDataLayer` to develop a centralized core data access component. Rename `Class1.cs` to `tpDataLayer.cs`.

In addition to the default namespaces, add the following namespaces:

```
//Added
using System.Collections.Generic;
using System.Xml.Linq;
using System.Linq;
using System.Threading;
using System.ServiceModel;
using System.ServiceModel.Channels;
```

Adding a WCF Service Reference

Next, add the `getContent` WCF service reference created in the previous step. Right-click the project in Solution Explorer and choose Add Service Reference. This will bring up the Add Service Reference dialog box (see Figure 5-25).

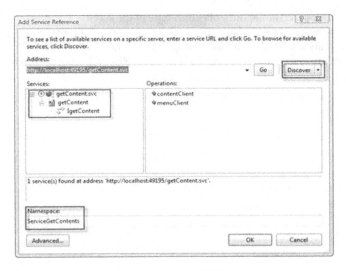

Figure 5-25. *Adding the* getContent *WCF service as a reference*

Add the getContent WCF service URL, and click the Discover button. Set the namespace as ServiceGetContent, and click the OK button. The ServiceReferences.ClientConfig file is created in the project, and it contains information regarding the service endpoint and binding as shown in the following code snippet:

```xml
<configuration>
    <system.serviceModel>
        <bindings>
            <basicHttpBinding>
                <binding name="BasicHttpBinding_IgetContent"
                        maxBufferSize="2147483647"
                        maxReceivedMessageSize="2147483647">
                    <security mode="None" />
                </binding>
            </basicHttpBinding>
        </bindings>
        <client>
            <endpoint
                address="http://localhost:49195/getContent.svc"
                binding="basicHttpBinding"
                bindingConfiguration="BasicHttpBinding_IgetContent"
                contract="ServiceGetContent.IgetContent"
                name="BasicHttpBinding_IgetContent" />
        </client>
    </system.serviceModel>
</configuration>
```

■**Note** The service endpoint address is referring to the locally hosted WCF service in the development environment on port 49195, which can be different for different machines. In practice, you will be publishing the WCF service to the production server.

To return a collection of type List, we need to change the Collection type of the service. For this, expand the Service References section in the tpDataLayer project, right-click the ServiceGetContents reference, and choose Configure service reference. In the opened dialog box, change the Collection type to System.Collection.Generic.List from System.Collections.ObjectModel.ObservableCollection as shown in Figure 5-26.

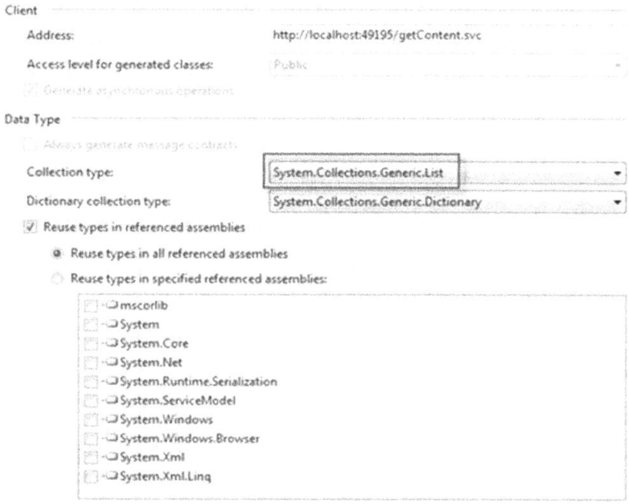

Figure 5-26. *Changing the Collection type of the data service to support the* List *collection type*

Note The ServiceReferences.ClientConfig file must be present in the XAP package upon deployment. As it is generated in tpDataLayer, it will not be automatically added to the XAP package. To utilize the service, you need to add the ServiceReferences.ClientConfig file to the TrainingPortal Silverlight application project manually.

TechnologyOpinion Default Namespace

We will use TechnologyOpinion as the namespace of all training portal–related Silverlight projects. Add TechnologyOpinion as the namespace, as shown in the following code:

```
namespace TechnologyOpinion
{
    public class tpDataLayer
    {.....}
}
```

Figure 5-27 shows the class diagram of the tpDataLayer component.

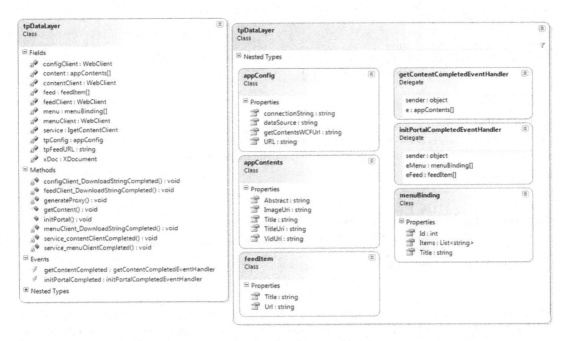

Figure 5-27. *Class diagram of the* tpDataLayer *data access component*

Defining Data Classes

To support different data operations for the portal, we will define the following four data classes under the data classes region:

- The appConfig class
- The menuBinding class
- The appContents class
- The feedItem class

appConfig Class

The appConfig class will be used by the TrainingPortal project to store different Enterprise Training Portal application configuration values retrieved from the tpConfig.xml file. These are the automatic properties dataSource, connectionString, URL, and getContentsWCFUrl.

```
public class appConfig
{
    public string dataSource { get; set; }
    public string connectionString { get; set; }
    public string URL { get; set; }
    public string getContentsWCFUrl { get; set; }
}
```

menuBinding Class

The menuBinding class is used by the panelMenu custom control for storing different training categories and tracking information retrieved from the application data source. The retrieved information will be used to build the left navigation pane.

```
public class menuBinding
{
    public int Id { get; set; }
    public string Title { get; set; }
    public List<string> Items { get; set; }
}
```

appContents Class

The appContents class is used by the thumbnails custom control to store available training items retrieved from the application data source, which will be displayed in the preview pane.

```
public class appContents
{
    public string Title { get; set; }
    public string Abstract { get; set; }
    public string TitleUri { get; set; }
    public string ImageUri { get; set; }
    public string VidUri { get; set; }
}
```

feedItem Class

The feedItem class is used by the Rss2Reader custom control to store available subscribed RSS URLs to display the selected RSS feed within the portal.

```
public class feedItem
{
    public string Title { get; set; }
    public string Url { get; set; }
}
```

Defining Private Fields

Under the private fields region, define the following required private fields:

```
//Private fields
private XDocument xDoc = new XDocument();
private appContents[] content;
private menuBinding[] menu;
private feedItem[] feed;
private string tpFeedURL;
//Webclient object for various HTTP Request
private WebClient menuClient = new WebClient();
private WebClient contentClient = new WebClient();
private WebClient configClient = new WebClient();
private WebClient feedClient = new WebClient();
private appConfig tpConfig = new appConfig();
//Proxy client for "getContents" WCF service
private ServiceGetContent.IgetContentClient service;
```

The defined variables are mainly related to retrieving the XML file using the WebClient object. To integrate with the WCF service, we also need to define the proxy client for the getContents WCF service.

Defining the initPortal Method

The public initPortal method is used by the TrainingPortal project to initialize the Enterprise Training Portal and retrieve the key application configuration information such as data source, data service, and subscribed RSS feeds. With the use of the WebClient object, we will retrieve the XML configuration file asynchronously (using the HTTP protocol). So we need to create a custom event handler that will be raised when the asynchronous data retrieval operation is completed.

To achieve this, first create a delegate, initPortalCompletedEventHandler, under the public fields region.

```
public delegate void
    initPortalCompletedEventHandler(object sender, menuBinding[] eMenu,
    feedItem[] eFeed);
```

Note that here we supply our custom data types menuBinding and feedItem as parameters along with first parameter, sender, of type Object, which provides a reference to the object that raised the event to the calling environment.

Next, create one event handler of type initPortalCompletedEventHandler:

```
public event initPortalCompletedEventHandler initPortalCompleted;
```

Now we create the initPortal method. This method has two parameters of type string that hold the URL to both configuration files.

```
public void initPortal(string tpConfigURL,string tpFeedsURL)
{
    //Getting tpConfig.xml configuration file using WebClient
    configClient.DownloadStringCompleted += new
            DownloadStringCompletedEventHandler
                (configClient_DownloadStringCompleted);
    configClient.DownloadStringAsync
            (new Uri(tpConfigURL, UriKind.RelativeOrAbsolute));

    //Getting tpFeeds.xml configuration file using WebClient
    feedClient.DownloadStringCompleted += new
            DownloadStringCompletedEventHandler
                (feedClient_DownloadStringCompleted);
    //Store local parameter to global variable
    tpFeedURL = tpFeedsURL;
}
```

In this method, we defined an event handler for the DownloadStringCompleted event of the configClient WebClient. This event is raised each time an asynchronous operation to download a resource as a string is completed. These operations are started by calling one of the DownloadStringAsync methods. Next, we make an asynchronous call to download the tpConfig.xml file. Similarly, we define an event handler for the DownloadStringCompleted event of the feedClient WebClient. We will raise the DownloadStringAsync event of feedClient later.

Let's implement the methods to extract the XML information.

configClient_DownloadStringCompleted Method

Once the tpConfig.xml file is retrieved in this method, we will create a simple LINQ query to parse the received XML and store the result in the tpConfig variable of the appConfig class.

```
void configClient_DownloadStringCompleted
    (object sender, DownloadStringCompletedEventArgs e)
{
    XDocument xDocConfig = XDocument.Parse(e.Result);
    //Define Query
```

```
var Config =
    (from g in xDocConfig.Descendants("TrainingPortal")
      select new appConfig()
    {
      dataSource = g.Attribute("Datasource").Value,
      connectionString =g.Element("Datasource").Element
          (g.Attribute("Datasource").Value).Element
            ("connectionString").Value,
        URL = g.Element("Datasource").Element
          (g.Attribute("Datasource").Value).Element("URL").Value,
        getContentsWCFUrl = g.Element("webservice").Element
          ("getContents").Element("serviceEndpoint").Value,
    });

//Store configuration
foreach (var item in Config)
{
  tpConfig.dataSource = item.dataSource;
  tpConfig.connectionString = item.connectionString;
  tpConfig.URL = item.URL;
  tpConfig.getContentsWCFUrl = item.getContentsWCFUrl;
}
 xDocConfig = null;

//Based on DataSource configuration, get the contents to build menu of the
//training portal from XML or SQL Server
switch (tpConfig.dataSource)
{
  case "XML":
    //Read tpContents.xml to build the left navigation pane
    menuClient.DownloadStringCompleted += new
        DownloadStringCompletedEventHandler
          (menuClient_DownloadStringCompleted);
     menuClient.DownloadStringAsync
        (new Uri(tpConfig.URL, UriKind.RelativeOrAbsolute));
     break;

  case "SQL":
    //Call to generateProxy
    generateProxy();
    //Call to Web Service to build the left navigation pane
    service.menuClientAsync(tpConfig.connectionString);
    service.menuClientCompleted += new EventHandler
      <TechnologyOpinion.ServiceGetContent.menuClientCompletedEventArgs>
        (service_menuClientCompleted);
    break;
  }
}
```

First we define the LINQ code to retrieve the data source and data service–related fields from the tpConfig.xml file.

In the case of the XML data source, we made an asynchronous call to get the XML file (tpContents.xml in this example) based on the retrieved tpConfig.URL field to build the left navigation pane. We also need to define the DownloadStringCompleted event handler to process the retrieved XML file.

In the case of the SQL type data source, we call the generateProxy method to initialize the proxy of the getContents WCF data service based on the retrieved tpConfig.getContentsWCFUrl field, and then call the service to build the left navigation pane. After an asynchronous call to the menuClient method of the data service, we set the `menuClientCompleted` event handler to process the retrieved XML file.

generateProxy Method

The `generateProxy` method initializes the proxy of the `getContents` WCF data service. This method will be called only if the data source type is `SQL`. The method updates the endpoint of the service to point to the new endpoint based on the retrieved `tpConfig.getContentsWCFUrl` field from the `tpConfig.xml` client file.

```
//This method creates the getContents service proxy
private void generateProxy()
{
    //Silverlight 2 supports only basic HTTP binding
    BasicHttpBinding serviceBinding = new BasicHttpBinding();
    //Endpoint address for service
    EndpointAddress serviceURI=new
        EndpointAddress(tpConfig.getContentsWCFUrl);
    //Creates service proxy based on endpoint from tpConfig.xml
    service = new TechnologyOpinion.
        ServiceGetContent.IgetContentClient(serviceBinding,serviceURI);
}
```

menuClient_DownloadStringCompleted Method

The `menuClient_DownloadStringCompleted` method, which is called only if the data source type is XML, parses the retrieved training content from the training content XML file to get the `Id`, `Title`, and `Items` fields using LINQ. These retrieved fields will be used by the `panelMenu.addMenuItem` method as a parameter to build the left navigation pane. At the end of the method, we make an asynchronous call to retrieve the `tpFeeds.xml` file to populate the RSS feeds drop-down control.

```
void menuClient_DownloadStringCompleted
    (object sender,  DownloadStringCompletedEventArgs e)
{
        xDoc = XDocument.Parse(e.Result.ToString());
        //Parsing xml
        menu =
        (from cat in xDoc.Root.Elements("Category")
        select new menuBinding()
            {
            Id = (int)cat.Attribute("Id"),
            Title = (string)cat.Attribute("Title"),
            Items = (from row in cat.Elements("Training")
            select (string)row.Element("Track")).Distinct().ToList()
            }).ToArray();
        //Get RSS feed URLs
        feedClient.DownloadStringAsync
            (new Uri(tpFeedURL,UriKind.RelativeOrAbsolute));
}
```

service_menuClientCompleted Method

The `service_menuClientCompleted` method, which is called only if the data source type is `SQL`, gets the `Id`, `Title`, and `Items` fields from each retrieved record. These retrieved fields will be used by the `panelMenu.addMenuItem` method as a parameter to build the left navigation pane. At the end of the method, we make an asynchronous call to retrieve the tpFeeds.xml file to populate the RSS feeds drop-down control.

```
void service_menuClientCompleted
  (object sender, TechnologyOpinion.ServiceGetContent.
   menuClientCompletedEventArgs e)
{
    menu = new menuBinding[e.Result.Count+1];
    foreach (var item in e.Result)
    {
        menu[item.Id] = new menuBinding();
        menu[item.Id].Id = item.Id;
        menu[item.Id].Title = item.Title;
        menu[item.Id].Items = item.Items;
    }
    //Get RSS feed URLs
    feedClient.DownloadStringAsync
        (new Uri(tpFeedURL, UriKind.RelativeOrAbsolute));
}
```

feedClient_DownloadStringCompleted Method

The feedClient_DownloadStringCompleted method parses the retrieved tpFeeds.xml file using LINQ and stores the feeds in an array of type feedItem.

```
void feedClient_DownloadStringCompleted
    object sender, DownloadStringCompletedEventArgs e)
{
    XDocument xDocFeed = XDocument.Parse(e.Result.ToString());
    feed = (from cat in xDocFeed.Root.Elements("feed")
        select new tpDataLayer.feedItem()
        {
        Title = cat.Element("Title").Value,
        Url = cat.Element("Url").Value,
        }).ToArray();
    xDocFeed = null;

    initPortalCompleted(this, menu, feed);
}
```

Since we have the left navigation menu and RSS feed items defined, we need to raise the initPortalCompleted event. The calling environment must have some kind of implementation of the initPortalCompleted event handler. We will implement that when we wire up all the custom controls along with the WCF service in the Page.xaml.cs file of the main TrainingPortal project.

Defining the getContent Method

The public getContent method is called by the itemClicked event of the tpMenu panelMenu control. The retrieved content is used for thumbnail generation.

The approach of the getContent method is very similar to the initPortal method. As we did for the initPortal method, we need to create a getContentCompletedEventHandler delegate and an event handler of type getContentCompletedEventHandler under the public fields region.

```
public delegate void
    getContentCompletedEventHandler(object sender, appContents[] e);
public event getContentCompletedEventHandler getContentCompleted;
```

As shown in the following code snippet of the getContent method, based on the retrieved data source (tpConfig.dataSource) type, XML or SQL, you will use LINQ or call the WCF data service, respectively, to get the training content.

```
public void getContent(string selectedItem, string selectedMenuId)
{
    switch (tpConfig.dataSource)
    {
        case "XML":
            //Parse the in-memory copy of tpContents.xml i.e. xDoc
            var rowData =
                (from cat in xDoc.Root.Elements("Category")
                where cat.Attribute("Id").Value ==
                    selectedMenuId.ToString()
                select new
                {
                    trainings = (from training in cat.Elements("Training")
                        where training.Element("Track").Value == selectedItem
                        select new appContents()
                        {
                            Title = training.Element("Title").Value,
                            Abstract = training.Element("Abstract").Value,
                            TitleUri = training.Element("TitleUri").Value,
                            ImageUri = training.Element("ImgUri").Value,
                            VidUri = training.Element("VidUri").Value,
                        })
                });

            foreach (var item in rowData )
            {
                content = item.trainings.ToArray<appContents>();
            }
            getContentCompleted(this, content);
            break;

        case "SQL":
            //Call to generateProxy
            generateProxy();
            //Call to Web Service
            service.contentClientAsync(selectedItem,
                selectedMenuId,tpConfig.connectionString);
            service.contentClientCompleted += new
                EventHandler<TechnologyOpinion.ServiceGetContent.
                contentClientCompletedEventArgs>
                (service_contentClientCompleted);
            break;
    }
}
```

Note that in the case of the XML data source type, the foreach loop converts System.Linq. IQueryable<AnonymousType#1> to getContents.appContents[]. After completion of the foreach loop, we raise the getContentCompleted event. The calling environment must implement the getContentCompleted event handler. We will implement this when we wire up all the custom controls in the Page.xaml.cs class of the main TrainingPortal project.

In the case of a SQL data source, we make an asynchronous call to the contentClient method of the getContents Web Service and define the service_contentClientCompleted event handler.

service_contentClientCompleted Method

This method is called only if the data source type is SQL. The service_contentClientCompleted method gets the Title, Abstract, TitleUri, ImageUri, and VidUri fields from each retrieved record. These retrieved fields are placed in the content array of type appContents.

Finally, we raise the getContentCompleted event. The calling environment must have some kind of implementation of the getContentCompleted event handler.

```
void service_contentClientCompleted(object sender,
    TechnologyOpinion.ServiceGetContent.contentClientCompletedEventArgs e)
{
    content = new appContents[e.Result.Count];
    int countTo = e.Result.Count;
    int incr = 0;
    foreach (var item in e.Result)
    {
        content[incr] = new appContents();
        content[incr].Title = item.Title;
        content[incr].Abstract = item.Abstract;
        content[incr].TitleUri = item.TitleUri;
        content[incr].ImageUri = item.ImageUri;
        content[incr].VidUri = item.VidUri;
        incr++;
    }

    getContentCompleted(this, content);
}
```

Deploying the tpDataLayer Class Library Component

You are all set to deploy the tpDataLayer class library. Now the data access class library component—tpDataLayer—is ready as a class library to deploy and can be referenced by the project's custom controls to perform training portal schema–specific data operations.

■**Note** The data access layer component is flexible enough and can be enhanced easily for additional data platforms (you need to recompile the project though). To keep the example simple, we kept the design of the data access layer as a single noncomplex component. However, based on enterprise needs, you can design the data access layer to be more abstracted and loosely coupled, where just changing XML and deploying the new data platform agent can enable an additional data platform.

Developing Custom Controls Enterprise Library

Custom controls will allow the Enterprise Training Portal to be modular, pluggable, and customizable. We need to develop four Silverlight class library projects—panelMenu, thumbnails, mediaPlayer, and Rss2Reader—as custom controls to build the interactive presentation layer of the training portal.

Figure 5-28 shows a complete high-level class diagram of the Enterprise Training Portal RIA.

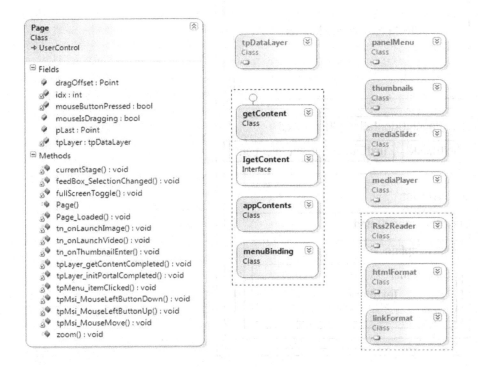

Figure 5-28. *High-level class diagram of the Enterprise Training Portal RIA*

Left Navigation Pane: panelMenu Custom Control

Add a new project to the solution by creating a new panelMenu Silverlight class library project to develop the left navigation pane UI component of the portal. It will build the left navigation pane dynamically from the data source defined in the tpConfig.xml file. As described in the design section, in this case it will read either the tpContents.xml file or the trainingPortalDB_Data.mdf SQL Server database file to get the navigation definition.

Next, we are going to follow all the steps outlined in the "Understanding Silverlight Custom Controls" section.

Building the generic.xaml File

Add a file named generic.xaml under the Theme folder and follow all the steps described in the section "Understanding Silverlight Custom Controls" to add ControlTemplate with the TargetType set to local:panelMenu.

Figure 5-29 presents the user interface layout design of the left navigation pane.

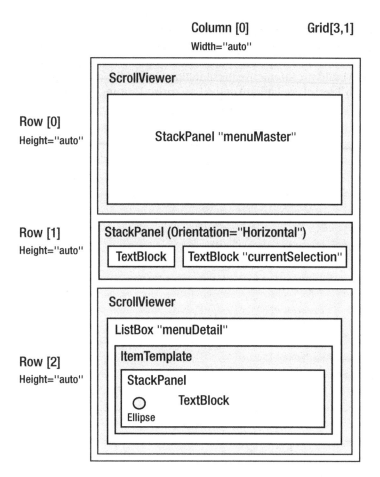

Figure 5-29. *User interface layout design of the left navigation pane*

Take the following steps to build the left navigation pane as shown in Figure 5-29:

1. We will use a Grid control as the main layout control. Under the ControlTemplate section, add a Grid control with no background and having three autoresizable rows.

2. In the first row of the Grid control, place the ScrollViewer control, and under that add a StackPanel layout control with the name menuMaster. The StackPanel control will hold dynamically created instances of the Button control based on the number of Category records (for database) and nodes (for XML) available in the training content database or XML file, respectively, at runtime. For this chapter, there will be four Button control instances for the four categories: Technology Articles, IT Management Articles, Technical Presentations, and Technical Videos. The Button control instances will be placed vertically, so set the StackPanel control Orientation property value to Vertical.

3. In the second row of the Grid control, place the StackPanel layout control, and inside that put two TextBlock controls. To display the title of the currently selected category with the check mark prefix, for the first TextBlock control set the Text property to a and FontFamily property to Webdings with FontSize set to 20. Name the second TextBlock control currentSelection, with the FontSize set to 13 to display the currently selected category at runtime.

4. In the third row, place the ScrollViewer control and under that a ListBox control with the name menuDetail. This ListBox control will display distinct tracks of the selected category with a bullet point as a prefix. To place a bullet point as a prefix, we will use ListBox.ItemTemplate and place a StackPanel layout control with Orientation set to Horizontal. Under the StackPanel control, we will place a 10×10 Ellipse control with the Fill property set to White and Stroke property set to Cyan to create a bullet point. Next place a TextBlock control to display tracks.

5. For both ScrollViewer controls, hide the border by setting BorderThickness to 0. To display an automatic vertical scrollbar when required, set the VerticalScrollBarVisibility value to Auto.

The following is the resultant XAML code for the generic.xaml file:

```xaml
<ResourceDictionary
    xmlns="http://schemas.microsoft.com/winfx/2006/xaml/presentation"
    xmlns:x="http://schemas.microsoft.com/winfx/2006/xaml"
    xmlns:vsm="clr-namespace:System.Windows;assembly=System.Windows"
    xmlns:local="clr-namespace:TechnologyOpinion;assembly=panelMenu">
    <Style TargetType="local:panelMenu">
        <Setter Property="Template">
            <Setter.Value>
                <ControlTemplate TargetType="local:panelMenu">
                    <Grid Background="{x:Null}" Width="Auto" Height="Auto" >
                        <Grid.RowDefinitions >
                            <RowDefinition Height="auto" ></RowDefinition>
                            <RowDefinition Height="auto"></RowDefinition>
                            <RowDefinition Height="auto"></RowDefinition>
                        </Grid.RowDefinitions>
                        <!-- First Row -->
                        <ScrollViewer VerticalScrollBarVisibility="Auto"
                                MaxHeight="250" BorderThickness="0" >
                            <StackPanel x:Name="menuMaster"
                                ScrollViewer.VerticalScrollBarVisibility="Auto"
                                Orientation="Vertical" >
                            </StackPanel>
                        </ScrollViewer>
                        <!-- Second Row -->
                        <StackPanel Height="Auto" Margin="0,20,0,10"
                                VerticalAlignment="Bottom" Grid.Row="1"
                                Orientation="Horizontal">
                            <TextBlock Height="Auto" Width="Auto"
                                    Text="a" TextWrapping="Wrap" Foreground="Cyan"
                                    FontFamily="Webdings" FontSize="20"/>
                            <TextBlock Height="Auto" x:Name="currentSelection"
                                    Width="Auto" Text="" Foreground="White"
                                    TextWrapping="Wrap" FontSize="13"/>
                        </StackPanel>
                        <!-- Third Row -->
                        <ScrollViewer VerticalScrollBarVisibility="Auto"
                                MaxHeight="200" BorderThickness="0"
                                Margin="0,-4,0,-8" Grid.Row="2">
                            <ListBox x:Name="menuDetail" Height="auto"
                                    Width="auto" Background="{x:Null}"
                                    Foreground="White">
                                <ListBox.ItemTemplate>
                                    <DataTemplate>
                                        <StackPanel Orientation="Horizontal" >
```

```
                                                <Ellipse x:Name="bullet"
                                                        HorizontalAlignment="Left"
                                                        Margin="2,2,4,2"
                                                        Width="10" Fill="White"
                                                        Height="10"
                                                        Stroke="Cyan" />
                                            <TextBlock Text="{Binding}"/>
                                        </StackPanel>
                                    </DataTemplate>
                                </ListBox.ItemTemplate>
                            </ListBox>
                        </ScrollViewer>
                    </Grid>
                </ControlTemplate>
            </Setter.Value>
        </Setter>
    </Style>
</ResourceDictionary>
```

Building the panelMenu.cs Class File

Rename `Class1.cs` to `panelMenu.cs`. Figure 5-30 shows the class diagram of the `panelMenu` class.

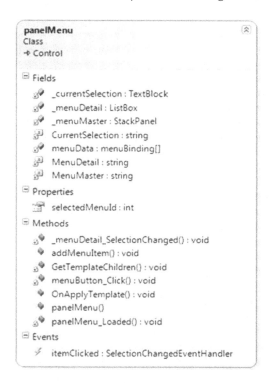

Figure 5-30. *Class diagram of the panelMenu class*

Follow these steps to build the panelMenu class:

1. To access the tpDataLayer project menuBinding class to get the details on the categories and tracks, add a reference to the tpDataLayer project and add the TechnologyOpinion namespace. Also add the System.Collections.Generic namespace, since later we are going to use the List<> data type. The following code snippet defines the overall panelMenu.cs class structure:

```
using System;
using System.Net;
using System.Windows;
using System.Windows.Controls;
using System.Windows.Documents;
using System.Windows.Ink;
using System.Windows.Input;
using System.Windows.Media;
using System.Windows.Media.Animation;
using System.Windows.Shapes;
//Additional references
using TechnologyOpinion;
using System.Collections.Generic;

namespace TechnologyOpinion
{

    //Define custom control contracts

    public class panelMenu:Control
    {
        //Define private fields
        //Define public fields
        Public panelMenu
        {
            ....
        }
        //Define public methods
        //Define TemplateHandlers
        //Define private methods
        //Define TemplateHandlers
        //Add event handlers
    }
}
```

2. Add custom control contracts. The TemplatePart represents a contract as an attribute that is applied to the class definition to identify the types of the named parts that are used in the control template and to place them under the VSM domain. Add the following three attributes to the panelMenu custom control:

```
[TemplatePart(Name = panelMenu.MenuDetail, Type = typeof(ListBox))]
[TemplatePart(Name = panelMenu.MenuMaster, Type = typeof(StackPanel))]
[TemplatePart(Name = panelMenu.CurrentSelection, Type = typeof(TextBlock))]
```

3. Add the following private class members and string constants aligned with the contract definition:

```
#region Private Fields

    private const string MenuMaster = "menuMaster";
    private const string MenuDetail = "menuDetail";
```

```
        private const string CurrentSelection= "currentSelection";

        private tpDataLayer.menuBinding[] menuData = new
            tpDataLayer.menuBinding[50] ;

        private StackPanel _menuMaster;
        private ListBox _menuDetail;
        private TextBlock _currentSelection;

    #endregion
```

Note We are going to follow a standard naming convention pattern across the project. String constants used for adding attributes to the custom control as well as for passing as parameters to the GetTemplateChild method will be in Pascal case. Actual elements will be defined in camel case with the prefix _.

---

4. Add the selectedMenuId as an int property within the public fields region:

```
#region Public Fields

    public int selectedMenuId { get; set; }

#endregion
```

5. Create the class constructor and set the FrameworkElement.DefaultStyleKey property to the type of the panelMenu control. Then call the OnApplyTemplate method to load the relevant control template, allowing its parts to be referenced within the class, as in the following code snippet:

```
public panelMenu()
{
    this.DefaultStyleKey = typeof(panelMenu);
    this.Loaded+=new RoutedEventHandler(panelMenu_Loaded);
    OnApplyTemplate();
}
```

6. Add the following two methods under the TemplateHandlers region:

```
#region TemplateHandlers

    //Add OnApplyTemplate and GetTemplateChildren methods

#endregion
```

7. First the OnApplyTemplate method. As shown in the following code snippet, we call the base version of the OnApplyTemplate method and then call the GetTemplateChildren method to retrieve the named element of the control template. Next, we wire an event handler for the SelectionChanged event of the _menuDetail list box control:

```
public override void OnApplyTemplate()
{
 base.OnApplyTemplate();
 GetTemplateChildren();
 //Assign event handler only if not Null
 if (_menuDetail != null)
   {
```

```
        _menuDetail.SelectionChanged += new
            SelectionChangedEventHandler
                (_menuDetail_SelectionChanged);
    }
}
```

8. Next the `GetTemplateChildren` method. As shown in the following code snippet, we need to retrieve three named elements from the control template—the `ListBox` control named `menuDetail`, the `StackPanel` control named `menuMaster`, and the `TextBlock` control named `currentSelection`.

```
private void GetTemplateChildren()
{
    _menuMaster= base.GetTemplateChild(MenuMaster) as StackPanel;
    _menuDetail = base.GetTemplateChild(MenuDetail) as ListBox;
    _currentSelection = base.GetTemplateChild(CurrentSelection) as TextBlock;
}
```

9. Add a region called `Public Methods` to define required public methods. First we need to define an event handler, `itemClicked`, of the same type as the `_menuDetail_SelectionChanged` event so that the control that is hosting this custom control can subscribe to this event, as in the following code snippet. This will allow the host to access the selected information when this event is raised.

```
public event SelectionChangedEventHandler itemClicked;
```

10. Next add the main method—`addMenuItem`—of this custom control. The main objective of this method is to store the retrieved information, add a category-related button dynamically, and assign a `Click` event to it. The following code snippet presents the `addMenuItem` method:

```
public void addMenuItem(int Id, string Title, List<string> Items)
{
    menuData[Id] = new tpDataLayer.menuBinding();
    menuData[Id].Title = Title;
    menuData[Id].Items = Items;
    Button menuButton = new Button();
    menuButton.FontSize = 13;
    menuButton.Content = Title;
    menuButton.Name = Id.ToString();
    menuButton.Click+=new RoutedEventHandler(menuButton_Click);
    _menuMaster.Children.Add(menuButton);
}
```

As you can see, the method required three parameters, Id, `Title`, and `Items` (which contains a collection of distinct tracks related to the category), aligned with the content database or content XML file definition.

The menuButton `Button` control `Content` property is set to the `Title` of the category. Each menuButton will dynamically assign a `Click` event handler as well. And finally, the `Name` property of the menuButton will be set to the Id of that category to identify which instance of menuButton raised the associated menuButton_Click event. We are also storing parameters to the menuData array using Id as the index for the array. With the use of the same Id, we can access information associated with the selected menuButton when it gets clicked. To build the left navigation pane, we add the dynamically created menuButton `Button` control as a child in the _menuMaster `StackPanel` control.

11. Define the event handler. As mentioned previously, we have three events that we need to define. Add them under the event handler region.

```
void panelMenu_Loaded(object sender, RoutedEventArgs e)
{
    this.ApplyTemplate();
}
```

When the panelMenu control is loaded, we call the ApplyTemplate method to load the relevant control template so that its parts can be referenced within the class.

```
void menuButton_Click(object sender, RoutedEventArgs e)
{
    Button btnRef = (Button)sender;
    selectedMenuId = int.Parse(btnRef.Name);
    _menuDetail.ItemsSource = menuData[selectedMenuId].Items;
}
```

Here we've used the same technique of casting the sender object to a Button control as we did with TextBlock control (representing the category name) for the My Album RIA in Chapter 2. We set the selectedMenuId property to the Name property of the selected Button control, which is actually a unique Id of the related category. At the end, we set the ItemSource property of the _menuDetail ListBox control to the Items field of menuData with the same selectedMenuId as an index of the array for the selected Button control.

```
void _menuDetail_SelectionChanged
    (object sender, SelectionChangedEventArgs e)
{
    itemClicked(this, e);
}
```

Earlier we defined the itemClicked event handler of the same type as the _menuDetail_ SelectionChanged event. During the event implementation, we call itemClicked to display the available training programs in the preview pane of the selected track item.

Deploying the panelMenu Custom Control

Now you are all set to deploy the panelMenu custom control. Follow the instructions provided in the "Adding a Custom Control in the Visual Studio Toolbox" section of the chapter to register the component in Visual Studio, or you can add it later as a reference when we develop the main training portal Silverlight project.

■**Note** Due to a shortage of space, from this point onward in this chapter I am not going to mention redundant information or steps that are required to develop all projects. For this, you can refer either to the downloadable source code for the book or the earlier sections of this chapter.

Preview Pane: thumbnails Custom Control

Add a new project to the solution by creating a new thumbnails Silverlight class library project, which will be used to develop the preview pane user interface component of the portal. It will build the preview pane thumbnails dynamically based on the training track selection in the left navigation pane. The thumbnails get populated from the training content data file based on the data source defined in the tpConfig.xml file. In our case, it will read either the tpContents.xml file or the trainingPortalDB_ Data.mdf SQL Server database file to get the navigation definition.

Building the generic.xaml File

Add a file named generic.xaml under the Theme folder and follow all the steps described earlier to add ControlTemplate with the TargetType set to local:thumbnails.

Figure 5-31 presents the user interface layout design of the left navigation pane.

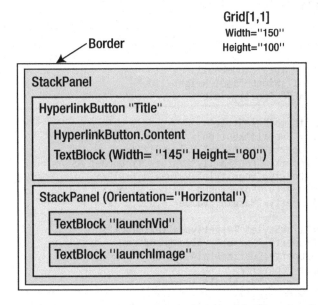

Figure 5-31. *User interface layout design of the thumbnails to develop the preview pane*

Please follow these steps to build the preview pane as shown in Figure 5-31:

1. We will use the Grid control as the main layout control. Under the ControlTemplate section, add a Grid control with Opacity set to 0.6 to make thumbnails slightly fade out when they are loaded. To have thumbnails match the Enterprise Training Portal color scheme, set BackGround to #99BDF4FF (which is a light cyan color).

2. Add the Grid.Resources section to include two styles. One is named thumbTitleStyle for the HyperLinkButton control, and the second is linkStyle for the TextBlock control.

3. Add a Border control to surround the Grid control with boundaries. Set the BorderBrush property to Cyan and BorderThickness to 2, and add an appropriate Margin.

4. Place a StackPanel control inside a 1×1 Grid control with Width="150" and Height="100" px.

5. In the StackPanel, place one HyperLinkButton control named Title to hold the title of the training item. Since the HyperLinkButton control does not have the TextWrapping property, we will use the TextBlock control in the HyperLinkButton.Content template. This allows us to span training titles over multiple lines. We use the HyperLinkButton control and its Title.NavigateUri property set to the Title field to display the training title with the link pointing to the original source of the training.

6. In the same StackPanel, place another StackPanel control with the Orientation property set to Horizontal. Inside this StackPanel, place two TextBlock controls named launchVid and launchImage, respectively. As their names suggest, these controls enable users to launch the appropriate video or image (which is a Deep Zoom image collection) related to that training subject in the training content display pane.

Here is the finished generic.xaml file:

```
<ResourceDictionary
    xmlns="http://schemas.microsoft.com/winfx/2006/xaml/presentation"
    xmlns:x="http://schemas.microsoft.com/winfx/2006/xaml"
    xmlns:vsm="clr-namespace:System.Windows;assembly=System.Windows"
    xmlns:local="clr-namespace:TechnologyOpinion;assembly=thumbnails"
    >
    <Style TargetType="local:thumbnails">
        <Setter Property="Template">
            <Setter.Value>
                <ControlTemplate TargetType="local:thumbnails" >
                    <Grid x:Name="LayoutRoot" Width="150" Height="100"
                        Background="#99BDF4FF" Opacity="0.6">
                        <Grid.Resources>
                            <Style x:Key="thumbTitleStyle"
                                TargetType="HyperlinkButton">
                                <Setter Property="FontSize" Value="12"/>
                                <Setter Property="FontFamily" Value="Trebuchet MS"/>
                                <Setter Property="FontStyle" Value="Normal"/>
                                <Setter Property="Foreground" Value="Blue"/>
                                <Setter Property="Margin" Value="3,0,0,0"/>
                            </Style>
                            <Style x:Key="linkStyle" TargetType="TextBlock">
                                <Setter Property="Cursor" Value="Hand"/>
                                <Setter Property="HorizontalAlignment"
                                    Value="Center"/>
                                <Setter Property="VerticalAlignment"
                                    Value="Center"/>
                                <Setter Property="FontSize" Value="13"/>
                                <Setter Property="Foreground" Value="Yellow"/>
                                <Setter Property="TextWrapping" Value="Wrap"/>
                                <Setter Property="Margin" Value="10,0,0,0"/>
                            </Style>
                        </Grid.Resources>
                        <StackPanel Width="150" Height="100">
                            <HyperlinkButton Height="80" Width="145" x:Name="Title"
                                TargetName="_blank"
                                Style="{StaticResource thumbTitleStyle}" >
                                <HyperlinkButton.Content>
                                    <Canvas>
                                        <TextBlock Width="145" Height="80"
                                            TextWrapping="Wrap"  Text="{Binding}"
                                            TextDecorations="Underline" />
                                    </Canvas>
                                </HyperlinkButton.Content>
                            </HyperlinkButton >
                            <StackPanel Height="20" Width="150"
                                Orientation="Horizontal">
                                <TextBlock Height="Auto" Width="Auto"
                                    Text="Play Video"  Style="{StaticResource
                                    linkStyle}"
                                    x:Name="launchVid"/>
                                <TextBlock Height="Auto" Width="Auto" Text="View"
                                    Style="{StaticResource linkStyle}"
                                    x:Name="launchImage"/>
                            </StackPanel>
```

```
            </StackPanel>
            <Border BorderBrush="Cyan" BorderThickness="2"
                    Margin="0,-1,0,1"/>
          </Grid>
        </ControlTemplate>
      </Setter.Value>
    </Setter>
  </Style>
</ResourceDictionary>
```

Building the thumbnails.cs Class File

Rename Class1.cs to thumbnails.cs. Figure 5-32 shows the class diagram of the thumbnails class.

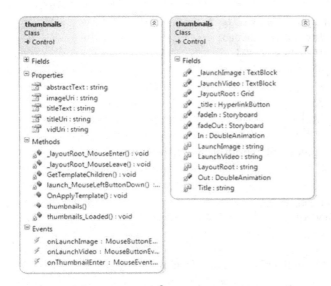

Figure 5-32. *Class diagram of the* thumbnails *class*

Follow these steps to build the thumbnails.cs class:

1. In addition to the default namespaces, you need to add the following namespaces:

```
//Additional namespaces
using System.Windows.Media.Imaging;
```

2. Add the following attributes to the thumbnails custom control:

```
[TemplatePart(Name = thumbnails.Title, Type = typeof(HyperlinkButton))]
[TemplatePart(Name = thumbnails.LaunchVideo, Type = typeof(TextBlock))]
[TemplatePart(Name = thumbnails.LaunchImage, Type = typeof(TextBlock))]
```

3. Add the following private class members and string constants aligned with the contract definition under the private fields region:

```
private const string Title = "Title";
private const string LaunchVideo = "launchVid";
private const string LaunchImage = "launchImage";
private const string LayoutRoot = "LayoutRoot";
```

```
private HyperlinkButton _title;
private TextBlock _launchVideo;
private TextBlock _launchImage;
private Grid _layoutRoot;
private Storyboard fadeIn=new Storyboard();
private Storyboard fadeOut = new Storyboard();
private DoubleAnimation In=new DoubleAnimation();
private DoubleAnimation Out = new DoubleAnimation();
```

4. Create five public properties that can be set for the thumbnails custom control. The titleUri property will contain a link to the original source of the training. The vidUri will have a link to the media file. We also create two public events of type MouseButtonEventHandler named onLaunchImage and onLaunchVideo, and one event of type MouseEventHandler named onThumbnailEnter.

```
public event MouseButtonEventHandler onLaunchImage;
public event MouseButtonEventHandler onLaunchVideo;
public event MouseEventHandler onThumbnailEnter;

public string titleUri { get; set; }
public string vidUri { get; set; }
public string imageUri { get; set; }
public string titleText { get; set; }
public string abstractText { get; set; }
```

5. The following is a code snippet of the self-explanatory class constructor:

```
public thumbnails()
{
    this.DefaultStyleKey=typeof(thumbnails);
    this.Loaded += thumbnails_Loaded;
    OnApplyTemplate();
}
```

6. Add the following two methods under the TemplateHandlers region:

```
public override void OnApplyTemplate()
{
    base.OnApplyTemplate();
    GetTemplateChildren();
    //Assign
    if (_launchVideo != null)
    {
        if (vidUri == null || vidUri=="")
            _launchVideo.Visibility = Visibility.Collapsed;
        else
            _launchVideo.MouseLeftButtonDown +=
                launch_MouseLeftButtonDown;
    }
    if (_launchImage != null)
    {
        if (imageUri == null || imageUri=="")
            _launchImage.Visibility = Visibility.Collapsed;
        else
            _launchImage.MouseLeftButtonDown +=
                launch_MouseLeftButtonDown;
    }
    if (_title != null)
```

```
        {
            _title.DataContext = titleText;

            if (titleUri != null )
                _title.NavigateUri = new
                    Uri(titleUri,UriKind.RelativeOrAbsolute);
        }
    if (_layoutRoot != null)
    {
        _layoutRoot.MouseEnter += new
            MouseEventHandler(_layoutRoot_MouseEnter);
        _layoutRoot.MouseLeave += new
            MouseEventHandler(_layoutRoot_MouseLeave);
        ToolTipService.SetToolTip(_layoutRoot, "Click to visit...");
    }
}
```

After calling the GetTemplateChildren method in this method, we need to wire up some events
to the retrieved elements. For both TextBlock controls _launchVideo and _launchImage, assign
the MouseLeftButtonDown event. For the _layoutRoot Grid control, assign the MouseEnter and
MouseLeave event. We will call the animation storyboards fadeIn and fadeOut from these
events of the _layoutRoot Grid control. Here we also set the NavigateUri property of the _title
HyperlinkButton control to TitleUri.

The following is a code snippet for the GetTemplateChildren method:

```
private void GetTemplateChildren()
{
    _title = base.GetTemplateChild(Title) as HyperlinkButton;
    _launchVideo = base.GetTemplateChild(LaunchVideo) as TextBlock;
    _launchImage = base.GetTemplateChild(LaunchImage) as TextBlock;
    _layoutRoot = base.GetTemplateChild(LayoutRoot) as Grid;
}
```

7. Now define the event handlers:

```
void thumbnails_Loaded(object sender, RoutedEventArgs e)
{
    this.ApplyTemplate();
    //Setting storyboard and animation
    //fadeIn
    In.From = 0.6;
    In.To = 1;
    In.SpeedRatio = 2;
    Storyboard.SetTarget(In, _layoutRoot);
    Storyboard.SetTargetProperty
        (In, new PropertyPath("(Grid.Opacity)"));
    fadeIn.Children.Add(In);
    //fadeOut
    Out.From = 1;
    Out.To =0.6;
    In.SpeedRatio = 3;
    Storyboard.SetTarget(Out, _layoutRoot);
    Storyboard.SetTargetProperty
        (Out, new PropertyPath("(Grid.Opacity)"));
    fadeOut.Children.Add(Out);
}
```

This event will provide the fadeIn and fadeOut animations by creating a Storyboard and DoubleAnimation type animation.

The _layoutRoot_MouseEnter and _layoutRoot_MouseLeave event handlers for _layoutRoot will start the animation storyboards as shown here:

```
void _layoutRoot_MouseLeave(object sender, MouseEventArgs e)
{
    fadeOut.Stop();
    fadeOut.Begin();
}

void _layoutRoot_MouseEnter(object sender, MouseEventArgs e)
{
    fadeIn.Stop();
    fadeIn.Begin();
    onThumbnailEnter(this, e);
}
```

The launch_MouseLeftButtonDown event handler contains a switch case on txtRef.Name. Based on the Name property of the TextBlock that has raised the event, it will perform the appropriate action to launch the training video or display the image with Deep Zoom capabilities.

```
void launch_MouseLeftButtonDown(object sender, MouseButtonEventArgs e)
{
    TextBlock txtRef = new TextBlock();
    txtRef = (TextBlock)sender;
    switch (txtRef.Name)
    {
        case LaunchVideo:
            onLaunchVideo(this,e);
            break;
        case LaunchImage:
            onLaunchImage(this,e);
            break;
    }
}
```

Deploying the thumbnails Custom Control

Now you are all set to deploy the thumbnails custom control. Follow the instructions provided in the earlier part of the chapter to register the component with Visual Studio, or you can add it later as a reference when we develop the main training portal Silverlight project.

Media Player: mediaPlayer Custom Control

Add a new project to the solution by creating a new mediaPlayer Silverlight class library project to develop the video media player control to play training video files within the training content display pane. We will implement basic media player functionality like play, pause, rewind, and forward functions as well as volume control functionality.

Building the generic.xaml File

Add a file named generic.xaml under the Theme folder and follow all the steps described earlier to add a ControlTemplate with the TargetType set to local:mediaPlayer.

Figure 5-33 presents the user interface layout design of the media player custom control.

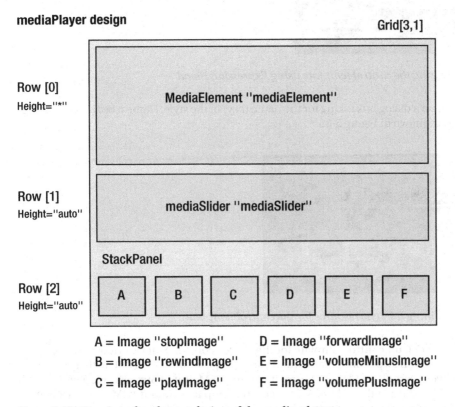

Figure 5-33. *User interface layout design of the media player*

Follow these steps to build the media player as shown in Figure 5-33:

1. We will use the Grid control as the main layout control. Under the ControlTemplate section, add a Grid control with no background and three rows. The Grid.Resources section contains two storyboard animations named fadeIn and fadeOut. We call these animations from mediaPlayer. cs on the MouseEnter event of each of the navigation Image controls (e.g., stopImage, playImage, etc.). Note that both storyboards have no TargetName property defined. We will set up this property at runtime when we call the storyboards.

2. The first row of the Grid control will contain the MediaElement control.

3. The second row contains a mediaSlider custom control. This control is actually derived from the Slider control (see Figure 5-4 earlier in the chapter). Here we just need to add drag functionality to the Slider control in such a way so it can skip forward or backward in the currently playing media. For that we just need to code the OnDragCompleted event of the HorizontalThumb Thumb control in the default control template of the Slider control. We can create this default control template with help of Expression Blend.

   Open Expression Blend, and create a new Silverlight application project. On the Page.xaml file, drag the Slider control from the toolbox. Right-click the control and choose Edit Control Parts (Template) ➤ Edit a Copy as shown in Figure 5-34.

Figure 5-34. *Editing the control template using Expression Blend*

This will bring up a dialog box asking for the name (key) of the style. Name it mediaSliderStyle and click OK, as shown in Figure 5-35.

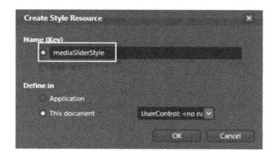

Figure 5-35. *Defining the style resource for the control template*

This will create a default control template for the Slider control. You can view it by switching to XAML view in Expression Blend. You will see a huge amount of XAML with a control template for every part of the Slider control including VSM. But in our case, we just need the HorizontalTemplate of the default Slider control template without VSM, as we are not changing or adding any new states to the mediaSlider control derived from the Slider control. So we will copy the XAML code for HorizontalTemplate only and will paste it into generic.xaml in the ResourceDictionary section.

4. Add the mediaSlider control to the second row of the Grid control. Note that here we apply mediaSliderStyle to the mediaSlider control that we just created using Expression Blend.

5. In the third row, the StackPanel control will contain six Image controls that together will act as a navigation pane. Note that in the following code snippet, we set the ToolTip property of each Image control to display populated property values upon the MouseEnter state. We also want to change the Cursor to Hand for all six Image controls. So we will apply the custom mediaButtonStyle Style. Here we will set the Opacity property to 0.5 to slightly fade out the images and set the Margin property to 5 between each image. Add this custom style into generic.xaml in the ResourceDictionary section.

The following is the complete XAML code of the mediaPlayer custom control:

```
<ResourceDictionary
    xmlns="http://schemas.microsoft.com/winfx/2006/xaml/presentation"
    xmlns:x="http://schemas.microsoft.com/winfx/2006/xaml"
    xmlns:vsm="clr-namespace:System.Windows;assembly=System.Windows"
    xmlns:local="clr-namespace:TechnologyOpinion;assembly=mediaPlayer">
```

```xml
<Style x:Key="mediaButtonStyle" TargetType="Image">
    <Setter Property="Margin" Value="5,0,0,0"/>
    <Setter Property="Cursor" Value="Hand"/>
    <Setter Property="Opacity" Value="0.5"/>
</Style>

<Style x:Key="mediaSliderStyle" TargetType="Slider">
    <Setter Property="Template">
        <Setter.Value>
            <ControlTemplate TargetType="Slider">
                <Grid x:Name="Root">
                    <Grid.Resources>
                        <ControlTemplate x:Key="RepeatButtonTemplate">
                        <Grid x:Name="Root" Opacity="0"
                            Background="Transparent"/>
                        </ControlTemplate>
                    </Grid.Resources>
                    <Grid x:Name="HorizontalTemplate"
                            Background="{TemplateBinding Background}">
                        <Grid.ColumnDefinitions>
                            <ColumnDefinition Width="Auto"/>
                            <ColumnDefinition Width="Auto"/>
                            <ColumnDefinition Width="Auto"/>
                        </Grid.ColumnDefinitions>
                        <Rectangle Height="3" Margin="5,0,5,0" Grid.Column="0"
                            Grid.ColumnSpan="3" Fill="#FFE6EFF7"
                            Stroke="#FFA3AEB9"
                            StrokeThickness="{TemplateBinding
                            BorderThickness}"
                            RadiusX="1" RadiusY="1"/>
                        <RepeatButton x:Name=
                            "HorizontalTrackLargeChangeDecreaseRepeatButton"
                            IsTabStop="False" Grid.Column="0"
                            Template="{StaticResource RepeatButtonTemplate}"/>
                        <Rectangle x:Name="LeftTrack" Grid.Column="0"
                            Fill="#00FFFFFF" />
                        <Thumb x:Name="HorizontalThumb" Height="18" Width="11"
                            IsTabStop="True" Cursor="Hand" Grid.Column="1"/>
                        <RepeatButton x:Name=
                            "HorizontalTrackLargeChangeIncreaseRepeatButton"
                            IsTabStop="False" Grid.Column="2"
                            Template="{StaticResource RepeatButtonTemplate}"/>
                        <Rectangle x:Name="RightTrack" Grid.Column="2"
                            Fill="#00FFFFFF" />
                    </Grid>
                </Grid>
            </ControlTemplate>
        </Setter.Value>
    </Setter>
</Style>

<Style TargetType="local:mediaPlayer">
    <Setter Property="Template">
        <Setter.Value>
            <ControlTemplate TargetType="local:mediaPlayer">
                <Grid>
                    <Grid.Resources>
```

```xml
                    <Storyboard x:Name="fadeIn">
                        <DoubleAnimation
                            Storyboard.TargetProperty ="Opacity"
                            From="0.5" To="1"SpeedRatio="2"/>
                    </Storyboard>
                    <Storyboard x:Name="fadeOut">
                        <DoubleAnimation
                            Storyboard.TargetProperty ="Opacity"
                            From="1" To="0.5" SpeedRatio="4"/>
                    </Storyboard>
                </Grid.Resources>
                <Grid.RowDefinitions>
                    <RowDefinition Height="*"/>
                    <RowDefinition Height="auto"/>
                    <RowDefinition Height="auto"/>
                </Grid.RowDefinitions>
                <StackPanel  HorizontalAlignment="Center" Grid.Row="2"
                    Orientation="Horizontal">
                    <Image x:Name="stopImage" ToolTipService.ToolTip="Stop"
                        Style="{StaticResource mediaButtonStyle}"/>
                    <Image x:Name="rewindImage"
                        ToolTipService.ToolTip="Rewind"
                        Style="{StaticResource mediaButtonStyle}"/>
                    <Image x:Name="playImage" ToolTipService.ToolTip="Play"
                        Style="{StaticResource mediaButtonStyle}" />
                    <Image x:Name="forwardImage"
                        ToolTipService.ToolTip="Forward"
                        Style="{StaticResource mediaButtonStyle}" />
                    <Image x:Name="volumeMinusImage"
                        ToolTipService.ToolTip="Decrease Volume"
                        Style="{StaticResource mediaButtonStyle}"  />
                    <Image x:Name="volumePlusImage"
                        ToolTipService.ToolTip="Increase Volume"
                        Style="{StaticResource mediaButtonStyle}"/>
                </StackPanel>
                <local:mediaSlider x:Name="mediaSlider" Grid.Row="1"
                    MaxWidth="500" Style="{StaticResource
                    mediaSliderStyle}"
                    Margin="0,5,0,5" >
                </local:mediaSlider>
                <MediaElement x:Name="mediaElement"
                    Grid.Row="0" AutoPlay="True" />
            </Grid>
        </ControlTemplate>
    </Setter.Value>
  </Setter>
 </Style>
</ResourceDictionary>
```

Building the mediaSlider.cs File

Rename Class1.cs to mediaSlider.cs. Figure 5-36 shows the class diagram of the mediaSlider class.

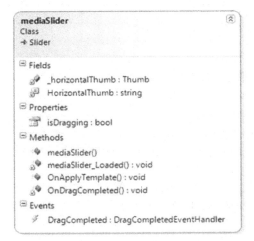

Figure 5-36. *Class diagram of the* mediaSlider *class*

Follow these steps to build the mediaSlider.cs class:

1. In addition to the default namespaces, you need to add the following namespace:

```
using System.Windows.Controls.Primitives;
```

2. Add the following attribute to the mediaSlider custom control:

```
[TemplatePart(Name = mediaSlider.HorizontalThumb,
    Type = typeof(Thumb))]
```

3. Add the following private class member and string constant aligned with the contract definition:

```
private const string HorizontalThumb = "HorizontalThumb";
private Thumb _horizontalThumb;
```

4. Add isDragging as a Boolean property within the public fields region and an event handler for the DragCompleted event:

```
public bool isDragging
{
    get { return _horizontalThumb.IsDragging; }
}
public event DragCompletedEventHandler DragCompleted;
```

5. The following is a code snippet of the class constructor:

```
public mediaSlider()
{
    this.DefaultStyleKey = typeof(mediaSlider);
    this.Loaded += new RoutedEventHandler(mediaSlider_Loaded);
    OnApplyTemplate();
}
```

6. Add the following two methods under the TemplateHandlers region:

```
public override void OnApplyTemplate()
{
    base.OnApplyTemplate();

    getTemplateChildren();
    if (_horizontalThumb != null)
    {
        _horizontalThumb.DragCompleted += new
            DragCompletedEventHandler(OnDragCompleted);

    }
}
```

We need to retrieve only one named element from our control template: Thumb HorizontalThumb in the getTemplateChildren method.

```
private void getTemplateChildren()
{
    _horizontalThumb = GetTemplateChild(HorizontalThumb) as Thumb;
}
```

7. Finally, define the following two event handlers:

```
void mediaSlider_Loaded(object sender, RoutedEventArgs e)
{
    this.ApplyTemplate();
}

private void OnDragCompleted(object sender, DragCompletedEventArgs e)
{
    DragCompleted(this, e);
}
```

Building the mediaPlayer.cs File

Right-click the project in Solution Explorer, choose Add ➤ Class, and name it mediaPlayer.cs.
Figure 5-37 shows the class diagram of the mediaPlayer class.

Figure 5-37. *Class diagram of the* mediaPlayer *class*

Follow these steps to build the mediaPlayer.cs class:

1. In addition to the default namespaces, you need to add the following namespace, as we make use of DispatcherTimer:

   ```
   using System.Windows.Threading;
   ```

2. Add the following attribute to the mediaPlayer custom control:

   ```
   [TemplatePart(Name = mediaPlayer.FadeIn, Type = typeof(Storyboard))]
   [TemplatePart(Name = mediaPlayer.FadeOut, Type = typeof(Storyboard))]
   [TemplatePart(Name = mediaPlayer.ForwardImage, Type = typeof(Image))]
   [TemplatePart(Name = mediaPlayer.FullScreenImage, Type = typeof(Image))]
   [TemplatePart(Name = mediaPlayer.MediaElement,
        Type = typeof(MediaElement))]
   [TemplatePart(Name = mediaPlayer.MediaSlider,Type = typeof(Slider))]
   [TemplatePart(Name = mediaPlayer.PlayImage, Type = typeof(Image))]
   [TemplatePart(Name = mediaPlayer.RewindImage, Type = typeof(Image))]
   [TemplatePart(Name = mediaPlayer.StopImage,Type = typeof(Image))]
   [TemplatePart(Name = mediaPlayer.VolumeMinusImage, Type = typeof(Image))]
   [TemplatePart(Name = mediaPlayer.VolumePlusImage, Type = typeof(Image))]
   ```

3. Add the following private class members and string constants aligned with the contract definition:

   ```
   //String for the media element template item.
   private const string MediaElement = "mediaElement";
   //String for the media slider template item.
   private const string MediaSlider = "mediaSlider";
   //String for the media player navigation control template item.
   private const string PlayImage = "playImage";
   ```

```
private const string StopImage = "stopImage";
private const string ForwardImage = "forwardImage";
private const string RewindImage = "rewindImage";
private const string VolumePlusImage = "volumePlusImage";
private const string VolumeMinusImage = "volumeMinusImage";
private const string FullScreenImage = "fullScreenImage";
private const string FadeIn = "fadeIn";
private const string FadeOut = "fadeOut";
private double volumeValue = 0.1;
//Animations
private Storyboard _fadeIn;
private Storyboard _fadeOut;
//The main media element for playing audio and video.
private MediaElement _mediaElement;
//The slider for showing video progress and drag feature.
private mediaSlider _mediaSlider;
//Images for media player navigation
private Image _play;
private Image _stop;
private Image _forward;
private Image _rewind;
private Image _volPlus;
private Image _volMinus;
private BitmapImage _pauseState;
private BitmapImage _playState;
//DispatcherTimer object to update slider as video progresses
private DispatcherTimer timer = new DispatcherTimer();
```

In this code snippet, we create a BitmapImage object for _pauseState and _playState rather than Image, as we need to toggle the image displayed in the _play Image control based on the current state of the _mediaElement control.

4. Add seven public properties and two public methods:

```
public Uri playImgUri
{
  set
    {_playState = new BitmapImage(value);
     _play.SetValue(Image.SourceProperty, _playState);
    }
}

public Uri pauseImgUri
{
  set
    {_pauseState = new BitmapImage(value);}
}

public Uri stopImgUri
{
  set
    {
      BitmapImage source = new BitmapImage(value);
      _stop.SetValue(Image.SourceProperty, source);
    }
}

public Uri forwardImgUri
```

```
{
  set
    {
      BitmapImage source = new BitmapImage(value);
      _forward.SetValue(Image.SourceProperty, source);
    }
}

public Uri rewindImgUri
{
  set
    {
      BitmapImage source = new BitmapImage(value);
      _rewind.SetValue(Image.SourceProperty, source);
    }
}

public Uri volPlusImgUri
{
  set
    {
      BitmapImage source = new BitmapImage(value);
      _volPlus.SetValue(Image.SourceProperty, source);
    }
}

public Uri volMinusImgUri
{
  set
    {
      BitmapImage source = new BitmapImage(value);
      _volMinus.SetValue(Image.SourceProperty, source);
    }
}

public void stopMediaPlayer()
{
_mediaElement.Stop();
}

public void setMediaPlayerSource(Uri mediaFile)
{
_mediaElement.Source = mediaFile;
}
```

In this code snippet, the method setMediaPlayerSource is the main method to set the Source property of the _mediaElement control. It requires a Uri object containing the URL to the media file.

5. The following is the code snippet of the class constructor:

```
public mediaPlayer()
{
    this.DefaultStyleKey = typeof(mediaPlayer);
    this.Loaded += new RoutedEventHandler(mediaPlayer_Loaded);
    OnApplyTemplate();
    timer.Interval = new TimeSpan(0, 0, 1);
}
```

The timer.Interval is set to 1 second by using the TimeSpan object. So every second, the event handler assigned for timer.Tick will be called. We will create an event handler for timer.Tick later in this section.

6. Next, we will add two methods under the TemplateHandlers region.

After calling the GetTemplateChildren method in the OnApplyTemplate method, we need to wire up some events to the retrieved elements. For the navigation elements (six Image controls), we assign three event handlers: MouseLeftButtonDown as Control_MouseLeftButtonDown, MouseEnter as Control_MouseEnter, and MouseLeave as Control_MouseLeave. For the Image _play control, we need to assign the MouseLeftButtonDown event handler as playPause_MouseLeftButtonDown. For the _mediaElement control, we assign the event MediaOpened. For the _mediaSlider control, we assign the event DragCompleted. We also need to assign the event timer_Tick to the DispatcherTimer timer control.

```
public override void OnApplyTemplate()
{
    base.OnApplyTemplate();

    GetTemplateChildren();

    //Assign event handlers
    timer.Tick += new EventHandler(timer_Tick);

    if (_mediaElement != null)
        _mediaElement.MediaOpened += new
            RoutedEventHandler(_mediaElement_MediaOpened);

    if (_mediaSlider != null)
        _mediaSlider.DragCompleted += new
            System.Windows.Controls.Primitives.
            DragCompletedEventHandler(_mediaSlider_DragCompleted);

    if (_play != null)
    {
        _play.MouseLeftButtonDown += playPause_MouseLeftButtonDown;
        _play.MouseEnter += Control_MouseEnter;
        _play.MouseLeave += Control_MouseLeave;
    }
    if (_stop != null)
    {
        _stop.MouseLeftButtonDown += Control_MouseLeftButtonDown;
        _stop.MouseEnter += Control_MouseEnter;
        _stop.MouseLeave += Control_MouseLeave;
    }
    if (_forward != null)
    {
        _forward.MouseLeftButtonDown += Control_MouseLeftButtonDown;
        _forward.MouseEnter += Control_MouseEnter;
        _forward.MouseLeave += Control_MouseLeave;
    }
    if (_rewind != null)
    {
        _rewind.MouseLeftButtonDown += Control_MouseLeftButtonDown;
        _rewind.MouseEnter += Control_MouseEnter;
        _rewind.MouseLeave += Control_MouseLeave;
    }
```

```
        if (_volMinus != null)
        {
            _volMinus.MouseLeftButtonDown += Control_MouseLeftButtonDown;
            _volMinus.MouseEnter += Control_MouseEnter;
            _volMinus.MouseLeave += Control_MouseLeave;
        }
        if (_volPlus != null)
        {
            _volPlus.MouseLeftButtonDown += Control_MouseLeftButtonDown;
            _volPlus.MouseEnter += Control_MouseEnter;
            _volPlus.MouseLeave += Control_MouseLeave;
        }

    }

    private void GetTemplateChildren()
    {
        _mediaElement = base.GetTemplateChild(MediaElement)
            as MediaElement;
        _mediaSlider = base.GetTemplateChild(MediaSlider) as mediaSlider;
        _play = base.GetTemplateChild(PlayImage) as Image;
        _stop = base.GetTemplateChild(StopImage) as Image;
        _forward = base.GetTemplateChild(ForwardImage) as Image;
        _rewind = base.GetTemplateChild(RewindImage) as Image;
        _volPlus = base.GetTemplateChild(VolumePlusImage) as Image;
        _volMinus = base.GetTemplateChild(VolumeMinusImage) as Image;
        _fadeIn = base.GetTemplateChild(FadeIn) as Storyboard;
        _fadeOut = base.GetTemplateChild(FadeOut) as Storyboard;
    }
```

In this code snippet, the last two lines retrieve the fadeIn and fadeOut storyboards that we defined in our control template of mediaPlayer under the Grid.Resources section.

7. Finally, we define the event handlers:

```
void mediaPlayer_Loaded(object sender, RoutedEventArgs e)
{
    this.ApplyTemplate();
}

void timer_Tick(object sender, EventArgs e)
{
    if (_mediaSlider.isDragging == false)
        _mediaSlider.Value = _mediaElement.Position.TotalSeconds;
}
```

This event changes the value property of _mediaSlider so that as the media in _mediaElement progresses, the thumb in the mediaSlider control will update its position. Here we are preventing _mediaSlider.Value from changing to stop HorizontalThumb in _mediaSlider moving when the user drags the thumb. We determine this feature by validating the isDragging property of the _mediaSlider control.

```
void _mediaElement_MediaOpened(object sender, RoutedEventArgs e)
{
    _mediaSlider.Maximum = _mediaElement.NaturalDuration.
        TimeSpan.TotalSeconds;
    timer.Start();
}
```

Here we set the _mediaSlider control's Maximum property to the length in seconds of
the media file, which is currently playing in _mediaElement by using the _mediaElement.
NaturalDuration property. We also start the timer object to begin moving the thumb in the
_mediaSlider control.

```
void _mediaSlider_DragCompleted(object sender,
    System.Windows.Controls.Primitives.DragCompletedEventArgs e)
{
    _mediaElement.Position = TimeSpan.FromSeconds(_mediaSlider.Value);
}
```

Here we set _mediaElement.Position to _mediaSlider.Value.

Add code for the event handler playPause_MouseLeftButtonDown as follows. Note that we also
change the tooltip for the control as we change the source of the image.

```
void playPause_MouseLeftButtonDown
    (object sender, MouseButtonEventArgs e)
{
    if (_mediaElement.CurrentState == MediaElementState.Playing)
    {
        _mediaElement.Pause();
        _play.SetValue(Image.SourceProperty, _playState);
        ToolTipService.SetToolTip(_play, "Play");
    }
    else
    {
        _mediaElement.Play();
        _play.SetValue(Image.SourceProperty, _pauseState);
        ToolTipService.SetToolTip(_play, "Pause");
    }
}
```

In the event handlers Control_MouseEnter and Control_MouseLeave, we call the _fadeIn and
_fadeOut animations so that when the user mouses over any navigation control, they fade in
and when the mouse leaves that control, they fade out to their original Opacity.

```
void Control_MouseEnter(object sender, MouseEventArgs e)
{
    Image imgRef = new Image();
    imgRef = (Image)sender;
    _fadeIn.Stop();
    _fadeIn.SetValue(Storyboard.TargetNameProperty, imgRef.Name);
    _fadeIn.Begin();
}

void Control_MouseLeave(object sender, MouseEventArgs e)
{
    Image imgRef = new Image();
    imgRef = (Image)sender;
    _fadeOut.Stop();
    _fadeOut.SetValue(Storyboard.TargetNameProperty, imgRef.Name);
    _fadeOut.Begin();
}
```

In the `Control_MouseLeftButtonDown` event, we will place a `switch` case on `imgRef.Name`. Based on the `Name` property of the control that has raised the event, we select the appropriate actions to perform. This way we avoid defining an individual event handler for each of the six navigation `Image` controls.

```
void Control_MouseLeftButtonDown
    (object sender, MouseButtonEventArgs e)
{
    Image imgRef = new Image();
    imgRef = (Image)sender;

    switch (imgRef.Name)
    {
        case StopImage :
        _mediaElement.Stop();
        _play.SetValue(Image.SourceProperty, _playState);
        break;

        case ForwardImage:
        _mediaElement.Position =
            _mediaElement.Position.Add(new TimeSpan(0, 0, 5));
        break;

        case RewindImage:
        _mediaElement.Position =
            _mediaElement.Position.Subtract(new TimeSpan(0, 0, 5));
        break;

        case VolumePlusImage:
        _mediaElement.Volume = _mediaElement.Volume + volumeValue;
        break;

        case VolumeMinusImage:
        _mediaElement.Volume = _mediaElement.Volume - volumeValue;
        break;
    }
}
```

Deploying the mediaPlayer Custom Control

Now you are all set to deploy the `mediaPlayer` custom control. Follow the instructions provided in the section "Understanding Silverlight Custom Controls" to register the component with Visual Studio, or you can add it later as a reference when we develop the main training portal Silverlight project.

RSS 2 Feed Viewer: Rss2Reader Custom Control

Add a new project to the solution by creating a new `Rss2Reader` Silverlight class library project to develop the RSS feed viewer UI component of the portal. This control will be populated with the data that we parse using LINQ and the `SyndicationFeed` class. The URL for the feed will be accessed from `tpFeeds.xml`.

We are going to follow all the steps outlined previously in the "Understanding Silverlight Custom Controls" section.

Building the generic.xaml File

Add a file named generic.xaml under the Theme folder and follow all the steps described earlier to add a ControlTemplate with the TargetType set to local:Rss2Reader.

Figure 5-38 presents the user interface layout design of the left navigation pane.

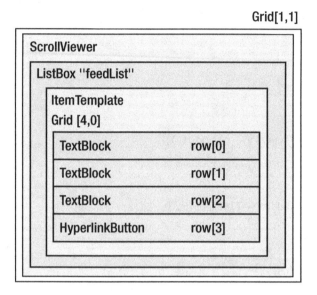

Figure 5-38. *User interface layout design of the RSS feed viewer*

Follow these steps to build the RSS feed viewer as shown in Figure 5-38:

1. We will use the Grid control as the main layout control. Under the ControlTemplate section, add a Grid control with no background and only one row, and add the Grid.Resources section to include the htmlFormat and linkFormat helper classes under the local namespace. We will develop these helper classes when we develop the Rss2Reader class.

2. Add a ScrollViewer control inside the Grid control. Add the ListBox control within the ScrollViewer control and name it feedList. Set the Background property of the ListBox control to {x:Null} and the BorderThickness property to 0.

3. In the ItemTemplate of the feedList ListBox control, add another Grid control with four rows. Set the Height property to Auto and MaxWidth property to 800. In the first three rows, place TextBlock controls, and in the last row place the HyperlinkButton control.

4. The Rss2Reader control will display only the Title, PublishDate, and Summary properties of the SyndicationFeed class and bind them with the Text property of three TextBlock controls. Bind the Links property of the SyndicationFeed class to the NavigateUri property of the HyperlinkButton.

5. Set the Converter to htmlFormatter when you bind the Summary in the third TextBlock control to remove all HTML tags, newline characters, and spaces. Set the Converter to linkFormatter when you bind the HyperlinkButton to display only the first link that will point to the post.

6. Set other properties of these four controls as shown in the following code snippet for the generic.xaml file:

```xml
<ResourceDictionary
    xmlns="http://schemas.microsoft.com/winfx/2006/xaml/presentation"
    xmlns:x="http://schemas.microsoft.com/winfx/2006/xaml"
    xmlns:local="clr-namespace:TechnologyOpinion;assembly=Rss2Reader"
    xmlns:vsm="clr-namespace:System.Windows;assembly=System.Windows">
    <Style TargetType="local:Rss2Reader">
        <Setter Property="Template">
            <Setter.Value>
                <ControlTemplate TargetType="local:Rss2Reader">
                    <Grid>
                        <Grid.Resources>
                            <local:htmlFormat x:Key="htmlFormatter"/>
                            <local:linkFormat x:Key="linkFormatter"/>
                        </Grid.Resources>
                        <ScrollViewer VerticalScrollBarVisibility="Auto"
                            HorizontalScrollBarVisibility="Auto"
                            BorderThickness="0"
                            Style="{StaticResource ScrollViewerStyle1}">
                        <ListBox x:Name="feedList" Background="{x:Null}"
                            BorderThickness="0" >
                            <ListBox.ItemTemplate>
                                <DataTemplate>
                                    <Grid MaxWidth="800"
                                        ScrollViewer.HorizontalScrollBarVisibility
                                        ="Auto" >
                                        <Grid.RowDefinitions>
                                            <RowDefinition Height="Auto"/>
                                            <RowDefinition Height="Auto"/>
                                            <RowDefinition Height="Auto"/>
                                            <RowDefinition Height="Auto"/>
                                        </Grid.RowDefinitions>
                                        <TextBlock Foreground="Cyan" Grid.Row="0"
                                            FontWeight="Bold"  Text ="{Binding
                                            Path=Title.Text}"
                                            TextWrapping="Wrap" FontSize="12" />
                                        <TextBlock Foreground="SkyBlue"
                                            Grid.Row="1"
                                            Text="{Binding Path=PublishDate}"
                                            TextWrapping="Wrap" FontSize="10"   />
                                        <TextBlock Foreground="White" Grid.Row="2"
                                            Text="{Binding Converter=
                                                {StaticResource htmlFormatter},
                                            Path=Summary.Text}"TextWrapping="Wrap"
                                            FontSize="11"/>
                                        <HyperlinkButton Foreground="Yellow"
                                            Grid.Row="3"
                                            VerticalAlignment="Top"
                                            HorizontalAlignment="Left"
                                            Content="Read more..."
                                            NavigateUri="{Binding Converter={
                                                StaticResource linkFormatter},
                                                Path=Links}"
                                            FontSize="12" TargetName="_blank"/>
                                    </Grid>
                                </DataTemplate>
                            </ListBox.ItemTemplate>
```

```
                                              </ListBox>
                                          </ScrollViewer>
                                      </Grid>
                                  </ControlTemplate>
                              </Setter.Value>
                          </Setter>
                      </Style>
                  </ResourceDictionary>
```

Note Here we have not used Expression Blend. To make the control more rich looking and integrate with VSM to make it more interactive, you can use Expression Blend and VSM as described earlier.

Building the Rss2Reader.cs Class File

Rename Class1.cs to Rss2Reader.cs. Figure 5-39 shows the class diagram of the Rss2Reader class library project.

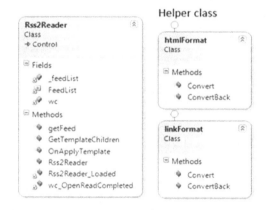

Figure 5-39. *Class diagram of the* Rss2Reader *class library project*

Follow these steps to build the Rss2Reader.cs class:

1. In addition to the default namespaces, you need to add the following namespaces:

```
//Additional namespaces
using System.Text.RegularExpressions;
using System.Windows.Browser;
using System.ServiceModel.Syndication;
using System.Windows.Data;
using System.Collections.ObjectModel;
using System.Linq;
using System.Xml;
using System.Windows.Controls.Primitives;
```

2. Add the following attribute to the Rss2Reader custom control:

```
[TemplatePart(Name = Rss2Reader.FeedList, Type = typeof(ListBox))]
```

3. Add the following private class members and string constant aligned with the contract definition:

```
private const string FeedList = "feedList";
private ListBox _feedList;
private WebClient wc = new WebClient();
```

4. The following is the code snippet of the class constructor:

```
public Rss2Reader()
{
    this.DefaultStyleKey = typeof(Rss2Reader);
    OnApplyTemplate();
    this.Loaded += new RoutedEventHandler(Rss2Reader_Loaded);
    wc.OpenReadCompleted += new
        OpenReadCompletedEventHandler(wc_OpenReadCompleted);
}
```

We will use the WebClient class and make asynchronous calls to access the RSS feed XML file using HTTP. To download feeds, we need to make an HTTP request. To support this functionality, within the class constructor we create the event handler that will notify when the asynchronous call is completed.

5. Add the following two methods under the TemplateHandlers region:

```
public override void OnApplyTemplate()
{
    base.OnApplyTemplate();
    GetTemplateChildren();
}

private void GetTemplateChildren()
{
    _feedList = base.GetTemplateChild(FeedList) as ListBox;
}
```

Here we need to retrieve only the ListBox control named feedList.

6. The public getFeed method will have one parameter of type Uri pointing to the RSS feed that we want to download and display. So we make an asynchronous call to the wc WebClient in this method.

```
public void getFeed( Uri feedAddress)
{
    wc.OpenReadAsync(feedAddress);
}
```

7. Now we define the event handlers:

```
void Rss2Reader_Loaded(object sender, RoutedEventArgs e)
{
    this.ApplyTemplate();
}

void wc_OpenReadCompleted(object sender, OpenReadCompletedEventArgs e)
{
    if (e.Error == null)
    {
        //Load feed into SyndicationFeed
        XmlReader reader = XmlReader.Create(e.Result);
```

```
            SyndicationFeed feed = SyndicationFeed.Load(reader);

            //Set up databinding
            _feedList.ItemsSource = (feed as SyndicationFeed).Items;
        }
    }
```

When the RSS feed read operation is completed, the wc_OpenReadCompleted event handler will parse the result using XmlReader and then set the _feedList ListBox control's ItemSource property.

8. We need to define two additional helper classes to format the data based on the portal requirement. Place them in the helper classes region.

   Both of these classes inherit from the IvalueConverter interface. It exposes methods that allow us to modify the data as it passes through the binding engine. In other words it allows us to convert the format of our data between the source and the target.

   The htmlFormat class removes all the HTML tags, newline characters, and spaces:

```
public class htmlFormat : IValueConverter
{
    public object Convert(object value, Type targetType, object parameter,
      System.Globalization.CultureInfo culture)
    {
      //Remove all HTML tags, newline characters, and spaces
      string returnValue = Regex.Replace(value as string, "<.*?>", "");
      returnValue = Regex.Replace(returnValue, @"\n+\s+", "\n\n");

      //Decode HTML entities
      returnValue = HttpUtility.HtmlDecode(returnValue);
      return returnValue;
    }
    //We need to implement IValueConverter interface member. ConvertBack
    public object ConvertBack(object value, Type targetType,
      object parameter,  System.Globalization.CultureInfo culture)
    {
      throw new NotImplementedException();
    }
}
```

   The linkFormat class gets the first link (this link will point to the post) from the SyndicationLink collection.

```
public class linkFormat : IValueConverter
{
  public object Convert(object value, Type targetType, object parameter,
    System.Globalization.CultureInfo culture)
  {
      //Get the first link that will point to the post
      return ((Collection<SyndicationLink>)value).FirstOrDefault().Uri;
  }
  //We need to implement IValueConverter interface member ConvertBack
  public object ConvertBack(object value, Type targetType, object parameter,
    System.Globalization.CultureInfo culture)
  {
      throw new NotImplementedException();
  }
}
```

Deploying the Rss2Reader Custom Control

Now you are all set to deploy the Rss2Reader custom control. Follow the instructions provided in the earlier part of the chapter to register the component with Visual Studio, or you can add it later as a reference when we develop the main TrainingPortal Silverlight project.

Image Viewer: MultiScaleImage Control

The image viewer includes the Silverlight Deep Zoom functionality. You need to use the MultiScaleImage control (available as part of the default Silverlight control) to enable the Deep Zoom functionality. We will add this control as part of the main Silverlight TrainingPortal application project within the main user control of the Page.xaml file.

In this section, you will see how to prepare images for Deep Zoom using the freely available Deep Zoom Composer. You can download the Deep Zoom Composer by visiting http://silverlight.net/GetStarted/ and clicking the Install Deep Zoom Composer link.

Understanding the Deep Zoom Composer

After successful installation of the Deep Zoom composer, the following steps will allow you to prepare images for the Deep Zoom functionality using the MultiScaleImage Silverlight control:

1. Open Deep Zoom Composer, create a new project, and name it whatever you want.

2. This will open the IDE of the tool where you will have three options for the workspace: Import, Compose, and Export. The Import workspace allows you to import and manage images in the project. The Compose workspace allows you to position and arrange your images. The Export workspace allows you to export your final composition to a Deep Zoom image or collection. Choose the Import option for the workspace.

3. Add images that you want to prepare for Deep Zoom by clicking the Import tab.

4. After completion of the import process, click Compose to switch to the Compose workspace. At the right side, you can see images that you added in the previous step. You need to drag them to the center of the workspace to compose them for Deep Zoom. Drag as many images as you want and arrange them. There are various tools available at the bottom of this workspace that will help in composing your images.

5. You can also alter the square, as shown in Figure 5-40, to adjust the default view of Deep Zoom images when they are loaded.

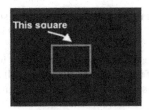

Figure 5-40. *Adjusting the default view of Deep Zoom images*

6. When you are finished with the composition, click the Export tab. Here you will see a pre-view of the composition that you finished in the previous step. You will be presented with two options to export. The first is PhotoZoom Export, which requires you to sign in with your Windows Live ID if you already have a PhotoZoom account. PhotoZoom is the free service that provides hosting of Deep Zoom albums. The second option is the Silverlight Export. In this tab, you need to name the composition. Then if you want, click Browse to set the export location. We are going to use the second option for our application.

7. The next section is Image Type, where you need to select between Export as Composition and Export as Collection. For our needs, you can select any one. Choose Image Format as JPEG from the drop-down box, as it will have a smaller size than the default format PNG.

8. In the last section, Output Type, we have two options. The first option is Export Images, which exports only images that can be used with the `MultiScaleImage` control. The second option is Export Images and Silverlight Project, which also generates a sample Deep Zoom project displaying your images as Deep Zoom images. For our needs, we will select the first option.

9. After successful export, you will get a dialog box providing information about the image folder where Deep Zoom images are saved. Click that folder to open the export location.

10. The export folder contains two folders and three XML files. We need all these items when we add or upload Deep Zoom images to use with our application. The XML file `dzc_output.xml` is the main file, and we will supply the URL of it when setting the `MultiScaleImage` control's `Source` property. Repeat the preceding steps to prepare your images for Deep Zoom.

Now we are all set for Deep Zoom. We will integrate this feature in the next section.

Developing the Main Silverlight Application Project: TrainingPortal

Create a `TrainingPortal` Silverlight application project by selecting the Silverlight Application project template with a web solution to host the Silverlight control for the testing.

Adding Exiting Custom Controls and the Data Access Component

Since we are going to use the `tpContents.xml` file as a training database, except for the `getContents` WCF data service, we need to add all the developed components (four custom controls and one data access component) to this newly created project.

To make your efforts organized and simple, create a `Bin` folder under the training portal solution folder `TrainingPortal`. Place all deployed custom control DLLs and the data class library DLL in this folder.

Now right-click the project, choose Add reference, and browse to the `Bin` folder that you just created. Select all the DLLs and click OK. The References section of the project will contain all four custom controls and the data access component. Figure 5-41 shows the added components under the References section.

To contain the resources that we use in the `TrainingPortal` project, we will create a `res` folder in the project and put each resource we create in this folder. Here I have placed six PNG images for the `vidStage mediaPlayer` control, one PNG image for the training portal icon, and a PNG image RSS feed icon as shown in Figure 5-41.

Added References   **Added Resource Files**

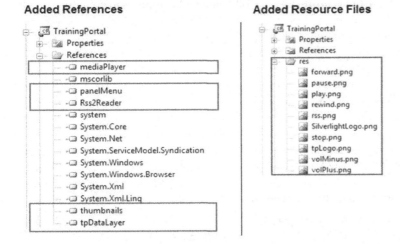

Figure 5-41. *Additional references and resource files for the* `TrainingPortal` *project*

Building the Page.xaml File

The `Page.xaml` XAML markup file represents the main user interface of the Enterprise Training Portal RIA and is derived from the `UserControl`.

1. In the XAML code view of `Page.xaml`, within the `UserControl` we need to add four XML namespaces for our custom controls as shown here:

```
<UserControl x:Class="TrainingPortal.Page"
    xmlns="http://schemas.microsoft.com/winfx/2006/xaml/presentation"
    xmlns:x="http://schemas.microsoft.com/winfx/2006/xaml"
    xmlns:TO1="clr-namespace:TechnologyOpinion;assembly=mediaPlayer"
    xmlns:TO2="clr-namespace:TechnologyOpinion;assembly=Rss2Reader"
    xmlns:TO3="clr-namespace:TechnologyOpinion;assembly=thumbnails"
    xmlns:TO4="clr-namespace:TechnologyOpinion;assembly=panelMenu" >
```

2. Now change the `Background` property of the `LayoutRoot` Grid control to `#FF023B4A`. Under the `Grid.Resources` section, add a simple storyboard `fadeIn` that you will call while loading thumbnails into the `ThumbBar` StackPanel control.

```
<Grid.Resources>
    <Storyboard x:Name="fadeIn">
    <DoubleAnimation
        Storyboard.TargetProperty ="Opacity"
        From="0.6"
        To="1"
        SpeedRatio="2"/>
    </Storyboard>
</Grid.Resources>
```

3. As defined in Figure 5-4, the Grid control has the following code for row and column definitions:

```
<Grid.RowDefinitions>
    <RowDefinition Height="120"/>
    <RowDefinition Height="*"/>
    <RowDefinition Height="120"/>
    <RowDefinition Height="22"/>
</Grid.RowDefinitions>

<Grid.ColumnDefinitions>
    <ColumnDefinition Width="200"/>
    <ColumnDefinition Width="*"/>
</Grid.ColumnDefinitions>
```

4. Add a Border control surrounding the Grid control:

```
<!--Border surrounding Grid "LayoutRoot"-->
<Border Grid.ColumnSpan="2" Grid.RowSpan="4" BorderThickness="3,3,3,3"
    BorderBrush="Cyan" Padding="0,0,0,0" Margin="0,0,0,0"/>
```

5. Add the TechnologyOpinion enterprise logo using the Image control:

```
<Image x:Name="logo" Margin="10,15,0,0" Height="118" Source="res/tpLogo.png"
    Stretch="Fill"  HorizontalAlignment="Center" VerticalAlignment="Top"
    Width="172" Grid.RowSpan="2"/>
```

6. Add the enterprise name, Technology Opinion, using the TextBlock control:

```
<!--Application company name -->
<TextBlock x:Name="companyName" Text="Technology Opinion" Margin="3,18,0,0"
    FontSize="16" Foreground="White" TextWrapping="Wrap" Width="181"
    Grid.Column="1" HorizontalAlignment="Left" VerticalAlignment="Top"/>
```

7. Add the application title, Enterprise Training Portal, using the TextBlock control:

```
<!--Application title -->
<TextBlock x:Name="portalTitle" HorizontalAlignment="Left" Margin="3,34,0,51"
    Width="Auto" FontSize="24" Text="Enterprise Training Portal"
    TextWrapping="Wrap" Foreground="Cyan" Grid.Column="1" />
```

8. Add the Silverlight logo using the Image control:

```
<!-- Powered by Microsoft Silverlight Logo -->
<Image x:Name="silverlightLogo" Source="res/SilverlightLogo.png" Stretch="None"
    Grid.Row="2" Margin="0,0,0,0" Height="84" Width="76"
    VerticalAlignment="Center"
    HorizontalAlignment="Center" RenderTransformOrigin="0.487,0.25"/>
```

9. Add the text "Powered by" above the Silverlight logo using the TextBlock control:

```
<!--Add "Powered by" text above Microsoft Silverlight Logo -->
<TextBlock Height="24" Margin="61.34,0.503,43.66,95.497"
    VerticalAlignment="Stretch" Grid.Row="2" Text="Powered by"
    TextWrapping="Wrap" Foreground="#FFFFFFFF" HorizontalAlignment="Stretch"/>
```

10. Add the enterprise copyright notice with a link to the enterprise web site using the Hyper-linkButton control:

```
<!-- Copyright notice -->
<HyperlinkButton x:Name="copyrightNote" Margin="0,2,0,2" Grid.Column="1"
    Grid.Row="3" Content ="© 2009 Technology Opinion LLC
    (www.TechnologyOpinion.com)    " NavigateUri=http://www.technologyopinion.com
    TargetName="_blank" Foreground="SkyBlue" HorizontalAlignment="Right"
    VerticalAlignment="Top"/>
```

11. Add a full screen/normal screen TextBlock control with the default Full Screen value as its Text property:

```
<!-- Fullscreen command -->
<TextBlock x:Name="goFullscreen" Height="20" HorizontalAlignment="Right"
    Margin="0,8,0,0" VerticalAlignment="Top" Width="135" Grid.Column="1"
    Text="Full Screen" TextWrapping="Wrap" Foreground="#FFFFFD11"
    FontSize="14"  MouseLeftButtonDown="fullScreenToggle" Cursor="Hand"/>
```

12. Add code for the feedBox ComboBox control along with the Image and Title that get displayed above it to select the RSS feed:

```
<!-- "feedBox" ComboBox -->
<ComboBox x:Name="feedBox" SelectionChanged="feedBox_SelectionChanged"
    Margin="98.5,0,24.5,8" Grid.Column="1" VerticalAlignment="Bottom" Height="22"
    Width="250" HorizontalAlignment="Center">
  <ComboBox.ItemTemplate>
    <DataTemplate >
      <StackPanel Orientation="Horizontal">
          <Image Source="res/rss.png" Margin="0,0,5,0" />
          <TextBlock Text="{Binding Path=Title}" FontSize="13" Foreground="Black" />
      </StackPanel>
    </DataTemplate>
  </ComboBox.ItemTemplate>
</ComboBox>

<!-- "feedBox" ComboBox Title -->
<TextBlock Margin="130,0,104,38" Grid.Column="1" Text="Get the latest Feeds"
    TextWrapping="Wrap" Foreground="#FFF6FF1C" FontSize="14"
    VerticalAlignment="Bottom" HorizontalAlignment="Center"/>

<!-- "feedBox" ComboBox Image-->
<Image Margin="102,27,257,41" Source="res/rss.png" Stretch="Fill"
    Grid.Column="1" RenderTransformOrigin="-0.321,0.071" Width="14"
    HorizontalAlignment="Center" Height="14" VerticalAlignment="Bottom"/>
```

13. And finally add code for Cell[1,1], which contains all the custom control instances along with the MultiScaleImage tpMsi control, enabling the Deep Zoom functionality:

```
<!--Following 6 items are in Cell[1,1]-->
<!--Border surrounding cell[1,1] -->
<Border Grid.Row="1" Grid.Column="1" BorderThickness="1" BorderBrush="Gray"
    Margin="5,19,19,19" Background="Black"/>
<!-- panelMenu "tpMenu"-->
<TO4:panelMenu x:Name="tpMenu" itemClicked="tpMenu_itemClicked" Width="172"
    Grid.Row="1" Margin="5,20,0,0" HorizontalAlignment="Center"/>
```

```
<!-- mediaPlayer "tpVidStage"-->
<TO1:mediaPlayer x:Name="tpVidStage" Visibility="Collapsed"  Grid.Row="1"
    Grid.Column="1" Margin="6,20,20,20"  />
<!-- Rss2Reader "tpFeed"-->
<TO2:Rss2Reader x:Name="tpFeed" Visibility="Collapsed" Grid.Row="1"
    Grid.Column="1" Margin="6,20,20,20" />
<!-- StackPanel "tpInfoPanel" -->
<StackPanel x:Name="tpInfoPanel" MaxWidth="800" Grid.Row="1" Grid.Column="1"
    Margin="6,20,20,20" HorizontalAlignment="Center" VerticalAlignment="Center" >
    <TextBlock x:Name="Title" FontSize="18" Foreground="Yellow" TextWrapping="Wrap"
        />
    <TextBlock x:Name="Abstract" FontSize="16" Foreground="White"
        TextWrapping="Wrap"/>
</StackPanel>
<!-- MultiScalImage "tpMsi" for DeepZoom -->
<MultiScaleImage x:Name="tpMsi" MouseLeftButtonDown="tpMsi_MouseLeftButtonDown"
    MouseLeftButtonUp="tpMsi_MouseLeftButtonUp" MouseMove="tpMsi_MouseMove"
    Visibility="Collapsed" Grid.Row="1" Grid.Column="1" Margin="6,20,20,20"/>
```

In this code snippet, as you type code for MultiScaleImage tpMsi events, IntelliSense will prompt you to create event handlers in the code-behind (Page.xaml.cs). Please do so.

Now if you look at the design view of the Page.xaml file, the training portal screen will look as shown in Figure 5-42.

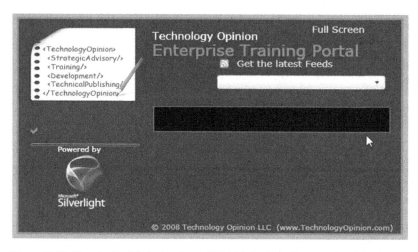

Figure 5-42. *Enterprise Training Portal RIA in design view mode of the* Page.xaml *file*

Building the Page.xaml.cs File

The Page.xaml.cs class is a code-behind of Page.xaml and will have methods and event handlers defined for custom controls.

Figure 5-43 shows the Page.xaml.cs class diagram of the TrainingPortal main Silverlight application project.

Figure 5-43. *Class diagram of the* Page.xaml.cs *class of the main* TrainingPortal *Silverlight application project*

Follow these steps to build the Page.xaml.cs class:

1. In addition to the default namespaces, you need to add the TechnologyOpinion namespace to access the tpDataLayer component:

```
using System;
using System.Collections.Generic;
using System.Linq;
using System.Net;
using System.Windows;
using System.Windows.Controls;
using System.Windows.Documents;
using System.Windows.Input;
using System.Windows.Media;
using System.Windows.Media.Animation;
using System.Windows.Shapes;
//Added
using TechnologyOpinion;
```

2. Create a global variable of type tpDataLayer named tpLayer. We also create one integer type idx that we will use when we generate thumbnails and name them:

```
TechnologyOpinion.tpDataLayer tpLayer = new
    TechnologyOpinion.tpDataLayer();
//Index for unique naming of thumbnails
int idx = 0;
```

3. In the Page constructor, we define the Loaded event and mouse wheel support for zoom in and out (Deep Zoom):

```
public Page()
{
    InitializeComponent();
    this.Loaded += new RoutedEventHandler(Page_Loaded);
    new MouseWheelHelper(this).Moved += delegate(object sender,
        MouseWheelEventArgs e)
    {
        double zoomFactor = 1.55;
        if (e.Delta < 0)
          zoomFactor = 1 / 1.55;
        zoom(zoomFactor, pLast);
    };
}
```

4. The Page_Loaded event initializes the portal by calling the initPortal method of tpLayer. We also define two required events, initPortalCompleted and getContentCompleted, here, as well as set seven required properties for the tpVidStage mediaPlayer control.

```
//Here we initialize our custom controls
void Page_Loaded(object sender, RoutedEventArgs e)
{
    //Initializing portal
    tpLayer.initPortal("tpConfig.xml","tpFeeds.xml");
    tpLayer.initPortalCompleted += new tpDataLayer.
      initPortalCompletedEventHandler(tpLayer_initPortalCompleted);
    tpLayer.getContentCompleted += new TechnologyOpinion.
      tpDataLayer.getContentCompletedEventHandler
        (tpLayer_getContentCompleted);

    //Setting tpVidStage mediaPlayer buttons
    tpVidStage.playImgUri = new
      Uri("res/play.png", UriKind.RelativeOrAbsolute);
    tpVidStage.pauseImgUri = new
      Uri("res/pause.png", UriKind.RelativeOrAbsolute);
    tpVidStage.rewindImgUri = new
      Uri("res/rewind.png", UriKind.RelativeOrAbsolute);
    tpVidStage.forwardImgUri = new
      Uri("res/forward.png", UriKind.RelativeOrAbsolute);
    tpVidStage.stopImgUri = new
      Uri("res/stop.png", UriKind.RelativeOrAbsolute);
    tpVidStage.volMinusImgUri = new
      Uri("res/volMinus.png", UriKind.RelativeOrAbsolute);
    tpVidStage.volPlusImgUri = new
      Uri("res/volPlus.png", UriKind.RelativeOrAbsolute);

}
```

5. In the initPortalCompleted event, we set the ItemSource property of the feedBox ComboBox control and populate the tpMenu panelMenu control by calling the addMenuItem method:

```
void tpLayer_initPortalCompleted(object sender,
  tpDataLayer.menuBinding[] eMenu,
 tpDataLayer.feedItem[] eFeed)
{
    //Generate menu
    foreach (var item in eMenu)
    {
        if (item != null)
        {
            tpMenu.addMenuItem
              (item.Id, item.Title, item.Items.ToList());
        }
    }

    //Fill the "feedBox" ComboBox by setting ItemSource
    feedBox.ItemsSource = eFeed;
}
```

6. The code for the goFullscreen TextBlock is the same as the Chapter 2 version of the full-screen command, as shown in the following snippet:

```
//Fullscreen toggle command
private void fullScreenToggle(object sender, MouseButtonEventArgs e)
{
    if (goFullscreen.Text == "Full Screen")
        goFullscreen.Text = "Normal Screen";
    else
        goFullscreen.Text = "Full Screen";

    Application.Current.Host.Content.IsFullScreen =
        !Application.Current.Host.Content.IsFullScreen;
}
```

7. As Cell[1,1] of the Grid LayoutRoot control contains many controls, we need to set Visibility to Visible for controls whenever a resource of its type needs to be displayed. For this we will create a simple method, currentStage, that will require one argument, controlToShow, of type FrameworkElement. This method will set Visibility to Visible for the control that we pass as a parameter. The remaining controls of Cell[1,1] will have Visibility set to Collapsed.

```
void currentStage(FrameworkElement controlToShow)
{
    //Hide all
    tpInfoPanel.Visibility = Visibility.Collapsed;
    tpFeed.Visibility = Visibility.Collapsed;
    tpMsi.Visibility = Visibility.Collapsed;
    tpVidStage.Visibility = Visibility.Collapsed;
    tpVidStage.stopMediaPlayer();
    //Currently visible
    controlToShow.Visibility = Visibility.Visible;
}
```

8. While we code the SelectionChanged event in Page.xaml for feedBox, VS automatically generates the corresponding code-behind in Page.xaml.cs. In this event, we will call the getFeed method of the tpFeed Rss2Reader control by supplying selectedFeed.Uri as a parameter.

```
//Feed ComboBox
private void feedBox_SelectionChanged(object sender,
    SelectionChangedEventArgs e)
{
    currentStage(tpFeed);
    tpDataLayer.feedItem selectedFeed =
      (tpDataLayer.feedItem)e.AddedItems[0];
    tpFeed.getFeed(new Uri(selectedFeed.Url, UriKind.RelativeOrAbsolute));
}
```

9. To add support for zoom in or out using the mouse wheel, we need to use the MouseWheel-Helper helper class from the Deep Zoom project that is automatically generated by the Deep Zoom Composer.

Note Remember, when we prepared images for Deep Zoom, in the last Export tab under the Output Type section, you saw the option Export Images and Silverlight Project. This generates a sample Deep Zoom project for displaying images as Deep Zoom images. We reuse the helper class MouseWheelHelper from that project and add it to the tpDataLayer class library project.

10. We need to define the following four variables to enable the Deep Zoom functionality:

```
#region DeepZoom variables
    public bool mouseIsDragging = false;
    public Point dragOffset;
    public Point pLast;
    bool mouseButtonPressed = false;
#endregion
```

The bool mouseIsDragging variable will help to determine whether the user is dragging the mouse over the tpMsi MultiScaleImage control or not. The Point dragOffset will capture the offset from where the drag is started. The Point pLast will store the last location of the tpMsi MultiScaleImage control after the drag is completed. The bool mouseButtonPressed variable will help to determine whether the mouse button is pressed over the tpMsi MultiScaleImage control or not.

11. For the zoom in and out feature of the tpMsi MultiScaleImage control, create the method zoom:

```
public void zoom(double zoom, Point pointToZoom)
{
    if (tpMsi.Visibility == Visibility.Visible)
    {
        Point pz = tpMsi.ElementToLogicalPoint(pointToZoom);
        tpMsi.ZoomAboutLogicalPoint(zoom, pz.X, pz.Y);
    }
}
```

12. In the tpMsi_MouseLeftButtonDown event handler, we will set pLast to tpMsi.ViewportOrigin. The ViewPortOrigin property of the MultiScaleImage control gets or sets the top-left corner of the area of the image to be displayed. We will also capture the drag offset in dragOffset here as shown in the following code snippet:

```
private void tpMsi_MouseLeftButtonDown
   (object sender, MouseButtonEventArgs e)
{
    mouseIsDragging = false;
    mouseButtonPressed = true;
    pLast = tpMsi.ViewportOrigin;
    dragOffset = e.GetPosition(this);
}
```

13. In the tpMsi_MouseMove event handler, we change ViewportOrigin to the new point where the user is dragging the image:

```
private void tpMsi_MouseMove(object sender, MouseEventArgs e)
{
    if (mouseButtonPressed)
        mouseIsDragging = true;

    if (mouseIsDragging)
    {
        Point newOrigin = new Point();
        newOrigin.X = pLast.X - (((e.GetPosition(tpMsi).X - dragOffset.X) /
          tpMsi.ActualWidth) * tpMsi.ViewportWidth);
        newOrigin.Y = pLast.Y - (((e.GetPosition(tpMsi).Y - dragOffset.Y) /
          tpMsi.ActualHeight) * tpMsi.ViewportWidth);
        tpMsi.ViewportOrigin = newOrigin;
    }
}
```

14. For when the user releases the image in the tpMsi control, we code the tpMsi_MouseLeftButtonUp as follows:

```
private void tpMsi_MouseLeftButtonUp
   (object sender, MouseButtonEventArgs e)
{
    mouseButtonPressed = false;
    pLast = e.GetPosition(this.tpMsi);
    double zoomFactor = 1.55;
    if (mouseIsDragging == false)
    {
        zoom(zoomFactor, pLast);
    }
  mouseIsDragging = false;
}
```

15. Create the tpMenu_ItemClicked event handler. We call the tpLayer.getContent method to get the content of the selected category and generate thumbnails in the tpLayer.getContentCompleted event handler.

```
private void tpMenu_itemClicked
  (object sender, SelectionChangedEventArgs e)
{
    //If condition to prevent itemClicked Event
      //raised on menu button click
    if (e.AddedItems.Count != 0)
    {
        fadeIn.Stop();
        fadeIn.SetValue(Storyboard.TargetNameProperty, "thumbBar");
        fadeIn.Begin();
        //Clear previous thumbnails
        thumbBar.Children.Clear();
        tpLayer.getContent(e.AddedItems[0].ToString(),
          tpMenu.selectedMenuId.ToString());
    }
}
```

16. The code for tpLayer_getContentCompleted is as follows. Here, we will dynamically define three event handlers to generate thumbnails instances.

```
void tpLayer_getContentCompleted(object sender,
  TechnologyOpinion.tpDataLayer.appContents[] e)
{
    //Now create thumbnails
    foreach (var item in e)
    {
            thumbnails tn = new thumbnails();
            tn.Name = "Thumb" + idx.ToString();
            tn.titleText = item.Title;
            tn.abstractText = item.Abstract;
            tn.imageUri = item.ImageUri;
            tn.vidUri = item.VidUri;
            tn.titleUri = item.TitleUri;
            //Right margin for spacing between thumbnails
            tn.Margin = new Thickness(0, 0, 8, 0);
            //Assign three event handlers
            tn.onLaunchImage += new
              MouseButtonEventHandler(tn_onLaunchImage);
            tn.onLaunchVideo += new
              MouseButtonEventHandler(tn_onLaunchVideo);
            tn.onThumbnailEnter += new
              MouseEventHandler(tn_onThumbnailEnter);
            //Add to thumbBar stackpanel
            thumbBar.Children.Add(tn);
            //Increment for unique naming
            idx++;
    }
}
```

17. These event handlers will load the appropriate resource in the appropriate container: the
    tn_onThumbnailEnter event handler will set the Title and Abstract text of the tpInfoPanel
    control, the tn_onLaunchVideo event handler will load video into the tpVidStage control, and
    the tn_onLaunchImage event handler will load the Deep Zoom image package into the tpMsi
    control.

```
void tn_onThumbnailEnter(object sender, MouseEventArgs e)
{
    currentStage(tpInfoPanel);
    thumbnails tnRef = (thumbnails)sender;
    Title.Text = tnRef.titleText;
    Abstract.Text = tnRef.abstractText;
}

void tn_onLaunchVideo(object sender, MouseButtonEventArgs e)
{
    currentStage(tpVidStage);
    thumbnails tnRef = (thumbnails)sender;
    this.tpVidStage.setMediaPlayerSource(new
        Uri(tnRef.vidUri, UriKind.RelativeOrAbsolute));
}

void tn_onLaunchImage(object sender, MouseButtonEventArgs e)
{
    currentStage(tpMsi);
    thumbnails tnRef = (thumbnails)sender;
    this.pLast = new Point(0, 0);
    this.tpMsi.ViewportOrigin = new Point(0, 0);
    this.tpMsi.ViewportWidth = 1.0;
    this.tpMsi.Source = new DeepZoomImageTileSource
        (new Uri(tnRef.imageUri, UriKind.RelativeOrAbsolute));
}
```

Centralized Deployment of the Enterprise Training Portal RIA

Now we are all set to deploy the Enterprise Training Portal centrally. We will follow the same steps
that we performed while deploying the My Album RIA (in Chapter 2) on the Microsoft Silverlight
Streaming Server. First, we'll create the deployment XAP package.

Figure 5-44 shows the overall deployment process. It includes the following steps:

1. Zip the XAP package, TrainingPortal.xap, and the two application configuration files,
   tpConfig.xml and tpFeeds.xml. Name the ZIP package TrainingPortal.zip and upload it
   to the Microsoft Silverlight Streaming Server. Refer to Chapter 2 for the required steps to
   deploy Silverlight RIAs on this server.

Note The service-oriented Enterprise Training Portal XAP package is very lightweight (about 300K) compared
to the My Album RIA package (about 1.8MB). Along with being flexible, the Enterprise Training Portal RIA becomes
a high-performing application at startup time.

---

2. Along with `Clientaccesspolicy.xml`, upload the content files to the TechnologyOpinion. com site (or the site from which you plan to deploy the content files) following the folder structure shown in Figure 5-44. The `Clientaccesspolicy.xml` file must be placed at the root level.

3. Update the `TrainingPortal.aspx` page to plug in the deployed training portal using the `iframe` element, as shown in Figure 5-44.

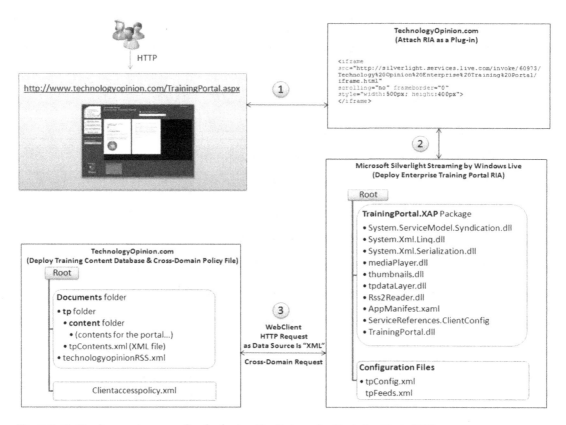

Figure 5-44. *Deployment process for deploying the Enterprise Training Portal RIA*

Use the following link to access the developed Microsoft Silverlight–based Enterprise Training Portal RIA shown in Figure 5-45: `http://technologyopinion.com/TrainingPortal.aspx`.

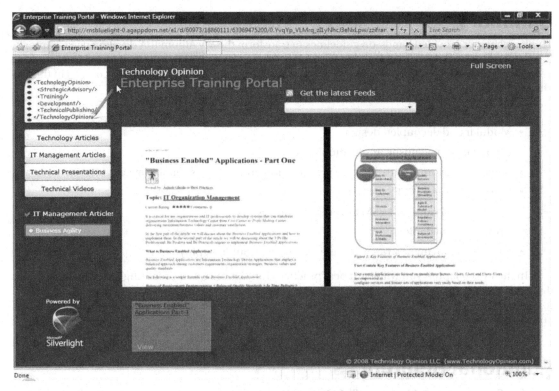

Figure 5-45. *Deployed Enterprise Training Portal RIA on TechnologyOpinion.com*

■**Note** Silverlight RIAs can be deployed centrally and in a distributed mode. You can deploy the same Enterprise Training Portal RIA in distributed mode, enabling distribution of the RIA on CD or DVD or installation on individual machines. There are only two things to remember for our application:

- You must use the local data storage (in this case, XML files) to support operations in disconnected/offline mode.

- You must change every resource in the tpConfig.xml file to use a relative URL instead of the absolute URL.

The distributed RIA does not need to connect to the central server to function. This approach will help enterprises to enable remote users to access RIAs installed in their machine or available on various media.

Summary

This long chapter provided hands-on guidelines to transform the My Album RIA developed in Chapter 2 to an enterprise-level Enterprise Training Portal. You learned how to apply enterprise-level features and capabilities to develop enterprise RIAs using Silverlight. Key features and capabilities covered in this chapter are as follows:

- Service-oriented architecture
- Modular and decoupled design
- Data platform–agnostic application design
- Reusable custom controls for the presentation and business service layers
- Use of LINQ and WCF services
- Use of Deep Zoom and VSM Silverlight features
- Cross-domain deployment
- Flexible deployment strategies: central and distributed deployment

In the next chapter, you will learn best practices for planning and preparing enterprises to deploy Silverlight-based RIAs. It also provides technical details on the key factors for the strategies to deploy Silverlight-based RIAs in the same domain and cross-domain by supporting globalization and localization.

Additional References
Links from the Microsoft Web Site

- Style Class, `http://msdn.microsoft.com/en-us/library/system.windows.style(VS.95).aspx`
- ControlTemplate Class, `http://msdn.microsoft.com/en-us/library/system.windows.controls.controltemplate(VS.95).aspx`
- Customizing the Appearance of an Existing Control by Creating a ControlTemplate, `http://msdn.microsoft.com/en-us/library/cc189093(VS.95).aspx`
- Styling and Skinning Your Objects, `http://silverlight.net/learn/tutorials/StylesTemplatesVSM.aspx`
- VisualStateManager Class, `http://msdn.microsoft.com/en-us/library/system.windows.visualstatemanager(VS.95).aspx`
- Emil Stoychev, "Creating a Silverlight Custom Control—The Basics," `http://www.silverlightshow.net/items/Creating-a-Silverlight-Custom-Control-The-Basics.aspx`
- Carol Snyder, "Different Kinds of Controls You Can Make in Silverlight," `http://blogs.msdn.com/silverlight_sdk/archive/2008/10/31/different-kinds-of-controls-you-can-make-in-silverlight.aspx`
- Expression Blend and Design team blog, "Deep Zoom Composer User Guide," `http://blogs.msdn.com/expression/archive/2008/03/05/deep-zoom-composer-user-guide.aspx`

CHAPTER 6

∎∎∎

Deploying Silverlight Applications

Finally, you have reached the finishing line after getting the application developed and tested successfully, and now you need to deploy it successfully. However, crossing the finishing line to win the game is not an easy job. For that, you need proper planning and preparation way before you get into the game. The deployment phase comes at the end of the software development life cycle (SDLC), but you need to plan and make coordinated efforts to execute the software deployment process from very early on in the project. The main objective of any application deployment process is to provide a secured, scalable, high-performing application execution platform and effective support and maintenance plan that can provide a great end-user experience.

In this book so far, we have developed Silverlight-based RIAs. Now it's time to discuss how to deploy Silverlight RIAs. Earlier, at a high level, I covered a few Silverlight technology deployment features and approaches such as Silverlight deployment package options, cross-domain deployment, how to host applications on the Microsoft Silverlight Streaming by Windows Live platform, and how to integrate Silverlight applications as plug-ins to your existing web sites. This chapter will define the deployment process, Silverlight deployment features, and Silverlight application deployment options/approaches in detail.

Defining the Deployment Process

In this section, we will quickly go through the key elements involved in defining and executing the deployment process for successful RIA development. The deployment process involves four main phases:

- Planning
- Definition
- Implementation
- Support and maintenance

Planning

In the Agile SDLC, the deployment planning phase begins from the day the project starts. Team-work plays a critical role for implementing and deploying SOA-based RIAs. In Chapters 3 and 4, we discussed seven key principles—flexibility, usability, simplification, reusability, scalability, main-tainability, security—and related dimensions of SOA-based RIAs. The planning of the deployment phase should consider and cover all the principles and related dimensions. The following items are covered as part of the deployment planning phase:

- Define key milestones of the deployment phase in alignment with the master project plan.
- Identify critical success factors.
- Identify user groups, user roles, and security policies.
- Analyze the geographical locations of the diversified end-user groups.
- Plan for network impact analysis and stress testing to perform performance analysis and security analysis.
- Plan for required technical and user training.
- Plan for required post-pilot support and system maintenance.
- Identify different risks and issues related to the deployment.

Definition

A deployment plan is a detailed definition of required steps and provides possible options that help to deploy the application successfully, achieving the defined organization strategic vision and deployment objectives. The deployment plan defines the overall deployment strategy, major mile-stones, roles and responsibilities, and budget allocation. The following items are covered as part of the deployment process definition phase and are aligned with the items of the deployment planning phase:

- Define deployment and operational requirements.
- Define the application deployment architecture and approach based on the application sys-tem/infrastructure architecture (physical tiers of the application and hardware definition) and application component and service architecture (logical application and service layers).
- Define the deployment approach based on globalization and localization requirements.
- Define the application installation package.
- Finalize user management policies.
- Define the system resource usage plan.
- Define the approach for performance/stress testing, network impact analysis, and security analysis.
- Define administration and system monitoring and instrumentation policies and approaches.
- Finalize the support model and the technical and end-user training approach, and define required materials.
- Define requirements for pilot to get early feedback on the product (this is an optional step).
- Define the postdeployment user feedback and survey approach.
- Define and monitor the risk and issue mitigation plan.

Implementation

It is important to consider deployment and support requirements during the definition and implementation of the application and system/infrastructure architecture, as well as during the design and development of application components and services. Enterprise architects and the development team need to coordinate efforts with the deployment and support teams to implement a successful deployment and system architecture.

System architects need to define the enterprise RIA deployment model based on the complexity of the application. They need to consider the following items while implementing the application deployment model:

- Platform scalability requirements in terms of number of users, number of concurrent users, performance expectation, data size, data volume, number of transactions, and network latency

- Scope of the customers—internal/external customers (intranet vs. Internet) and types of connectivity

- The organization's long-term vision, product roadmap, and technology roadmap in terms of the future usage of the systems, geographically diversified customers, and identity management

- IT governance rules and regulation policies (such as cross-border data sharing) and security measures

- Same-domain vs. cross-domain deployment

- Backup, archive, data retention, discovery, and disaster recovery requirements

- Application component and application service version management and upgrade policies

- Implementation of instrumentation and reporting requirements for monitoring

Application solution architects need to define application architecture that supports the agreed-upon enterprise RIA deployment model. They need to consider the following items during implementation of the application:

- The seven key principles and related dimensions defined in Chapters 3 and 4

- Globalization and localization feature and capability requirements

- The organization's long-term vision, product roadmap, and technology roadmap in terms of the future usage of the systems, geographically diversified customers, and identity management

- IT governance rules and regulations polices (such as cross-border data sharing) and security measures

- Same-domain vs. cross-domain deployment

- Backup, archive, data retention, and discovery requirements

- Metadata model

- The ability to support different types of client machine, operating system, and browser

- Instrumentation and logging capabilities

- Proper error management to provide user-friendly information upon unavailability of services on both the server side and client slide (e.g., Silverlight is not installed on user's machine)

Deployment, support, administration, and training teams will be performing the following activities during the deployment implementation phase:

- Effective continuous communication and status reporting on the progress of the deployment plan and actual deployment

- Development of required documentation such as user guides, training materials, technical documentation, FAQs, and instruction documents

- Running a pilot to get early user feedback

- Development of required support tools and support processes that help the organization support team to identify, analyze, debug, and isolate a problem and resolve it

- Implementing a support process and rapid action force to provide effective customer support

- Arranging training sessions—train the trainers as well as train the users

Support and Maintenance

Support and maintenance plays a very vital role after the deployment of the application, especially for the agile development model, in which you accommodate changes in your next release based on user feedback.

The following activities are involved in the support and maintenance phase:

- Continuously monitor and review system usage reports and logs to identify potential issues and usage patterns.

- Run post deployment end-user survey and feedback sessions to get productive feedback to improve the system.

- Provide effective customer support (technical and nontechnical) via rapid action force.

- Provide constructive feedback to the architecture and development team on possible improvements of the application and application hardware.

Deploying Silverlight Applications

The remaining sections of this chapter are focused on detailing how to package, test, and deploy Silverlight applications. You'll also see some tips on providing a better user experience by providing effective error management.

Silverlight Deployment Package Definition

Table 6-1 summarizes the mandatory and optional components to run any Silverlight 2 application on the browser successfully.

Table 6-1. *Silverlight Component for Running the Silverlight 2 Application Successfully*

Mandatory/Optional	Silverlight Components	When Is It Installed/Downloaded?
Mandatory	Silverlight core runtime library (such as System.dll, System.core.dll, and so forth)	Installed as Silverlight 2 runtime browser plug-in (not application specific)
	Silverlight main application package (XAP file), including in-package files such as AppManifest.xaml, application assembly, and other optional assemblies and resource files	Downloaded as a startup package when the user accesses the Silverlight application
Optional	Silverlight SDK library files (in-package or on-demand .NET library files such as System.Xml.Linq.dll)	Downloaded at startup (for in-package files) and at runtime when referenced (for on-demand files)
	Application class library assembly files (in-package or on-demand custom class library files developed as part of the Silverlight project)	Downloaded at startup (for in-package files) and at runtime when referenced (for on-demand files)
	Other referenced XAP packages, which are part of a partitioned application	Downloaded at runtime when referenced

Core Runtime Library

Silverlight 2 core runtime library is a set of core .NET Framework library components that are required on the client's machine to run any Silverlight 2 RIA. These components are installed on the client machine as part of the Silverlight 2 runtime installer. As a result, an individual application does not need to include them as part of the startup XAP package file. This helps to reduce the application startup package size and thus improves the application startup performance by reducing the startup download time.

In the "Custom Error Handling for Better User Experience" section of this chapter, we will develop a user-friendly approach to acknowledge that the Silverlight 2 runtime is not installed on the user's machine. We'll recommend to the user that he or she installs it to run Silverlight applications successfully.

Silverlight Application Package (XAP File)

The Silverlight 2 package is automatically generated as part of the project's build process in Visual Studio 2008. As mentioned in Chapter 2, the Silverlight application package is a standard compressed file with the extension .xap that contains all the required application startup files.

Figure 6-1 shows the SmartTabs Silverlight application project profile demonstrating the deployment profile—deployment package file name, application manifest file name, and startup application assembly name with the namespace definition.

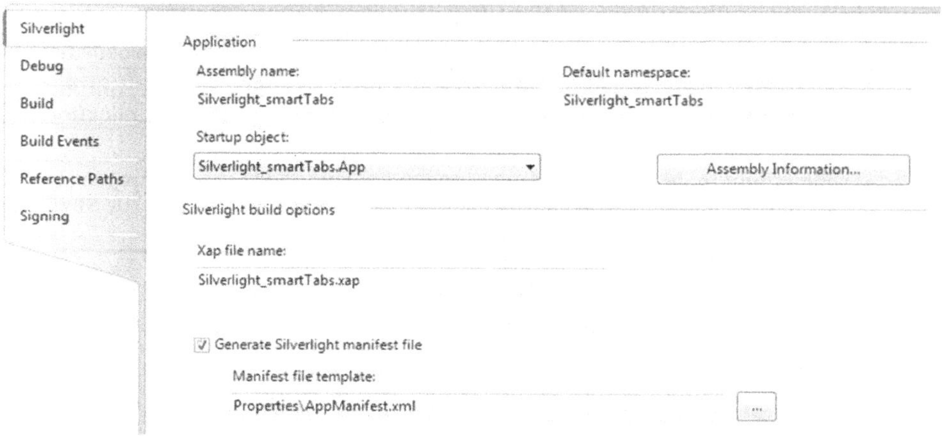

Figure 6-1. *Silverlight SmartTabs project properties window*

Figure 6-2 shows the SmartTabs Silverlight application package file (XAP file), opened as a ZIP file, containing the mandatory files AppManifest.xaml (application manifest file) and Silverlight_ smartTabs.dll (application class assembly), the optional .NET library files System.Windows.Controls. dll and System.Xml.Linq.dll, and the configuration file ServiceReferences.ClientConfig.

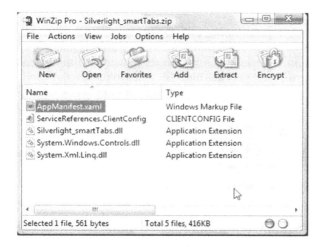

Figure 6-2. *Silverlight SmartTabs application XAP package file*

AppManifest.xaml: Application Manifest File

The application manifest file is an XAML file that Visual Studio creates when it creates the Silverlight project. It mainly includes a list of assembly files that need to be downloaded upon application startup by defining the Deployment object. Figure 6-3 shows the application manifest file of the Silverlight SmartTabs application we developed in Chapter 4.

```
<Deployment xmlns="http://schemas.microsoft.com/client/2007/deployment"
            xmlns:x="http://schemas.microsoft.com/winfx/2006/xaml"
            EntryPointAssembly="Silverlight_smartTabs" EntryPointType="Silverlight_smartTabs.App"
            RuntimeVersion="2.0.31005.0">
  <Deployment.Parts>
    <AssemblyPart x:Name="Silverlight_smartTabs" Source="Silverlight_smartTabs.dll" />
    <AssemblyPart x:Name="System.Windows.Controls" Source="System.Windows.Controls.dll" />
    <AssemblyPart x:Name="System.Xml.Linq" Source="System.Xml.Linq.dll" />
  </Deployment.Parts>
</Deployment>
```

Figure 6-3. *AppManifest.xaml of the SmartTabs application*

As shown in Figure 6-3, the main <Deployment> element contains attributes such as RuntimeVersion, which defines the Silverlight runtime version that is required on the client machine, and EntryPointAssembly and EntryPointType, which point toward the Silverlight application startup assembly.

The <AssemblyPart> element can appear one or more times as a child element of <Deployment. Parts>. Each <AssemblyPart> element includes information about an assembly (with x:Name and Source attributes) that is part of the Silverlight XAP application package. As you can see in Figure 6-3, the first <AssemblyPart> element defines the startup SmartTabs application assembly Silverlight_ smartTabs.dll. The other two optional assemblies, System.Windows.Controls.dll and System.Xml. Linq.dll, are Silverlight SDK component libraries, and for this project they are part of the XAP application package.

Application Startup Assembly File

Once the Silverlight application plug-in is downloaded, the startup application class assembly (Silverlight_smartTabs.dll in our example) containing the Startup event initiates all initialization actions. These initialization actions include displaying the application user interface (driven by the Page class) and other optional application initialization processes, such as retrieving data from a data source and beginning any asynchronous downloads of other on-demand referenced assembly files and resource files.

Optional Files

The XAP file contains the following optional files:

- *Silverlight SDK library files*: These are additional .NET Framework library files, such as System.XML.Linq.dll, that we can package so that they will be downloaded at application startup. Alternatively, they can be downloaded when referenced. Only referenced files from the SDK library are required as part of the package or are downloaded on demand.

- *Application class library assembly files*: These are custom class libraries created to introduce reusability. If you have an application class library assembly file, it can be downloaded upon startup or will be downloaded when referenced.

- *Resource files*: The application may refer to different types of resource files such as images and videos. Usually resource files are large (especially image and video files). You can reference these as on-demand, and they will be downloaded when referenced. You can see in Figure 6-2 earlier that the ServiceReferences.ClientConfig resource file is part of the Smart-Tabs application XAP package file.

- *Additional XAP packages*: In order to support enterprise-level development and maintenance and provide high-performing applications, application partitioning is one way to develop SOA-based RIAs. Using this approach, we can define distributed application modules and deploy them individually. Silverlight enables application partitioning and supports the definition and development of different application modules as separate deployment packages (XAP files) that can be referenced on-demand dynamically. This book does not cover the application partitioning feature in detail. A good article on the subject is contained in Hanu Kommalapati's blog at http://blogs.msdn.com/hanuk/archive/2008/05/19/silverlight-for-the-enterprises-application-partitioning.aspx.

In-Package and On-Demand Files

By now it should be crystal clear that RIAs are usually media-rich applications, and that it is important to consider different options during application and deployment design to improve overall application performance, stability, and security. Silverlight supports the in-package and on-demand file deployment options to balance initial startup performance and rich media functionality.

At minimum, AppManifest.xaml, the application class, and other library assemblies and resource files that are required when initializing the application must be part of the Silverlight XAP file. These are called *in-package files*. The package needs to be uploaded on the hosting server.

All other remaining files are optional, and the design team has to decide whether to keep them as part of the application package as in-package files or deploy them on the application hosting server. These files are *on-demand files* and will be downloaded to the client machine when referenced by the application at runtime. The on-demand files can be downloaded with a direct URI reference or using the asynchronous download feature.

At design time, you can control the assembly file (.NET library file or custom class library file) deployment behavior—in-package or on-demand—by setting the Copy Local property of each assembly. If the property value is set to True, the assembly will be part of the XAP deployment package as an in-package file and will be defined in the AppManifest.xaml file. Upon setting it to False, you need to deploy it to the hosting server, and it will be downloaded at runtime asynchronously or when referenced. Figure 6-4 demonstrates the Copy Local property for the System.XML.Linq assembly.

Figure 6-4. *Defining in-package/on-demand behavior using the Copy Local property of the assembly file*

At design time, you can control the deployment behavior—in-package or on-demand—of resource files (such as image files, video files, and text files) by setting the Build Action property of each resource file. The Build Action property defines how the added file relates to the build and deployment processes. It is an extensible property, and additional options can be added very easily. For Silverlight projects, three Build Action options—None, Resource, and Content—are mainly used. Figure 6-5 shows possible Build Action property values of the 01.jpg image file.

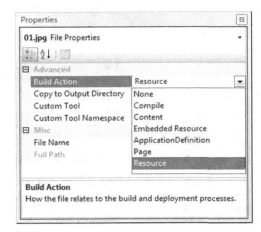

Figure 6-5. *Setting the Build Action property of a resource file*

If the property value is set to None, the resource file will not be part of the XAP deployment package or part of the main application assembly. The file will be deployed as an on-demand file on the hosting server. If the property value is set to Resource, during the application project build process the resource file will be embedded in the assembly file. If the property value is set to Content, the resource file is part of the XAP file and can be referenced by multiple assemblies of the project.

Hosting Silverlight Applications

If planned and designed properly, deploying Silverlight 2 applications in a secured enterprise environment is very straightforward compared to deploying Silverlight 1 applications. As shown in Figure 6-6, to deploy and consume a Silverlight 2 application successfully, you need to follow these steps on the server and client side:

- *Server side*:
  1. Deploy the Silverlight application package (XAP file).
  2. Deploy additional resource files (video files, image files, other files, assembly files).
  3. Deploy additional services (with required cross-domain policy files).
  4. Deploy required database (with required cross-domain policy files).
  5. Add the Silverlight plug-in or reference the deployed Silverlight application in your ASP.NET or HTML web page.

- *Client side*:

    1. Install the Silverlight 2 runtime.

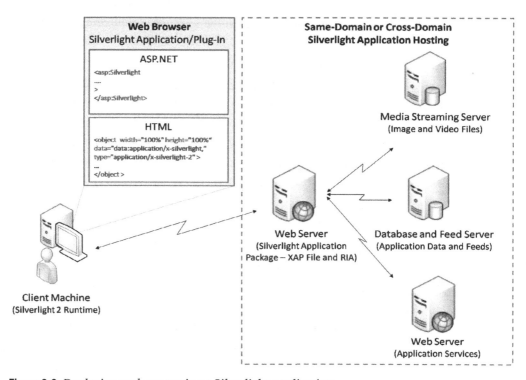

Figure 6-6. *Deploying and consuming a Silverlight application*

Server-Side Silverlight RIA Deployment

At minimum, you need to host the Silverlight XAP file on the web server. In more complex scenarios, you may have additional resource files, assembly files, databases, and web services to be deployed in the same-domain or cross-domain environment.

The simplest deployment option is to manually copy the deployment package and related resource files to the web server under the `ClientBin` directory.

Setting the IIS MIME Type

If you are using IIS 6 or earlier on the web server, you need to add the MIME type related to the Silverlight application deployment package XAP file type. You can right-click the IIS manager to open the Properties window. Click the MIME Type button to add a new MIME type for the file type XAP with the MIME type `application/x-silverlight-app`.

■**Note** If you are using IIS 7, the XAP Silverlight package file type is already related to the `application/x-silverlight-app` MIME type. No additional steps are required.

Same-Domain and Cross-Domain Deployment

It is critical to consider different security aspects as part of your deployment strategy. RIAs and social networking are dynamic in nature and need to access different services and data across domains, which exposes you to possible computer security vulnerability such as *cross-site scripting* (XSS) and *cross-site request forgery* (CSRF or XSRF).

XSS is a type of vulnerability where, with the help of client-side scripting of web applications, hackers can gather sensitive user data by accessing stored cookies and session information.

CSRF exploits trusted web sites or services, where hackers can perform unauthorized actions to get data and information from the trusted web sites and services by gaining unauthorized control on the logged-in user's web application session. The CSRF threat enables malicious access to web-based controls of the application and executing unauthorized commands to cross-domain applications and services.

As mentioned on Wikipedia:[1]

Cross-site scripting exploits the trust a user has for a particular site [whereas] cross-site request forgery exploits the trust that a site has for a particular user.

Note Get more information on XSS by visiting `http://en.wikipedia.org/wiki/Cross-site_scripting` and CSRF by visiting `http://en.wikipedia.org/wiki/Cross-site_request_forgery`.

To provide a secured environment that prevents CSRF threats, Silverlight supports same-domain and policy-based cross-domain networking to deploy Silverlight-based enterprise RIAs. Except for images and media, Silverlight allows only site-of-origin (i.e., within the same domain) communication to prevent cross-site request forgery vulnerabilities such as a malicious Silverlight control performing unauthorized actions to cross-domain applications and services. Here the term "same domain" covers the domain name, protocol, and port. As a result, the following scenarios are considered to be cross-domain deployment:

- Same protocol and domain name but different ports—as an example, `http://www.technologyopinion.com` and `http://www.technologyopinion.com:81`

- Same domain name and port but different protocol—as an example, `http://www.technologyopinion.com` and `https://www.technologyopinion.com`

- Same port and protocol but different domain names—as an example, `http://www.technologyopinon.com` and `http://www.apress.com`

Application services must explicitly opt in, detailing the scope of the cross-domain service access by a Silverlight application from all or specific domains by publishing policy files.

Silverlight enables cross-domain integration by providing two types of declaration policy method:

- `crossdomain.xml` policy file
- `clientaccesspolicy.xml` policy file

---

1. Wikipedia, `http://en.wikipedia.org/wiki/Cross-site_scripting`

The crossdomain.xml Policy File

This approach is very similar to the Adobe Flash policy. Silverlight supports a subset of the crossdomain.xml schema developed by Macromedia (now owned by Adobe). The following is a sample snapshot of the crossdomain.xml file:

```
<?xml version="1.0"?>
<!DOCTYPE cross-domain-policy
    SYSTEM "http://www.macromedia.com/xml/dtds/cross-domain-policy.dtd">
<cross-domain-policy>
  <allow-http-request-headers-from domain="*" headers="*"/>
</cross-domain-policy>
```

This policy file must be copied to the root of the domain where the service is hosted. As an example, if the service is hosted at http://servicesfortechnologyopinion.com, the crossdomain.xml policy file must be available at http://servicesfortechnologyopinion.com/crossdomain.xml. By deploying this file at the host service location, the service is publically available and can be accessed by any application from any other domain.

However, the following are two disadvantages of using crossdomain.xml as the security policy file to enable cross-domain access:

- For Silverlight, you must use the "*" value for the domain attribute and thus allow access to all external domains (<allow-http-request-headers-from domain="*" headers="*"/>). If you would like to enable access to only specific domain(s), say, only to the technologyopinion.com domain, you cannot achieve this using the crossdomain.xml policy file. Here the headers attribute is an optional attribute.

- With the use of this method, you can decide who has access (in Silverlight's case, it is all external domains). You do not have capabilities to specify what can be accessed.

The clientaccesspolicy.xml Policy File

Use of the clientaccesspolicy.xml as a security policy file is a Silverlight-specific approach. Its detailed schema supports a more selective and controlled approach, overcoming the disadvantages discussed for the crossdomain.xml file.

The following is a sample snapshot of the clientaccesspolicy.xml file:

```
<?xml version="1.0" encoding="utf-8"?>
<access-policy>
  <cross-domain-access>
    <policy>
      <allow-from http-request-headers="*">
        <domain uri="http://technologyopinion.com"/>
      </allow-from>
      <grant-to>
        <resource path="/servicesforTO/" include-subpaths="true"/>
      </grant-to>
    </policy>
  </cross-domain-access>
</access-policy>
```

This policy file must be copied to the root of the domain where the service is hosted. As an example, if the service is hosted at http://servicesfortechnolgoyopinion.com, the clientaccesspolicy.xml policy file must be available at http://servicesfortechnologyopinion.com/clientaccesspolicy.xml. By deploying this file at the host service location, the following rules are set:

- The service can be accessed only from the technologyopinion.com domain. We achieve this by setting the uri attribute of the <domain> element to http://technologyopinion.com. If you set it to the wildcard *, the services will be accessible from any cross-domain application.

- Only resources that are located at /servicesforTO/ can be accessed. We achieve this restriction by setting the path attribute of the <resource> element to /servicesforTO/. The default value is /, which enables full access.

Using the Policy Files

When a Silverlight application web client identifies the requirement to access the cross-domain service, it will first look at the existence of the clientaccesspolicy.xml file at the root of the deployed service. If it exists, it will authorize against the policy file and upon successful authorization can access and utilize the cross-domain deployed service. If the clientaccesspolicy.xml file does not exist at the root of the service's domain, next it will look for the crossdomain.xml file and authorize against it to gain access.

In this book, we use the clientaccesspolicy.xml policy file to enable cross-domain communication.

Embedding Silverlight Plug-ins into the Web Page

In the previous section, we looked at the Silverlight application security settings. Now it's time to embed the Silverlight application plug-in into your web page. Enterprises can embed the Silverlight plug-ins into web applications using the following three options:

- ASP.NET Silverlight server control

- HTML <object> element

- Silverlight.js JavaScript helper file

Upon creating a Silverlight 2 application project using Visual Studio 2008 SP1, if the user selects "Add a new ASP.NET Web project to the solution to host Silverlight" as the hosting platform option, a separate ASP.NET web site project with two additional test web pages (.aspx and .html) are added to host the Silverlight application/user control. The naming convention of these test pages is based on the Silverlight application name—<Name of the Silverlight Application>TestPage.aspx for the ASPX file and <Name of the Silverlight Application>TestPage.html for the HTML file.

ASP.NET Silverlight Server Control

The Silverlight 2 SDK installed along with the Microsoft Silverlight Tools for Visual Studio 2008 SP1 includes the Silverlight server control to host Silverlight plug-ins. The following code snippet demonstrates this control, added in the myAlbumTestPage.aspx file to host the My Album Silverlight application developed in Chapter 2:

```
<form id="form1" runat="server" style="height:100%;">
    <asp:ScriptManager ID="ScriptManager1" runat="server"></asp:ScriptManager>
    <div  style="height:100%;">
        <asp:Silverlight
            ID="Xaml1"
            runat="server"
            Source="~/ClientBin/myAlbum.xap"
            MinimumVersion="2.0.31005.0"
            Width="100%"
            Height="100%" />
    </div>
</form>
```

As shown in this code snippet, in addition to common attributes, the Silverlight control has a Source attribute containing the location of the Silverlight application XAP file (in this example, it is ~/ClientBin/myAlbum.xap) and a MinimumVersion attribute, which defines the minimum Silverlight runtime version that is required on the client machine to run the Silverlight application successfully.

HTML <object> Element

The HTML <object> element enables us to embed the Silverlight plug-in into the HTML web page. The following code snippet demonstrates the Silverlight control added in the myAlbumTestPage.html file to host the My Album Silverlight application developed in Chapter 2:

```
<object data="data:application/x-silverlight-2,"
        type="application/x-silverlight-2"
        width="100%"
        height="100%">
  <param name="source" value="ClientBin/myAlbum.xap"/>
  <param name="minRuntimeVersion" value="2.0.31005.0" />
</object>
```

As shown in this code snippet, you need to define attributes of the <object> element in order to run the Silverlight plug-in in all browsers with optimal performance.

- The data attribute is required for some browsers to avoid performance issues. The value ends with a comma, which indicates that the second parameter is an empty value.

- The type attribute defines the MIME type of Silverlight to allow the browser to identify the plug-in and the required Silverlight version.

- The width and height attributes are required (with fixed pixel values or with relative percentages) to run across different types of browsers properly.

A <param> child element with its name attribute set to source is required. The value attribute of this element contains the location of the Silverlight XAP file (in this example, it is ClientBin/myAlbum.xap).

The <param> child element with the name attribute set to minRuntimeVersion defines the minimum Silverlight runtime version that is required on the client machine to run the Silverlight plug-in successfully. Set the Silverlight version number as a value of the value attribute of this element.

Silverlight.js JavaScript Helper File

You can use the Silverlight.js JavaScript helper file and use the createObject and createObjectEx functions defined in this file to embed the Silverlight plug-in in a web page. This approach would be useful if there is a need to have multiple plug-in instances in a single web page by specifying a unique identifier for each embedded Silverlight plug-in.

However, it is recommended you use the ASP.NET Silverlight server control or HTML <object> element approach to integrate enterprise SOA-based Silverlight 2 plug-ins in your web pages. This book will not cover this approach in detail. A reference to the Microsoft MSDN site where you can get more details on this subject is provided in the "Additional References" section.

Custom Error Handling for Better User Experience

Clients' machines must have the Silverlight runtime installed in order to run Silverlight plug-ins successfully. However, it is very likely that a user's machine may not have Silverlight installed. In this scenario, instead of providing the default Microsoft message to install Silverlight, it would be friendlier if we provided a branded explanatory message and a link to the Silverlight runtime installer to make the user's machine Silverlight application compatible.

Both recommended Silverlight plug-in integration approaches—the ASP.NET `Silverlight` server control and the HTML `<object>` element—support custom error handling if the Silverlight runtime is not installed on a user's machine. This section describes how to implement custom error management for Silverlight 2 RIAs.

ASP.NET Silverlight Server Control Error Management

The ASP.NET `Silverlight` server control exposes the `PluginNotInstalledTemplate` object that we can use to provide a custom branded error handling message when the selected Silverlight version (defined by the `MinimumVersion` attribute of the `Silverlight` control) is not installed on the user's machine. The `PluginNotInstalledTemplate` object contains the HTML content to display the custom message. The following code snippet demonstrates the use of the `PluginNotInstalledTemplate` object:

```
<form id="form1" runat="server" style="height:100%;">
    <asp:ScriptManager ID="ScriptManager1" runat="server"></asp:ScriptManager>
    <div  style="height:100%;">
        <asp:Silverlight
            ID="Xaml1"
            runat="server"
            Source="~/ClientBin/myAlbum.xap"
            MinimumVersion="2.0.31005.0"
            Width="100%"
            Height="100%">

            <PluginNotInstalledTemplate>
                <div>
                        Write HTML markup to render in the browser providing
                            custom enterprise branded message with
                            Silverlight installation link
                </div>
            </PluginNotInstalledTemplate>

        </asp:Silverlight>

    </div>
</form>
```

HTML <object> Element Error Management

You need to add the HTML markup representing the branded message with its Silverlight installation link after all `<param>` child elements of the HTML `<object>` element. If the required version of Silverlight is not installed on the user's machine, the custom message will be displayed; otherwise, the message will be skipped.

The following code snippet demonstrates the custom error handling for Silverlight when the HTML `<object>` element is used to embed the Silverlight plug-in:

```
<object data="data:application/x-silverlight-2,"
        type="application/x-silverlight-2"
        width="100%"
        height="100%">

  <param name="source" value="ClientBin/myAlbum.xap"/>
  <param name="minRuntimeVersion" value="2.0.31005.0" />

  <div>
```

```
      Write HTML markup to render in the browser providing
      custom enterprise branded message with Silverlight installation link
   </div>
</object>
```

Silverlight Applications Supporting Globalization and Localization

Implementation of globalization and localization plays a critical role in the success of Web 2.0 RIAs supporting Enterprise 2.0. Enterprises must consider the globalization factor in the design and implementation of Silverlight-based RIAs. During the deployment, enterprises must consider the localization factor and support application localization requirements in their deployed Silverlight RIAs.

What Is Globalization?

Globalization is defined as the following:[2]

> *Globalization (or **globalisation**) in its literal sense is the process of transformation of local or regional phenomena into global ones.*

Any global application must support requirements of global and diversified user groups with different culture and requirements. At a minimum, global applications should be designed and developed to support the requirements of local culture-based language, numbers, currency, and date formats. With these requirements in mind, we can define globalization for RIAs as follows:

> *Globalization is the application design and development process that incorporates local culture-specific requirements such as local language support in the user interface design and support for local numbers, currency, and date formats in the data representation.*

The key enterprise-level design concept behind globalization is to implement externalization. The localized information should not be part of the core application component; rather, it should be externalized, and at runtime, based on the user's locale information, the localized resources should be retrieved.

Silverlight 2 is based on the .NET Framework 3.5 and thus supports globalization features using traditional .NET Framework techniques. We can use the CultureInfo class of the System. Globalization namespace to retrieve information about the specific culture. The CultureInfo class provides culture-specific information such as languageCode-regionCode (e.g., en-US for English language and US region), character set, currency symbol, and number and date (calendar) format.

What Is Localization?

Localization is defined as the following:[3]

> *Localization is the process of adapting software for a specific region or language by adding locale-specific components and translating text.*

---

2. Wikipedia, http://en.wikipedia.org/wiki/Globalization
3. Wikipedia, http://en.wikipedia.org/wiki/Internationalization_and_localization

Based on the design concepts implemented as part of the globalization process, localization is the physical process of implementing culture-specific language requirements, which mainly involves the process of translating text and images into the local language to provide a localized presentation layer. For Silverlight applications, one of the standard ways of implementing localization is to develop culture- or locale-specific resource files, including translated text and images.

Hub-and-Spoke Model

The .NET Framework uses satellite assemblies to package and deploy resources and uses the traditional hub-and-spoke model to locate the appropriate resources in those satellite assemblies at runtime based on the user's locale-specific culture information. The hub is the main application assembly containing the application executable and the neutral culture or default culture. The neutral or default culture assembly refers to only the default language (e.g., en for English) and is not associated with any region (e.g., US or UK).

Each satellite assembly is a spoke and contains resources for one specific culture. This concept also allows enterprises to deploy additional culture-specific satellite assemblies even after they have deployed the Silverlight application without recompiling and redeploying the whole application.

As mentioned earlier, with the hub-and-spoke model concept, the .NET Framework resource manager follows a structured pattern to load the proper resource file based on the client locale and deployed satellite assemblies for that application. Figure 6-7 demonstrates the structured execution path of the resource manager to identify and load the appropriate resource file.

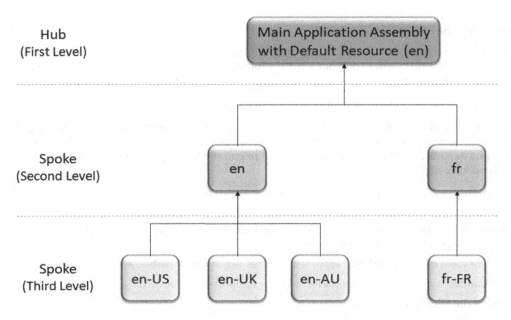

Figure 6-7. *The .NET Framework resource manager follows the hub-and-spoke model to identify and load the appropriate satellite assembly.*

As shown in Figure 6-7, if we start from top to bottom, the first level is the hub, which is a main application assembly containing the neutral/default culture resource assembly (in this example, the default resource assembly is for the English language—en). The spoke is the next two levels. The second level contains one or more neutral language-specific resource assemblies and no region (similar to the hub resource assembly file). In this example, the second level contains neutral resource assemblies for English (en) and French (fr). The third level, which contains the culture-specific assemblies, would have resources associated with the language and region. In this example, for the English language, we have assemblies specific to the US region (en-US), UK region (en-UK), and Australia region (en-AU), and for the French language we have assemblies specific to the France region (fr-FR).

The resource management execution model follows the bottom-up approach. Based on the retrieved culture information of the client, it will start to find the appropriate satellite assembly starting from culture specific (third level) to neutral language specific (second level) to the default assembly (first level) and loads the appropriate resources. If no specific match is found, it will load the default resources. Following are three examples to help you understand the concept:

- For the local culture specific to the English language (en) and US region (US), in this example the resource manager will identify and load the culture-specific satellite assembly (third level–en-US).

- For the local culture specific to the French language (fr) and Canada region (CA), in this example, the resource manager will identify and load the neutral French language–specific satellite assembly (second level—fr), since the application does not have any French language and Canada region–specific satellite assembly available.

- For the local culture specific to the German language (de) and Germany region (DE), in this example, the resource manager will identify and load the default resource assembly (first level—en), since the application does not have any German culture-specific satellite assembly available.

Deploying Global Silverlight Applications

At a minimum, to enable multiple cultures for your Silverlight project, you need to first add proper resource files (default and culture specific) to your project. Second, in the AssemblyInfo.cs file, define the neutral/default culture:

```
[assembly: NeutralResourcesLanguage("en")]
```

Here we have defined English (en) as the default culture. Now you need to unload the Silverlight project and edit the project properties to define supported cultures by adding a SupportedCultures tag and comma-separated cultures. After that, you can reload the Silverlight project again. You can achieve this by following these steps:

1. Right-click the Silverlight project and select the Unload Project option. The project is unloaded.

2. Right-click the unloaded project and select the Edit <Projectname> option. You will see the project file properties in editable mode.

3. Under PropertyGroup, find the SupportedCultures tag. If not available, add it.

4. Add comma-separated cultures that need to be supported by the Silverlight project.

5. Reload the Silverlight project.

Now you are all set to deploy the Silverlight application as a global application supporting different cultures. Upon compiling the project, the default culture becomes part of the main application assembly. The main application assembly with the default resources and other added satellite assemblies will be inserted into the Silverlight XAP file. Each satellite assembly is defined under the `Deployment.Parts` section of the `AppManifest.xml` file.

The main disadvantage of this approach is that all satellite assembly files are part of the default Silverlight XAP file and thus will be downloaded at startup. A Silverlight application with many defined cultures will increase the XAP package file size and thus degrade the application startup performance.

Silverlight also allows us to develop a localized, culture-specific application package for each culture. This approach will reduce the XAP package size and thus improve the application's startup performance. The Visual Studio Configuration Manager is used to define and create localized application packages. This book does not provide details on how to create localized packages. If you are interested in getting more details on this subject, a reference to the Microsoft MSDN site is provided in the "Additional References" section.

Summary

In this chapter, you learned that it is important to coordinate efforts among the system architects, application architects, development groups, deployment groups, and support groups from the very initial phase of the project for smooth deployment. If planned, designed, and implemented properly, it is straightforward to deploy enterprise-level Silverlight RIAs. Enterprises need to consider the following strategic items during the design, implementation, and deployment processes to deploy enterprise-level Silverlight RIAs in a secured, scalable, high-performing, and supportable environment:

- Define and analyze additional components (Silverlight SDK assemblies, custom class libraries, and resource files) and make a strategic decision to define in-package and on-demand files. A balanced decision considering application needs and startup download package size will help to optimize application performance and user experience.

- Hosting of Silverlight applications and related application services must align with your organization vision. Aligning with the organization infrastructure landscape, implement a proper encrypted and secured communication channel with the required bandwidth for information exchange, media streaming, and business process integration. Based on the definition of the system architecture, define required cross-domain policies for successful Silverlight application deployment.

- Keep in mind this well-known phrase when deploying—"Think global and act local." For any enterprise, Silverlight-based RIAs must be global applications facilitating diversified local culture-specific needs at least in terms of local language support and local number, currency, and date formats. Silverlight supports localization with a standard .NET Framework's satellite assembly approach. Proper definition of the language and region-specific culture resource files and localized deployment strategy will enable effective localization of Silverlight RIAs.

In the next chapter, you will learn basics of and key architecture considerations for the development of mobile applications and explore future capabilities of the Silverlight platform in this area of development.

Additional References

Links from the Microsoft Web Site

- MSBuild Team Blog, "How to: Add a Custom Build Action to Visual Studio," `http://blogs.msdn.com/msbuild/archive/2005/10/06/477064.aspx`

- Visual Studio Integration (MSBuild), `http://msdn.microsoft.com/en-us/library/ms171468.aspx`

- Making a Service Available Across Domain Boundaries, `http://msdn.microsoft.com/en-us/library/cc197955(VS.95).aspx`

- How to: Add Silverlight to a Web Page by Using JavaScript, `http://msdn.microsoft.com/en-us/library/cc265155(VS.95).aspx`, 2008

- Localizing Silverlight Applications, `http://msdn.microsoft.com/en-us/library/cc838238(VS.95).aspx`

PART 3

Silverlight for Mobile

■ ■ ■
Mobile Applications and Silverlight

Globalization, advancement in the wireless technology infrastructure, and increased market competition have forced enterprises to break the physical boundaries of the organization and implement the concept of the *virtual organization*. Enterprise mobility is a strategic component of virtualized global organizations. Even though Microsoft hasn't released Silverlight for Mobile yet, I cannot end this book on the development of enterprise RIAs without discussing the following:

- The role of mobile applications in Enterprise 2.0

- Basic concepts and architecture components for mobile applications in general

- The latest updates on Silverlight for Mobile and potential capabilities of Silverlight to develop RIAs for the mobile platform

This chapter starts with an overview of enterprise mobility and its key components to understand the role of mobile applications in Enterprise 2.0. Later the chapter will focus on the development of mobile applications by covering the basics of developing enterprise-level mobile applications, main architecture components, key design considerations, and different data synchronization models for mobile applications. Microsoft Silverlight could become a key strategic technology component to implement enterprise mobility. I will end the chapter by covering potential capabilities of Silverlight for developing mobile applications.

■**Note** When I started writing this book, it seemed pretty certain that Microsoft was going to release the first preliminary version of Silverlight for Mobile—Silverlight 1 for Mobile—which in the end remained a private release. Microsoft is now focused on releasing Silverlight 2 for Mobile sometime in 2009, so at the time of writing, there is no product to work with.

Enterprise Mobility for Enterprise 2.0

We can define enterprise mobility as the following:

> *Enterprise mobility* represents the ability of organizations to transform from a traditional organization to a virtual organization. Enterprise mobility enables globally distributed and diversified interorganization and intraorganization teams to access, collaborate on, and process information and execute different business processes utilizing wireless satellite networking–based information systems and services.

Innovation and calculated risks toward implementing enterprise mobility will help organizations to remain strategically ahead in the market. Enterprise mobility will improve the overall productivity, customer satisfaction, and ROI of the virtual organization. System and application virtualization, virtual meeting space, and mobile applications supporting online/offline mode are key components of enterprise mobility and thus virtual organizations.

System and Application Virtualization

System virtualization and application virtualization are two key buzz words for Enterprise 2.0, and they introduce modularity, mobility, scalability, and maintainability in the development and deployment of applications and services.

System virtualization provides system-level virtualization (including the operating system), while application virtualization decouples application installation and execution from the core operating system. Microsoft (http://www.microsoft.com/systemcenter/appv/default.mspx), VMware (http://www.vmware.com/), and Citrix (http://www.citrix.com) are a few of the leading providers of different product suites for enabling system and application virtualization.

Virtual Meeting Space

Meetings are essential to build consensus and make strategic decisions to achieve organizations' objectives. Face-to-face meetings are more effective and efficient, which is a challenge for virtual organizations since team members are located at different locations and working in different time zones across the world. The virtual meeting space is an innovative approach to overcoming this problem.

The virtual meeting space concept started with teleconferences. Teleconferencing allows voice collaboration over the telephone. Next, computer desktop sharing enabled team members at dispersed locations to share applications, documents, and presentations over a network. Microsoft SharedView (http://connect.microsoft.com/site/sitehome.aspx?SiteID=94) and Cisco WebEx (http://www.webex.com/) are a couple examples of desktop collaboration tools.

The next natural progression is video conferencing, whereby you can collaborate using audio and video across the network, enabling virtual meetings. Recent advancement in wireless technology has enabled full-featured video collaboration studios to provide real-time face-to-face meetings among virtually located teams. HP Halo (http://www.hp.com/halo) is a great example of creating an advanced virtual meeting space for effective audio and video collaboration.

Mobile Applications

Mobile applications are a prerequisite for any organization supporting a globally distributed community. Mobile application development and infrastructure setup is one of the strategic directions for any organization. Initially, organizations started with very basic mobile applications that provided functionality such as maintaining tasks and organizing an address book for mobile devices. Later, the scope expanded to e-mail management on mobile devices. Research In Motion (http://www.blackberry.com/) dominates the market by providing efficient e-mail management on its BlackBerry devices.

The Apple iPhone (http://www.apple.com/iphone/) has ushered in the second generation of mobile devices. Along with advanced mobile devices, a second-generation mobile technology platform such as Silverlight will help to bring revolutionary changes in the mobile market. Organizations will be able to develop RIAs and smart client applications for mobile devices, virtually connecting team members effectively and increasing overall productivity. The advanced mobile applications will ultimately help organizations to achieve increased ROI by providing effective enterprise mobility.

Basics of Mobile Applications

Mobile applications are unique in nature in terms of usage scenarios and required technology capabilities:

- From a usability and requirements point of view, users need access to an organization's systems to perform different types of operations while they are on the move. While connected (online), users expect to be able to carry out a wide range of operations mainly related to accessing and processing different types of information available in different formats and perform data validation and transactions to execute business processes. While disconnected (offline), users would prefer to have access to critical information (locally cached) and perform a limited set of critical operations that later can be synchronized with the main system while they are connected to the network.

- From a technology prospective, mobile devices are usually portable and lightweight with very limited technical capabilities in terms of processing power, available processing and storage memory, browser capabilities, bandwidth availability, and continuous connectivity (signal strength). Compared to desktops and laptops, mobile devices have a much smaller screen size (with different sizes for different types of mobile devices) and lower resolution. In addition, mobile devices have extra capabilities such as voice integration and messaging features that can be utilized to develop simplified, yet effective mobile applications.

In Chapters 3 and 4 we discussed the seven key principles—usability, flexibility, simplicity, reusability, scalability, maintainability, and security—for developing, deploying, and distributing SOA-based, loosely coupled, collaborative RIAs. The question is, can we develop SOA-based mobile applications and apply the same principles to develop, deploy, and distribute them?

The answer: mobile applications can be SOA-based RIAs following the seven key principles. You can use the same design concepts, technology, and development tools for desktop, web, and mobile application development. However, the requirements and environment for mobile applications are different from those for desktop and web applications. The ideal approach would be to use a device-agnostic common application framework and develop loosely coupled components and services to support different requirements for different flavors (mobile, web, and desktop versions) of the same application rather than creating separate applications.

Now let's take a look at the basics of mobile applications in terms of the seven key principles that can help to achieve the previously mentioned application implementation goals.

Usability and Simplicity

You should consider the three dimensions—effectiveness, efficiency, and satisfaction—of usability (discussed in Chapter 4) during the requirements analysis, technology selection, architecting/designing, and implementation of mobile applications to provide maximum customer satisfaction.

User Interface Design Challenges

During mobile application user interface design, you need to consider key questions such as "Can I get to it?", "Can I figure it out?", "Is it fast enough?", "Does it have what I want?", and "Are my identity and information secured?". These are related to the three dimensions of usability. Getting answers to these types of questions will play a key role in terms of screen design due to some unique challenges we face during mobile application design and implementation.

During the user interface design process for mobile applications, designers should consider and accommodate the following unique characteristics of mobile devices:

- Mobile screens are much smaller in size with less screen resolution compared to regular desktop/laptop screens.

- There are no consistent standards on mobile screen size and screen resolution; you will find a variety of screen sizes and screen resolutions across different mobile devices.

- Many mobile devices come with touch screen capability. As a result, mobile applications should support mobile devices with and without touch screen capabilities.

- Both portrait and landscape mobile screens need to be supported.

- Keyboards of mobile devices are not consistent and much smaller in size than conventional keyboards.

Along with these unique characteristics, the usage of mobile devices is also unique. Mobile devices are usually used to remain connected while you are away from your office or home and do not have easy access to your regular computer system. You need to access only key information (data and documents) to maintain your awareness and perform only critical but simplified operations to void your absence. You do not need to access all your information nor perform all your regular operations while you are away from the workplace.

To support the preceding considerations and features, you need to define a lightweight, simplified user interface that can provide a high-performing experience with the limited operating resources, memory resources, and bandwidth of mobile devices.

Flexibility and Reusability

As discussed in Chapter 4, flexible applications have three main characteristics—they are platform independent, loosely coupled and customizable, and have support for agility. These cover most of the criteria that make an SOA-based application.

It is important to perform a thorough analysis of users' expectations, requirements, business processes, and security requirements to identify common patterns and functionalities. With the use of an advanced technology platform such as Silverlight, you can capitalize on the identified common patterns. The common patterns help you implement modular and abstracted components, lightweight and decoupled application services, and a set of templates and standards as a part of the core framework. This will give you a flexible and reusable development platform across mobile and desktop RIAs.

Different mobile devices also have different flavors of browsers with different capabilities. You should consider and analyze mobile browser capabilities for the mobile devices your application needs to support. Based on the browser capabilities, you should design the presentation layer and services integration.

Scalability and Maintainability

High scalability and reliability of enterprise wireless networking are critical success factors for supporting enterprise mobility. Wireless network behavior is different from traditional wired network behavior, and you have different types of challenges to support. In addition to the three key dimensions of the scalability—volume, software, and hardware—discussed in Chapter 4, for enterprise mobility you also need to consider the *carrier* as the fourth dimension.

Enterprises need to implement a scalable environment that can provide maximum wireless signal strength at every location, which is called *carrier scalability*, to provide high-performing mobile application services. The enterprise needs to consider these four dimensions to support low-profile mobile devices, remote locations, and a high volume of mobile users.

A highly scalable and high-quality software and infrastructure environment will improve the overall reliability of mobile applications with high performance and high accessibility at any location. Increased reliability helps to improve overall supportability and thus maintainability of mobile applications. Enterprises should also consider continuous monitoring and proper instrumentation of mobile applications to predict future usage, future problems, and future end users' needs. Thus the monitoring dimension helps organizations to maintain and improve the quality of their products.

Mobile Device Management (MDM) tools installed on mobile devices help enterprise administrators to maintain and monitor those devices, as well as to manage the software and distribution of upgrades across different types of mobile devices. MDM tools also aid in reporting errors from mobile devices to a centralized location, thereby helping to improve overall fault management.

Security

Enterprises need to implement challenging but feasible enterprise mobility security policies. These policies need to align with enterprise IT security policies to implement mobile device security, information security during data transmission, and enterprise network security. You can implement five dimensions—information security, identity management, software security, infrastructure security, and regulatory compliance—of IT security (discussed in Chapter 4) to facilitate enterprise mobility in a secured environment.

Use of MDM tools, password protection, virus protection, lost device protection (disabling or formatting mobile devices), device encryption, and data encryption are a few examples of different ways to provide mobile device security.

The enterprise should consider alignment of the mobile application environment with enterprise security standards such as firewall implementation and access to enterprise servers through a Virtual Private Network (VPN) to provide an end-to-end secure environment. Signal and data transmission security is essential for the wireless network. The enterprise should also consider applying security standards such as Advanced Encryption Standard (AES), identity management, and data encryption.

Architectural Considerations

This section details key architecture considerations for developing mobile applications. The team should consider the following factors when finalizing the architecture and implementing the design and development of any mobile application:

- Features and capabilities of mobile devices to support—operating systems and browser support and availability of processing and storage memory

- Wireless network coverage area

- Overall available average signal strength and bandwidth

- Enterprise product roadmap, technology roadmap, infrastructure setup, and security policies

- Business requirements, user expectations, and mobile application scope—application feature availability in online/offline mode

- Developed application deployment features—application footprint, technology platform used for development, data storage requirements

- Cost of deployment and maintenance

Mobile Application Types

You can develop four types of mobile applications: rich client, smart client, web client, and RIA. Which type of mobile application is chosen depends on the requirements of the application, the capabilities of mobile devices that need support, the size of application installation and resource requirements, available bandwidth, and coverage of wireless network.

Rich Client Mobile Applications

Rich client mobile applications, as well as related data and configurations, are installed on the mobile device. Mobile games and other basic applications are examples of rich client applications. The following are characteristics of rich client mobile applications:

- All processing work is performed within the mobile device.
- No network connectivity is required to run the application. All application features are available to mobile users in online/offline mode.
- There are no dependencies on mobile device browser capabilities, signal strength, and bandwidth.
- The application is distributed to all mobile users. The complete application is installed and configured on the mobile device.
- Application-related data is stored within the mobile device.
- Administrators can maintain and monitor the application with the use of MDM tools.
- Application security is dependent on default mobile device security and data encryption.

Smart Client Mobile Applications

As with rich clients, smart client mobile applications are also installed on the mobile device. Related data and configurations are stored locally within the mobile device as a local cache. The key difference between the rich client and the smart client is that the latter's main data repository is a central data repository. The smart client application data synchronization service will synchronize the local cache with the central data repository periodically while connected. One of the best examples of a smart client application is the e-mail management application. The following are characteristics of smart client mobile applications:

- Most of the processing work is performed within the mobile device.
- Constant network connectivity is not required to run the application. All or some application features are available in offline mode.
- Users can enable offline application mode even if they are connected to the network.
- While working on the application in offline mode, there are no dependencies on mobile device browser capabilities, signal strength, and bandwidth.
- In connected mode, data will synchronize with central data storage (two-way synchronization) using the synch service client.
- While working in connected mode, the synchronization performance depends on the signal strength, bandwidth, and size of data to be synchronized.
- The application is distributed to all mobile users. The complete application is installed and configured on the mobile device.
- Application-related data is stored within the mobile device as a local cache.
- Administrators can maintain and monitor the application with the use of MDM tools.

- Application security is dependent on default mobile device security and data encryption. Data synchronization security depends on implemented data transmission security and enterprise network security.

Web Client Mobile Applications

The web client mobile application is a browser-based application installed on central servers. The application accesses the data from the centrally hosted database. Related configurations might be stored locally within the mobile device. Unlike the rich and smart client applications, the web client application is functional only in connected mode. The following are characteristics of web client mobile applications:

- All processing happens on the server side.
- Constant network connectivity is required to run the application. No application features are available in offline mode.
- Application performance depends on browser capabilities, application design, enterprise-deployed environment, signal strength, bandwidth, network latency, size of data, and number of required round-trips.
- The application is browser based and deployed centrally on the servers, so there is no need to distribute it to all mobile users.
- There is no local data cache. The required configuration can be stored on the mobile device.
- Administrators can centrally maintain and monitor the application.
- Application security is dependent on default data transmission security and enterprise network security.

Rich Internet Mobile Applications

Similar to the web client application, the rich Internet mobile application is a browser-based application installed on central servers. This type of application accesses data from a centrally hosted database. Related configurations might be stored locally within the mobile device. The key difference between the rich Internet application and the web client mobile application is that the former is developed using platforms such as Silverlight to support Enterprise 2.0 requirements. All characteristics of the web client mobile application are applicable to the rich Internet mobile application. The following are additional or enhanced characteristics of rich Internet mobile applications:

- Most of the processing work is performed on the server side.
- An advanced plug-in is required to be installed on the mobile device to run the application. All existing mobile devices cannot otherwise support rich Internet mobile applications.
- All existing browsers are not compatible with these types of applications.
- Based on the application design and mobile device capabilities, a rich Internet mobile application may support limited functionality in offline mode using the local cache.
- While working in the application in offline mode, there are no dependencies on the signal strength and bandwidth.
- In connected mode, the data may synchronize with central data storage (two-way synchronization) using a synch service client.
- While working in connected mode, the synchronization performance depends on the signal strength, bandwidth, and size of data to be synchronized.

- Based on the application design, configuration is stored on the mobile device.
- Administrators can centrally maintain and monitor the application.

Based on the preceding discussion, Table 7-1 details the comparison between mobile application types and the seven key principles of SOA. The comparison indicates in relative terms how successfully you can achieve the SOA principle. "High" means you can achieve the specific SOA principle maximum relative to other mobile application types, whereas "Low" means you have the least chance of achieving the principle.

Table 7-1. *Mobile Application Types and the Seven Key Principles of SOA*

SOA Principle	Mobile Application Types			
	Rich Client	**Smart Client**	**Web Client**	**Rich Internet**
Usability	High	High	Medium	High
Simplicity	Medium	Low	High	High
Flexibility	Medium	Medium	High	High
Reusability	Low	Medium	Medium	High
Scalability	Low	Medium	High	High
Maintainability	Low	Low	High	Medium
Security	High	High	High	High

Communication Patterns

Mobile applications need to perform communication between mobile devices (clients) and the enterprise server to execute different actions and events, send notifications and messages, and perform information exchange and data synchronization. There are two main communication models—push model and pull model—based on the enterprise system architecture, application implementation approach, and business requirements.

Push Model

In the push architecture model, central servers will automatically deliver messages to all or selective client devices to communicate specific information or perform specific actions. If the targeted mobile devices are not connected or available within the network range, the messages for those devices remain undelivered and in a queue. The next time the device establishes the connection, the queued message will be delivered automatically.

Figure 7-1 defines the push architecture model for performing communication between the server and mobile devices.

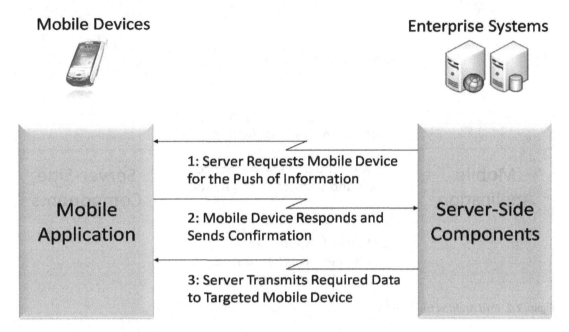

Figure 7-1. *Push architecture model*

As shown in Figure 7-1, first the server requests the mobile device for the push of the required information. If the device is within the coverage area and is connected to the network, the server receives the confirmation. Next, the server transmits the required data to the targeted mobile device.

It is apparent from the preceding discussion that the implementation of the push model is slightly complex, and we need to think of security considerations to help us define the right push model. The users targeted for automated communication can be determined by an enterprise user provisioning system (e.g., Active Directory for all organization employees) or by a subscription model. A push can increase the overall network traffic, depending on the number of mobile users requested by the push and the number of users connected to the network. The enterprise should consider this factor during system architecture design.

The key benefit of the push model is that mobile users do not need to check for updates or undelivered information. You can also implement strict policies via the push model; for example, if a user has not installed a critical patch after a set duration, you disable the device upon next connection to the network. Usually, enterprises implement the push model for critical features and applications such as application version management, security patches, device monitoring features, e-mail management, personal calendar, and contact management.

Pull Model

The pull architecture model and implementation is much simpler compared to the push model. In the pull architecture model, the user (and thus mobile device) initiates the data transmission request from the server. Figure 7-2 defines the pull architecture model for performing communication between the mobile device and the server.

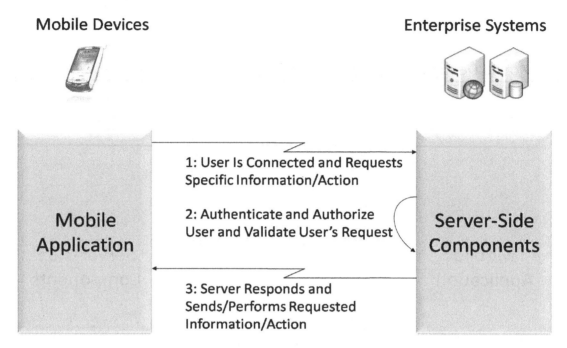

Figure 7-2. *Pull architecture model*

As shown in Figure 7-2, while the user is connected to the network, he or she (and thus the mobile device) initiates a request to receive information. When the server receives and validates the request, it transmits the requested data to the targeted mobile device.

It is apparent from the preceding discussion that the pull model is a user-controlled approach and is easy to implement. The enterprise will need to implement a security model to authenticate and authorize the user and validate the user's request. Since it is a user-controlled approach, the overall network traffic is usually limited (all users do not make requests at the same time) and thus will be easier to maintain and monitor.

The key disadvantage of the pull model is it is user controlled, and there is no guarantee that all users have received the required information or updated the mobile device by a given time. However, most of the day-to-day mobile application operations and events are user driven, and thus the pull model is the best approach for implementing a communication pattern for noncritical operations.

Synchronization Models

The smart client and rich Internet mobile applications support application functionality while the user is not connected to the network or chooses to work in offline mode. While the user is disconnected from the network, he or she can perform different actions (as well as make changes to information). Similarly, while the user is in disconnected mode, there can be several changes in the server-side database or a few server-side requests submitted for specific users. Synchronization agents manage the actions taken using either asynchronous or synchronous mode. In addition, there are three major architectural synchronization models: store-and-forward, database synchronization, and file replication.

Store-and-Forward Synchronization Model

The store-and-forward synchronization model represents asynchronous messaging queue features between client and server for error-free actions and information exchange. It's a well-proven information-exchange messaging model usually used to implement stable and reliable enterprise mobility. This model keeps actions and related information as messages in the queue on the server or client side while disconnected. When a connection is established between the client and server, the queued messages are transmitted asynchronously as part of a transaction to keep the message and related information intact. If the connection is lost in the middle of the transaction or, due to some server- or client-side problem, the message could not be transmitted successfully, the message and related data is not lost; upon the next connection, the same message will be transmitted.

Figure 7-3 demonstrates the high-level architecture of the store-and-forward synchronization model. As shown in the diagram, you can implement the push model or automatic synchronization model.

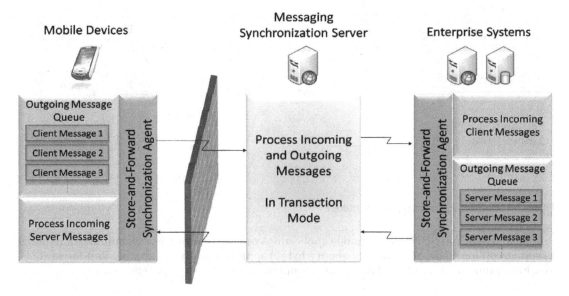

Figure 7-3. *Store-and-forward synchronization model*

Smart client and rich Internet mobile applications can use the store-and-forward synchronization model to support offline mode.

Database Synchronization Model

The database synchronization model performs traditional database synchronization and replication using different technologies or any available synchronization framework/platform. If changes are made in the database on the client or server while the client is in offline mode, upon connection a conflict occurs, and the synchronization agent will synchronize the updated records. You can implement the default last-in-first-win or first-in-first-win synchronization models or implement a custom conflict resolution model for user-driven synchronization.

If there is more than one user performing the transaction to update the same record at the same time, in the last-in-first-win conflict resolution model, the last committed transaction will remain as the final accepted value. In the first-in-first-win conflict resolution model, the database record is usually locked for the user who first tries to attempt the change, and the updated value will be saved. If other users attempt to change the value at the same time, they cannot update that particular record.

Figure 7-4 demonstrates the high-level architecture of the database synchronization model.

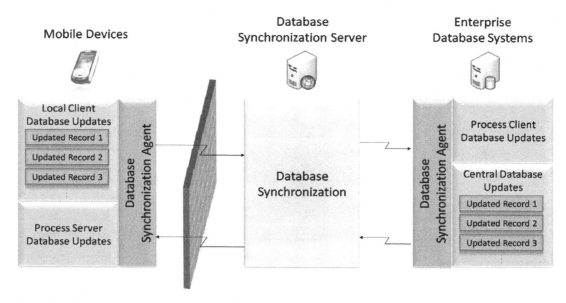

Figure 7-4. *Database synchronization model*

Smart client and rich Internet mobile applications can use the database synchronization model to support offline mode. You can implement a hybrid approach involving the store-and-forward synchronization model and the database synchronization model to provide effective solutions.

Files/Document Synchronization Model

The files/document synchronization model ensures that the client and the server have the same versions of files that were changed in connected or offline mode on the server or client side. Based on the application requirements and synchronization solution you are using, you may or may not need a file synchronization server.

Figure 7-5 demonstrates the high-level architecture of the file/document synchronization model.

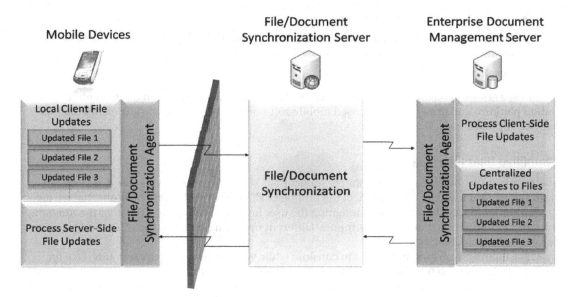

Figure 7-5. *File/Document synchronization model*

Smart client and rich Internet mobile applications can use the file/document synchronization model to support offline mode. You can implement a hybrid approach involving the store-and-forward synchronization model, the database synchronization model, and the file/document synchronization model to provide effective solutions.

Mobile Application Design Considerations

As discussed earlier, because mobile applications are unique in nature, you need to consider different factors and apply a different strategy during the design and development of mobile applications than you would for desktop or web applications. This section will provide a brief overview of different factors the design team should consider during mobile application design and development.

Making a Decision: Defining the Platform

We discussed three core architecture platform components for mobile applications—mobile application types (rich client, smart client, web client, rich Internet), communication patterns (push and pull models), and synchronization models (store-and-forward, data synchronization, file/document synchronization). First of all, the architect and design team needs to define the mobile application platform and decide on the core architecture platform components.

The technical team should do the following:

- Perform extensive requirements analysis.

- Evaluate the existing wireless network infrastructure and possibilities to expand it as part of the current development phase or in the near future.

- Define the number of users to support and areas to cover (to understand the availability of network and bandwidth).

- Understand the capabilities of the mobile devices to be used.

- Define mobile operating systems and browsers to support.

- Understand security implications.
- Align the proposed approach with the organization's strategic product and technology road maps.
- Develop required prototypes.

Based on the preceding analysis, the technical team can make a decision on the mobile application platform and present the proposed mobile solution architecture to the leadership team to receive approval.

Simplified User Interface Design

It is important to follow the "keep it simple" concept of SOA (discussed in Chapter 4) and design a simplified user interface that can meet the unique challenges of mobile applications that we discussed earlier in this chapter. When designing the user interface, you should consider the operating systems and browsers that you will support. Different operating systems and different browsers have different capabilities.

The following are do's and don'ts to consider while you are designing the user interface for mobile applications to provide a clear, concise, and readable user interface:

Do's

First the do's:

- Make the user interface simple and consistent.
- Ensure the interface fits and adjusts to different screen sizes and screen orientations.
- Ensure user actions are compatible with keyboard, stylus, and touch screen input.
- Design for easy navigation from one screen to another.
- Aim to limit the number of text-entry screens. You want such screens to be fewer compared to those in an application for a regular computer system (as it is difficult to type on mobile devices).
- Use a font size and font type suitable for mobile device screen sizes.
- Include proper background and foreground color contrast.
- Consider different language support (impact of globalization and localization).
- Focus on "users, users, and users." User requirements should be analyzed and validated before implementation.

Don'ts

Now the don'ts:

- Make the user interface very rich, heavy, jazzy, and complex.
- Include large horizontal and vertical scrollbars.
- Provide long and complex wizard-like approaches with multiple round-trips to servers.
- Require frequent refreshes of the complete screen.
- Display too much information on a small screen.

Mobile Devices Resources Management

Mobile devices have limited resources in terms of processing power (CPU), processing memory, storage memory, network connectivity, bandwidth, and battery strength compare to regular PCs. These limitations make support for more than one type of mobile device complex for a single application, because different mobile devices come with different resource capabilities.

The application design team needs to first define the matrix of supported mobile devices vs. device configuration (resources) to determine the minimum available device resources that need to be supported by the mobile application. The following is a list of high-impact items that consume one or more resources heavily and thus can have a negative impact on the availability of overall resources:

- Rich, heavy, jazzy, or complex user interface
- Media-driven (e.g., audio and video) applications
- Frequent client-server round-trips
- High number of required data transactions
- Complex business and validation logic execution
- Complex algorithms to support different business processes
- Large documents
- Heavy synchronization features
- Large application footprint
- Client-side processing
- Voice features

The following mobile application features will consume more resources based on the usage of these features by users:

- Voice features
- Video or camera
- Media player and photo album feature
- Internet usage
- Backlight feature

The application design team must analyze the features required for the mobile application and should make efforts to define a simplified application that balances the required features, richness of experience, and complex business issues.

Communication Protocols: SOAP and JSON

Wireless data transmission between mobile devices and a centralized server is critical for smart client, web client, and rich Internet mobile applications. SOAP and JSON are widely used messaging protocols for wireless data transmission. Both are lightweight and, depending on the situation, one is usually better than the other for providing data transmission.

As you saw in Chapter 4, SOAP, which is based on XML, allows us to use structured messages. As a reminder, a SOAP-based message consists of an envelope and optional header, a body, encoding rules, and an RPC representation. By contrast, JSON is a lightweight data-interchange language using a text format. It is based on a subset of JavaScript.

Compared to SOAP, JSON is more simplified and lightweight and is most suitable for simple and straightforward data transmission. SOAP represents a more descriptive and structured message format that is more suitable for complex data transmission and developing generic SOA-based reusable services.

Preparing for Possible Disasters

Mobile devices deal with many unpredictable, potentially disastrous scenarios compared to desktops. Some examples of such scenarios are the following:

- The mobile device loses power and the device is shut down.
- The mobile device is running on low battery power and some high-power consuming features are disabled.
- The user switches off the mobile device.
- The mobile device is in an out-of-network area.
- Low signal strength results in operation timeout.
- The user takes the device offline.
- The user interrupts the existing operation to utilize other features of the mobile device.

The application design team needs to consider different types of problematic scenarios and implement a disaster recovery and self-healing plan for when the application cannot finish its actions.

Silverlight for Mobile Applications

Silverlight is designed for us to develop and deploy cross-platform, cross-browser, and cross-device RIAs. This capability focuses on support for traditional computer machines and mobile handheld devices with different hardware configurations, operating systems, and web browsers. As you learned in earlier chapters, Silverlight 2 is an enterprise-enabled technology platform for developing SOA-based RIAs. This section focuses on how Silverlight can support enterprise mobility by developing SOA-based RIAs for mobile devices.

Silverlight Is Based on the .NET Framework

The main advantage of the Silverlight technology platform is that it is based on .NET Framework 3.5. As a result, the XML-based, loosely coupled presentation layer can be built upon WPF XAML, and all the processing can be implemented by integrating code-behind managed .NET assemblies and web services. The integration of Silverlight for Mobile with the .NET platform makes it easy to develop mobile applications that can support the seven principles of SOA-based applications.

This inherent capability makes Silverlight the right development platform for enterprises to develop RIAs for PCs and mobile devices.

Same Silverlight Applications for Desktop RIAs and Mobile RIAs

The following aspects of Silverlight provide opportunities for supporting the different and unique considerations that desktop RIAs and mobile RIAs have:

- Use of XAML for user interface design
- Vector graphics capabilities for developing a flexible user interface supporting different screen sizes and screen resolutions

- Loosely coupled and service-oriented implementation capabilities
- Reusable managed code integration

In addition Microsoft provides the same set of development tools—Visual Studio, Expression Blend, Deep Zoom Composer—for desktop and mobile RIAs. Visual Studio will also facilitate a Silverlight mobile application emulator for debugging Silverlight-based RIAs.

Based on the preceding discussion, it is safe to say that after a careful evaluation and analysis of requirements and an SOA-based architecture definition, an enterprise can develop and deploy a single RIA that can support both desktops and mobile devices. If the requirements are too different, Silverlight enables developers to reuse different components and services for desktop and mobile RIAs.

Where Do We Stand with Silverlight for Mobile?

Now the key question is, after exploring the promising capabilities of the Silverlight technology platform, where does Microsoft stand on Silverlight for Mobile today?

Silverlight 1 for Mobile

When I started writing this book, it seemed certain that Microsoft was going to release the first version of Silverlight for Mobile—Silverlight 1 for Mobile. Promising mobile RIA demonstrations based on Silverlight 1 for Mobile were presented during the Mix 2008 and TechEd 2008 conferences. Along with the support for Windows mobile phones, Nokia announced support for Silverlight 1 in its Series 60 mobile devices.

Silverlight 1 for Mobile was mainly based on JavaScript (as was the original Silverlight 1 release for the desktop), with more focus on media presentation, and was not fully integrated with the Visual Studio development tools. Even with the preliminary basic version of Silverlight 1 for Mobile, the different demonstrations presented promising capabilities for implementing RIAs for mobile devices.

However, Microsoft decided to keep Silverlight 1 for Mobile as a private test release. It is not available publicly for production development and deployment of Silverlight 1 for Mobile RIAs.

SOME SILVERLIGHT 1 FOR MOBILE–RELATED LINKS

To view a presentation on Silverlight 1 for Mobile presented during Mix 2008, visit http://sessions.visitmix.com/, click MIX08, and search for "Silverlight Mobile."

To get more information on the Nokia Series 60 device with the support for Silverlight, visit http://www.nokia.com/A4136001?newsid=1197788.

Silverlight 2 for Mobile

As mentioned on the Microsoft Silverlight web site at http://silverlight.net/learn/mobile.aspx, Microsoft is aiming to publicly release the next version of Silverlight for Mobile—Silverlight 2 for Mobile—sometime in 2009. Silverlight 2 for Mobile will be compatible with Silverlight 2 for the desktop and will utilize all the features mentioned previously for developing managed SOA-based RIAs for the mobile devices.

Based on the available information, Nokia Series 60 mobile devices (and probably Samsung mobile devices on which the PDC 2008 demonstration was based), along with Windows-based mobile phones, will support Silverlight 2 for Mobile initially. The requirement will be to have the Silverlight 2 plug-in installed on the mobile devices (as on desktop machines). Mobile device operating systems that allow us to install the Silverlight plug-in will be able to safely run Silverlight-based RIAs.

From the enterprise point of view, it is always good to use a consistent set of development tools that support a broad range of application types to develop applications and services that can be reused across applications. Using the Silverlight development platform, enterprises can achieve this objective. It will be possible to develop and debug Silverlight-based desktop RIAs and mobile RIAs using the same set of Visual Studio development tools. However, as mentioned, mobile applications are unique in nature and are generally used for purposes different from those of desktop machines. Thus it is critical to consider all the design considerations for mobile applications discussed in this chapter before making the decision to use the same RIAs for both types of devices.

SOME SILVERLIGHT 2 FOR MOBILE–RELATED LINKS

Continue visiting the Silverlight site (`http://silverlight.net/learn/mobile.aspx`) to get the latest information and updates on Silverlight for Mobile.

Get information on different demonstrations presented during PDC 2008 on the MSDN Team Blog for the Mobile Developer Group by visiting `http://blogs.msdn.com/mobiledev/archive/2008/11/03/let-s-review-the-pdc-silverlight-2-for-mobile-demos.aspx`.

Visit `http://sl.weatherbug.com/` to see a demonstration of WeatherBug, a Silverlight 2 for Mobile application. This application was presented originally during MIX 2008 using Silverlight 1 for Mobile.

Summary

As enterprises embrace the Enterprise 2.0 concept and become global, the necessity of implementing a virtual enterprise to support employees and customers around the world is increasing. Advanced wireless technology, network capabilities, and virtual and mobile application development platforms enable implementation of enterprise mobility. We started this chapter by exploring the concept of enterprise mobility for Enterprise 2.0 and discussed the key components—application and system virtualization, virtual meeting space, and mobile applications—of enterprise mobility.

The latter part of the chapter mainly focused on giving you an overview of mobile applications and architectural considerations for developing mobile applications. As explained, mobile applications are different in many ways (screen size, screen resolution, device resources, usage scenarios, operating system and browser capabilities, network connectivity, and available bandwidth) from regular PCs. Advanced mobile devices and mobile application development tools enable enterprises to develop and deploy SOA-based mobile applications following the seven principles of SOA-based applications.

Enterprise architects and the development team should perform a thorough analysis and develop the required prototypes and user acceptance testing before deploying mobile applications on a large scale. Based on user requirements and expectations, the team should decide whether to develop a rich client, smart client, web client, or rich Internet mobile application. A simplified user interface that supports the required mobile device platform is the recommended approach. The footprint and complexity of mobile applications should be balanced with what features a mobile device supports, and the application should utilize the minimum of resources possible to provide a high-performing user experience.

At the end of the chapter, we looked at the future of Silverlight for Mobile. As demonstrated by a number of applications in different conferences using Silverlight 1 and Silverlight 2, I am confident that Silverlight 2 for Mobile will be a promising, scalable, rich Internet mobile application development platform for enterprises looking to support enterprise mobility. Silverlight 2 for Mobile is scheduled to be released in 2009; I can hardly wait until then to start developing mobile RIAs using Silverlight 2 for Mobile.

In the next and final chapter of the book, I will give some practical advice and tips on how to adopt Silverlight technology in your enterprise.

PART 4

Final Words

CHAPTER 8

■ ■ ■

Adopting Silverlight

As you learned earlier in this book, organizations need to sustain increasing user and stakeholder expectations, as well as meet security and data governance rule and regulation requirements, by transforming from traditional organizations to globalized virtual organizations supporting enterprise mobility.

With the use of innovative and advanced technology such as Silverlight, organizations can achieve these goals effectively and efficiently. Choosing the right technology and adopting it at the right time in the right way that can fit the existing organization vision and culture is a critical success factor to achieve the previously mentioned goals.

So far, we discussed Silverlight technology and how to develop service-oriented enterprise RIAs using Silverlight and the .NET platform in the context of enterprise capabilities. It is just as important to understand how to adopt Silverlight in your organization as it is to understand the capabilities of Silverlight and developing Silverlight-based RIAs. This book will end with a nontechnical, organization management–level discussion that covers how you can successfully plan and adopt Silverlight in your organization.

This last chapter will start with summarizing Silverlight and its capabilities. Then it will discuss current challenges facing Silverlight and cover how organizations can make a decision on whether to select Silverlight as a key technology component. The chapter will wrap up with key issues that organizations need to consider to adopt Silverlight as part of their technology and product roadmaps.

Silverlight in a Nutshell

Silverlight is truly an Enterprise 2.0–ready technology platform enabling development of RIAs. The powerful integration of Silverlight with the .NET Framework and design and development tools such as Visual Studio and Expression (Expression Blend, Expression Encoder, and Deep Zoom Composer) enables IT organizations to develop and deliver service-oriented, high-quality RIAs that return maximum ROI in the long term.

The following are key features of Silverlight 2:

- Silverlight provides a platform to develop cross-browser (Microsoft Internet Explorer, Mozilla Firefox, Apple Safari, and Google Chrome), cross-platform (Microsoft Windows, Apple Mac, Linux), and cross-device (desktop, laptop, and handheld devices) enterprise RIAs.

- Silverlight is based on Microsoft .NET Framework 3.5.
  - As a subset of WPF, the Silverlight user interface framework is based on .NET Framework 3.5, WPF, and XAML. Visual Studio and the Silverlight toolkit contains more than a hundred XAML-based user controls in the areas of layout management (e.g., Canvas, StackPanel, and Grid), form controls (e.g., TextBox, CheckBox), data manipulation (e.g., DataGrid, ListBox), functional controls (e.g., Calendar, DatePicker, ScrollViewer), and media controls (e.g., MediaElement) to develop rich, interactive applications. Third-party vendors also provide an enhanced rich set of Silverlight user controls.
  - Support for CLR and availability of .NET BCL components enable the integration of Microsoft .NET managed code-behind using default Microsoft .NET class libraries in Silverlight 2 projects.
  - Asynchronous loosely coupled data integration capabilities enable development of complex, media-rich, SOA-based enterprise RIAs.
  - Integration with WCF and Web Services via REST, WS*/SOAP, POX, RSS, and standard HTTP enables the application to perform various data transactions with external data sources (e.g., XML, relational databases) and feeds (e.g., RSS).
  - ADO.NET data services, LINQ, LINQ to XML, and XLinq can be used for the data transformation.
  - Local data caching with isolated data storage capabilities supports client-side data processing.
  - DLR supports dynamic compilation and execution of scripting languages like JavaScript and IronPython to develop Silverlight-based applications.
- Silverlight provides effective media management supporting secured multimedia streaming.
  - Adaptive media streaming helps to improve synchronization of media by automatically adjusting bit rates based on the network bandwidth.
  - Digital rights management (DRM) for media streaming enables protected distribution of digital media.
- Silverlight supports rich graphics and animation.
  - 2D vector graphics are supported.
  - Deep Zoom provides an effective and easy-to-implement zoom-in and zoom-out feature.
  - With the use of the Deep Zoom Composer, professionals can smoothly enable navigation of large amounts of visual information, regardless of the size the data, and optimize the bandwidth available to download it.
  - Object animation and embedded code-based animation provides high-performing graphics and animation support.
  - Seamless integration with Microsoft Expression Blend allows development of compelling graphics with minimal effort.
- Silverlight provides networking support.
  - Silverlight is capable of background threading and asynchronous communication.
  - JSON-based services integration is supported. LINQ to JSON support enables querying, filtering, and mapping JSON results to .NET objects within a Silverlight application.
  - Policy-based application development and deployment can occur with cross-domain networking using HTTP and sockets.

- Support for different deployment options (in-package and on-demand) and cross-domain deployment capabilities enable users to access Silverlight RIAs in a high-performing and secured environment.

- Silverlight supports the open source and cross-platform Eclipse development platform by providing Eclipse Tools for Microsoft Silverlight (eclipse4SL—http://www.eclipse4SL.org).

- The Silverlight XAML schema vocabulary specification [MS-SLXV] released under the Open Specification Promise (OSP) improves interoperability.

From the preceding list, it is crystal clear that Silverlight 2 provides a platform to develop cross-browser, cross-platform, and cross-device enterprise RIAs with enhanced networking support, including policy-based cross-domain deployment to support different types of application deployment scenarios. With these features, as you learned earlier in this book, Silverlight 2 can certainly support the seven key SOA principles—usability, flexibility, simplicity, reusability, scalability, maintainability, and security—for building easy-to-deploy enterprise RIAs as a service.

Adopting Silverlight in Your Organization

Before adopting any new technology component, organizations have to perform comprehensive strategic and technical analysis. This analysis should provide convincing results and a promising technology adoption plan to the leadership and stakeholder teams. The analysis should answer the following questions that assess business values and short-term and long-term ROI:

- What to adopt?
- Why to adopt?
- How to adopt?
- When to adopt?

The outcome of the analysis must align with the organization's strategic vision in order to adopt the new technology. Along with the key milestones involved in the adoption process, the results should define how to integrate the new technology component in the organization's product roadmap and technology roadmap.

Let's see what should be included when performing an analysis to introduce the Silverlight technology as a new technology component to your organization.

Understanding the Current Challenges of Silverlight

Silverlight has a few technical and logistical challenges that you need to understand and evaluate before your organization adopts it. This section also provides some answers on how to mitigate certain challenges and risks.

New Technology

Some organizations are followers that don't like taking a risk with what they see as a new technology. However, Silverlight 2, which was released only a few months before this writing, is pretty mature and has shown promising results and impressive commercial acceptance in a wide range of markets because Silverlight 1 paved the way. This makes organizations think twice before they wait for it to be a bit more mature and proven in the market.

New technology comes up with its own challenges and risks such as the following:

- Lack of expertise and support

- Lack of sophisticated and advanced controls and integrated development, testing, and support tools

- Uncertainty of meeting security policies

- Risk of failure

- Large initial investment

- No proven record and model on the path to success

- Deployment and maintenance challenges

This book has proved that Silverlight is a new but mature technology that can be adopted in your organization with low risk. One of the key reasons for me to make this kind of statement is that Silverlight is built upon the well-proven and mature .NET Framework.

Enterprise Capabilities of Silverlight Technology

As covered in Chapters 3 and 4, Silverlight features enterprise capabilities and supports the seven key SOA principles—usability, flexibility, simplicity, reusability, scalability, maintainability, and security—for building easy-to-deploy enterprise RIAs as a service. Thus we can confidently claim Silverlight is an Enterprise 2.0–ready technology platform.

Not Yet a Truly Cross-Device and Cross-Platform Technology Platform

Silverlight for Mobile has not yet been released. Silverlight's not being a truly cross-device platform can be one of the excuses for adopting an alternative technology in its place. However, the first release of Silverlight for Mobile is planned for sometime in 2009. The first test release of Silverlight 1 for Mobile has shown some promising features and support from third-party vendors (e.g., Nokia support for Silverlight). At PDC 2008, Microsoft showed some interesting mobile applications using Silverlight 2 for Mobile.

Similarly, there is no official release of Silverlight for the Linux and UNIX operating systems, limiting its ability to be a truly cross-platform platform. However, the Moonlight open source product is on the way (it's currently in beta release), which will enable Silverlight on Linux and UNIX operating systems.

Note Get more information on the Moonlight project by visiting `http://www.mono-project.com/Moonlight`.

Providing Silverlight-Enabled Machines

One of the challenges for any organization is to make existing machines compatible with the new technology component and take into consideration possible licensing costs.

Microsoft has taken care of this problem already:

- As mentioned earlier, Silverlight is based on the .NET Framework. So if your organization is running any .NET 3.5 applications, you are capable of running Silverlight applications.

- The Silverlight 2 runtime installer is significantly small in size (less than 5MB) and takes about 10 seconds to install. There is no prerequisite (except Silverlight plug-in installation) to run any Silverlight RIA. It does not even require the .NET Framework on your machine, since the Silverlight installer includes all the necessary components.

- There is no licensing cost involved to enable your machine to run Silverlight RIAs. The Silverlight 2 runtime installer is free and available to all users.

Limited Silverlight User Control Library

Silverlight is made to develop rich, interactive Internet applications. The current release includes sufficient XAML controls to develop effective, rich media–enabled applications for the enterprise. However, its control toolkit is not as plentiful as other Microsoft development platform toolkits (e.g., Windows Form/WPF controls, ASP.NET controls).

As explained earlier in the book, Silverlight is not the answer for all. If you use the right technology for the right requirement, Silverlight can take a unique place in your organization's IT platform.

Making a Decision on Adopting Silverlight

How can you measure and decide that Silverlight is the best fit for Enterprise 2.0? There are a number of different techniques you can use to evaluate your need for Silverlight. As a first step, my favorite high-level analysis approach for deciding whether anything is suitable for my needs is the use of a checklist or logical decision-making flowchart. This helps to provide a quick, high-level positive or negative outcome before spending a lot of time on an in-depth analysis.

Performing a Requirements Analysis of the Application

A requirements analysis is a key component for decision making when selecting a technology platform. Different survey techniques for end users and stakeholders can help you perform this analysis. Table 8-1 is a sample high-level requirements analysis checklist for measuring requirements of the Silverlight-based RIA.

Table 8-1. *Requirements Analysis Checklist*

✔	Is the application an RIA?
✔	Does the application need to support media (audio, video), documents, and information (all at the same time)?
✔	Does the application need to support dynamic content?
✔	Does the application user interface need to be customizable at runtime?
✔	Does the application need to support different languages?
✔	Do the end users use different types of devices and different types of platform (Internet browser and operating system)? If yes, what devices and platforms need to be supported?
✔	Does the application need to be developed and deployed quickly and support agile SDLC?

If the answer is yes to most of the questions in the checklist, Silverlight can fit the application requirements. The last question is a bit more detailed, and a detailed answer will help to align the deliverables with the time line.

Note The provided checklist is a sample checklist only. You should expand the checklist to support your organization's needs and circumstances.

Measuring Technology Platform Suitability for Your Organization

Based on the application requirements and organization IT implementation strategy, Table 8-2 presents a high-level technical analysis checklist for measuring capabilities of a technology platform.

Table 8-2. *Technical Analysis Checklist*

✔	Does the technology allow development of a rich user interface with support for vector graphics?
✔	Does the technology seamlessly support media (audio and video) and content (data and documents)?
✔	Is it possible to design an abstracted user interface?
✔	Is it flexible and easy enough to change the user interface and service definition, and would it be easy to redeploy?
✔	Is the application footprint on client machines lightweight?
✔	Does application development support easy customization of the user interface?
✔	Does the technology allow single-byte and multibyte character sets to support localization?
✔	Does the richness of the user interface not have a negative impact on the application's performance?
✔	Does the technology support agile software development models?
✔	Is the technology browser independent?
✔	Is the technology device and operating system platform independent?
✔	Can the technology support reusable UI components to support different types of devices with different screen resolutions and sizes?
✔	Can you develop customizable application services?
✔	Can service definition, business logic, configuration, and resources be externalized for the customization?
✔	Can you develop a service featuring a plug-in/plug-out capability?
✔	Can the end user enable/disable and/or customize the service's features?
✔	Can you implement abstraction and modular components and services using object-oriented design principles?
✔	Can you implement all required security policies?

If your organization needs a technology that includes support for these capabilities, Silverlight 2 is the best fit for your organization.

Note The provided checklist is a sample checklist only. You should expand the checklist to support your organization's needs and circumstances.

Making a Decision on Silverlight

If you receive a positive outcome from the high-level requirements and technical analysis, you need to perform an in-depth analysis (which may include a few items we will discuss in the next section) to make the decision of whether to adopt Silverlight.

If you make a decision to adopt Silverlight for your organization, you should have a detailed impact analysis on existing applications and infrastructure and a definite adoption plan with key milestones aligning with your product and technology roadmap to present to the leadership team.

Key Considerations for Adopting Silverlight

A strategic, well-thought-out execution of an adoption plan will allow easy adoption of any change, such as adopting Silverlight in your organization. You should take the following items into consideration while adopting Silverlight in your organization.

Learn to Listen to Heartbeats

As part of an organization and a professional, you have to learn to listen to heartbeats. If you cannot make customers and stakeholders happy in the first release, there is rarely a chance you'll have successful future releases. Usually the application time line is very aggressive and agile. That's why it is critical to learn to listen to the heartbeats of the stakeholders and customers by working strategically and closely with them to discover the features that can provide the most business value.

Start Small

Careful prioritization of requirements based on understanding user and stakeholder requirements will help to define the phased implementation plan (applying the balancing act between requirements and the given time line) for a Silverlight-based RIA.

The "start small" approach can be effective if done properly. To follow this approach, the first release of a Silverlight-based RIA should be focused on delivering maximum business value to gain enough confidence and satisfaction among customers and stakeholders to move forward with future incremental releases. Once you understand the features by heart, you can prioritize them by the business values they deliver in a phased approach.

Don't Make Assumptions

Sometimes making the wrong assumptions can kill the whole application. Especially when developing in agile mode, you do not have the time to correct an application developed on such assumptions.

The key to success is to start with a small scope and work closely with customers and stakeholders to validate all assumptions and understand the requirements properly. Prototyping techniques can provide a quick visual overview of future application releases, which can help to validate assumptions and requirements.

Prototypes/Proof of Concepts: Good Approach for Agile SDLC

Development of prototypes/proof of concepts and getting immediate user feedback on them is the best approach for winning user acceptance before deploying the product. Especially while you are introducing a new technology with new requirements or migrating existing applications to a new technology platform, initial prototypes or proof of concepts help to validate assumptions, technical capabilities, and requirements.

Prototyping is also a good approach for effective change management. An early view of the future application release as well as close involvement of users from the beginning of the project can make users comfortable with the upcoming change.

The Right Technology for the Right Purpose

Silverlight is mainly suitable for developing RIAs where applications are media-centric and require a rich, interactive user interface. It is not made for complex business logic with very complex data management screens (for example, with complex `Grid` controls).

Make practical design decisions, not emotional ones, based on the application's requirements. You do not need to develop the whole application in Silverlight. A modular design approach would enable you to develop different parts of the application using the most suitable technology.

Don't Overengineer

It is very easy to overengineer any requirement and design for the application. As explained earlier, a simplified and balanced approach will increase overall usability and thus productivity and maintainability of the application. An application developed in agile mode usually has many iterations, with every iteration part of an aggressive deliverable time line. It is difficult to deliver, upgrade, scale, maintain, and support an application with a complex design using an iterative approach.

Silverlight supports development of simplified, loosely coupled, service-oriented RIAs. You can follow best practices provided by Microsoft and other experts as well as the guidelines provided in this book to develop simplified Silverlight-based enterprise RIAs.

Microsoft is continuously releasing best patterns and practices for the usage of different technologies in application design and development. In addition to this book, check out the links on understanding best patterns and practices to develop Silverlight-based RIAs in the "Additional References" section.

Test, Test, and Test

Continuous testing and continuous improvement can increase product quality significantly. Rigorous testing must be part of your project plan. You need to perform different types and different levels of testing before releasing any RIAs.

The enterprise-level capabilities of the technology platform enable development of sophisticated, distributed, service-based RIAs supporting different platforms and devices. These types of applications are more likely to break because of a large number of unknowns and the requirement to support a wide range of scenarios.

You have to implement a different strategy for testing RIAs, which means you have to perform different levels of testing. Use as much automation and simulation as you can to expedite the testing. Perform negative testing scenarios, such as what happens when Silverlight is not available on the end user's machine (you can create this test scenario by disabling Silverlight add-ons in the browser).

For more information on the Silverlight Unit Test Framework, see the "Additional References" section at the end of this chapter.

Summary

This chapter focused on organization management and discussed different options on how to adopt Silverlight in your organization. After summarizing key features of Silverlight, the text discussed how to adopt Silverlight in your organization by understanding the current challenges of Silverlight, performing requirements and technical analysis, and giving some practical advice. Thorough analysis, prototyping, simplified design, and proper testing will make for a smooth development and deployment experience.

As explained, Silverlight is a mature Enterprise 2.0–capable technology platform for developing service-oriented RIAs. A proper planning, design, and application implementation approach will make you successful in deploying high-performing and high-quality Silverlight-based RIAs that can deliver maximum customer satisfaction and ROI. Don't forget to prioritize requirements and simplify your design to develop and deploy high-performing, stable, and maintainable service-based RIAs.

I wish you good luck adopting Silverlight in your enterprise.

Additional References

Links from the Microsoft Web Site

- Enterprise Architecture, Patterns, and Practices, `http://msdn.microsoft.com/en-us/library/aa286494.aspx`

- Composite Application Guidance for WPF, `http://msdn.microsoft.com/en-us/library/cc707819.aspx` (continue visiting this site to get updates on Silverlight)

- Patterns in the Composite Application Library, `http://msdn.microsoft.com/en-us/library/cc707841.aspx`.

- Unit Test Framework for Microsoft Silverlight 2, `http://code.msdn.microsoft.com/silverlightut`.

Index

You Need the Companion eBook

Your purchase of this book entitles you to buy the companion PDF-version eBook for only $10. Take the weightless companion with you anywhere.

We believe this Apress title will prove so indispensable that you'll want to carry it with you everywhere, which is why we are offering the companion eBook (in PDF format) for $10 to customers who purchase this book now. Convenient and fully searchable, the PDF version of any content-rich, page-heavy Apress book makes a valuable addition to your programming library. You can easily find and copy code—or perform examples by quickly toggling between instructions and the application. Even simultaneously tackling a donut, diet soda, and complex code becomes simplified with hands-free eBooks!

Once you purchase your book, getting the $10 companion eBook is simple:

❶ Visit **www.apress.com/promo/tendollars/**.

❷ Complete a basic registration form to receive a randomly generated question about this title.

❸ Answer the question correctly in 60 seconds, and you will receive a promotional code to redeem for the $10.00 eBook.

THE EXPERT'S VOICE™

2855 TELEGRAPH AVENUE | SUITE 600 | BERKELEY, CA 94705